Big Data Shocks

LIBRARY INFORMATION TECHNOLOGY ASSOCIATION (LITA) GUIDES

Marta Mestrovic Deyrup, Ph.D.
Acquisitions Editor, Library Information and Technology Association, a division of the American Library Association

The Library Information Technology Association (LITA) Guides provide information and guidance on topics related to cutting-edge technology for library and IT specialists.

Written by top professionals in the field of technology, the guides are sought after by librarians wishing to learn a new skill or to become current in today's best practices.

Each book in the series has been overseen editorially since conception by LITA and reviewed by LITA members with special expertise in the specialty area of the book.

Established in 1966, LITA is the division of the American Library Association (ALA) that provides its members and the library and information science community as a whole with a forum for discussion, an environment for learning, and a program for actions on the design, development, and implementation of automated and technological systems in the library and information science field.

Approximately 25 LITA Guides were published by Neal-Schuman and ALA between 2007 and 2015. Rowman & Littlefield took over publication of the series beginning in late 2015. Books in the series published by Rowman & Littlefield are:

Digitizing Flat Media: Principles and Practices
The Librarian's Introduction to Programming Languages
Library Service Design: A LITA Guide to Holistic Assessment, Insight, and Improvement
Data Visualization: A Guide to Visual Storytelling for Librarians
Mobile Technologies in Libraries: A LITA Guide
Innovative LibGuides Applications
Integrating LibGuides into Library Websites
Protecting Patron Privacy: A LITA Guide
The LITA Leadership Guide: The Librarian as Entrepreneur, Leader, and Technologist
Using Social Media to Build Library Communities: A LITA Guide
Managing Library Technology: A LITA Guide
The LITA Guide to No- or Low-Cost Technology Tools for Libraries
Big Data Shocks: An Introduction to Big Data for Librarians and Information Professionals

Big Data Shocks

An Introduction to Big Data for Librarians and Information Professionals

Andrew Weiss

ROWMAN & LITTLEFIELD
Lanham • Boulder • New York • London

Published by Rowman & Littlefield
An imprint of The Rowman & Littlefield Publishing Group, Inc.
4501 Forbes Boulevard, Suite 200, Lanham, Maryland 20706
www.rowman.com

Unit A, Whitacre Mews, 26-34 Stannary Street, London SE11 4AB

British Library Cataloguing in Publication Information Available

Library of Congress Cataloging-in-Publication Data Available

ISBN 9781538103227 (hardback : alk. paper) | ISBN 9781538103234 (pbk. : alk. paper) | ISBN 9781538103241 (electronic)

♾ ™ The paper used in this publication meets the minimum requirements of American National Standard for Information Sciences Permanence of Paper for Printed Library Materials, ANSI/NISO Z39.48-1992.

Printed in the United States of America

To Akiko, Mia, and Cooper for their love, support, and patience

Contents

Figures

Table

Preface

Big Data Shocks

COPING WITH MODERNITY

It is said that modernity stems from a state of mind, from a sense that we are somehow different—and cut off as a result—from those who lived before us. Modernity is more than just an accumulation of the technological advancements we incorporate into our daily lives. Instead, modernity is always existing in the fragile here and now, dependent upon purely subjective perceptions and a lingering feeling of separation. It can be argued that the concept of modernity has existed in the Western world for the past several hundred years, since the age of the Enlightenment (Kirsch, 2016). Perhaps that is why, despite living in this supposedly postmodern world that no longer always speaks directly to futurism or the hope of science and technology (leaving us, it is argued, with fragmented collections of nonuniversal facts, or in the hands of fundamentalism of all stripes), the word *modernity* nevertheless persists and even *resists* the irony of its supposed demise. So, where else to begin a discussion of the impact of "big data" than with the concept of modernity itself and the shock and sense of lost connection to the past that is often associated with it?

The title of this book, *Big Data Shocks*, speaks to that moment when we become aware of such changes. These shocks play out across the world in different patterns—some in violence, some in internal change, some in decline of traditional values, and some in a reactionary adherence or even reversion to fundamentalist values. We speak—when we speak of such shocks—in the language of culture clash, of tradition and modernity, of new worlds and stone ages, of utopias and dystopias, and of Luddites and futurists. These and more are inherent in the concept of change, and the shocks they portend affect all of us.

"SHOCKS TO THE SYSTEM": INFORMATION OVERLOAD AND TIPPING THE SCALES OF THE FRAGILE MIND

The amount of information now generated in the digital age is mind boggling. According to David Farrier (2016), "Humans created 5 billion gigabytes of digital information in 2003; in 2013 it took only 10 minutes to produce the same amount of data." It is indeed one of the great shocks of our time. But even though the scale and rapidity of the information age has grown in size beyond the human capacity to visualize it, the fundamental shock brought on by the growth of information has *always* been with us.

Scholars and writers have wrestled with the problem of information overload since the written word became commonplace. Even those in our earliest written histories and literature, as noted in Ecclesiastes, have known about the dangers of excessive information: "And further, by these, my son, be admonished: of making many books *there is* no end; and much study *is* a weariness of the flesh" (Ecclesiastes 12:12). This is not an idea isolated to religious dogma either. Advances in writing have always come with a price that modern society seems to see as a minor issue. The problem with writing, according to Plato, was that it discouraged memorization. The mind could no longer be made stronger through memorization techniques common in the preliteracy era and in our oral traditions. Instead, scholars and scribes would come to control the facts of a republic, causing problems in a society's collective memory and giving rise to the erasure of facts, the revision of experiences, and tyranny itself. No longer would collective memory be humanized. Instead, it would become externalized and abstracted from the human condition. The human in us would be exiled from the information that resided outside of the "memory palaces" the mind had constructed.

The dilemma remains to this day. It may even be exacerbated by the proliferation of mobile and social media technology, which promises that we never need to remember anything so long as it is stored in a smartphone, tablet, or other wearable device. Our own sense of memory becomes more malleable, and facts less reliable as anchors to reality as they are infinitely edited and altered. Additionally, the mind is able to remember what it deems to be necessary so long as the scale is manageable, yet these days the increased rapidity and scale of the data we encounter daily all but disqualifies memorization as a viable mechanism for incorporating new information. Indeed, information has perhaps moved beyond the human scale and may be useful anymore only to machines designed to parse it.

Ultimately, as we move to an era of information that exists and functions beyond our own capacities and rely ever more on machinery to cope, will we lose something? Will we lose our humanity even more? Will the benefits outweigh the drawbacks, and how will we know this? Such concepts and essential questions will be examined in depth in each of the four main sections of this book, entitled "First Shocks," "Reality Shocks," "Library Shocks," and "Future Shocks." In some ways, it is hoped that the reader comes away with as many questions about the impact of big data on our lives as answers. Since the era of big data is really just taking off, much of what is discussed is in flux and may change by the time the book is published.

SHOCKS AND AWE

Section 1: First Shocks

The first section of this book, entitled "First Shocks," delves into the definition of data itself, tracing how it shifted from a medieval term related to biblical exegesis to the contemporary usage of computational-based numerical quantities of information that provide digital and computer modeling for many disciplines. But the initial shock factor of big data begins with scale. As a result, an outline of the transformation from data to big data will be examined. The volume and rapidity of data generation also meets the realization that this is just the beginning: the exponential growth of information will surely continue for decades to come. This section will also look at some of the approaches and tools being developed to harness the growth in data—especially through data mining and tracking—and the positive impacts that these have on various disciplines. Finally, the section will round out discussion by looking at how big data is utilized specifically in the wider segments of our society, including government and politics, education, the media, STEM (science, technology, engineering, and mathematics) fields, the humanities, and of course libraries.

Section 2: Reality Shocks

The second section, "Reality Shocks," examines the issues of big data as they relate to the world at large. There is a growing realization that privacy can be easily lost, despite being a core tenet of librarianship, and our own expectations of privacy have been altered and compromised by the rise of big data. Additionally, the source for this large amount of data is user online behavior monitored through social media, the growing internet of things, and voluntary opt-in surveillance accepted for token benefits. This overall erosion of privacy has led to a greater awareness of the widespread practice of political monitoring and spying. Information overload, another issue related to the proliferation of big data, will also be examined. As the scale of data and information increases, we need to analyze how that scale can impact human cognitive ability. Ultimately, it comes down to developing and preserving methods, strategies, and resolutions necessary to ensure that privacy and personal freedom endure even as the tools for big data are utilized for public and private good.

Section 3: Library Shocks

The third section looks at how big data directly impacts libraries. In particular, the chapters examine the growing area of open science, public funding mandates for open data, and the potential impact that widespread access to this information might have. Funder mandates have the potential to positively impact societies, especially in the relationship to climate science, public health, and the problems that might be solved through crowd sourcing or crowd sharing. Data management is also important as data becomes generated at large scale by more researchers and students. Harnessing it as well as preserving it becomes priorities for modern libraries. The humanities have embraced the era of big data as well. As digital humanities and libraries have a lot of important overlapping areas and goals, information literacy becomes ever more important as well. Finally, the section will examine a number of library case studies related to information literacy, data management and assessment of student data for the sake of examining important student learning outcomes.

Section 4: Future Shocks

Finally, the fourth section speculates on what's to come for libraries as they adapt to the rigors and promises of the big data era. The first part will examine how libraries can develop tools, policies, and methods for harnessing big data and, to coin a new term, "big assessment," which would help them track users, especially students, and monitor their progress. The chapter will also examine the proficiencies that all current and future librarians need to understand as big data and big assessment become more prevalent in theory and practice. The second chapter will examine the future of the library itself, speculating upon the feasibility of "smart libraries" and how they would fit within the development of big-data-driven smart societies.

On a final note, although no definitive answers exist for many of the issues raised by this book, clear trends do seem to be opening up for us. The technology is still new, and the amount of growing data is still in its early stages, but it is hoped that enough light will be shed on these problems to help readers anticipate future problems and arrive at viable solutions.

REFERENCES

Farrier, D. (2016). Deep time's uncanny future is full of ghostly human traces. Aeon. https://aeon.co.

Kirsch, A. (2016). Are we really so modern? *New Yorker*. http://www.newyorker.com.

Acknowledgements

The author would like to acknowledge the following people and organizations for their generous cooperation in the creation of this book: Dr. Martin Hilbert, Dr. Nova Spivak, Dr. Courtney Stewart, Dr. Elisabetta Poltrioni, Katy McKen, Suzanna Ward at the Cambridge Structural Database, and Emily Rogers at the Franklin Institute.

Special acknowledgement also goes to the editorial staff at Rowman & Littlefield for their help in shaping and developing the book, especially Katie O'Brien, Darren Williams, and, "last-but-not-least," Charles Harmon.

Among colleagues at CSUN, many thanks to Mark Stover, dean of the Oviatt Library, for allowing me to freely pursue subjects and areas of inquiry, wherever they might lead; to Ahmed Alwan and Eric Garcia for their discussions regarding assessment and diversity that have ultimately helped to shape parts of this book; to Luiz Mendes for his conscientious guidance and encouragement; and to Steve Kutay for his always interesting and thought-provoking conversations that spurred me to write about many of the topics in this book.

Last, a special acknowledgement to Akiko, for keeping me focused on what matters most.

Part I

First Shocks

Chapter One

What Is Data?

BEGINNINGS, APOCRYPHAL, AND OTHERWISE

"On Disproving Quintessence," or the Beginnings of Modern, Data-Driven Inquiry

Over his lifetime, Galileo Galilei published thirteen books and pamphlets, masterworks that impacted various scientific fields including astronomy, engineering, mathematics, and physics. Additionally, his work established methods of observation and experimentation that are still considered the foundations of modern science itself. In *Sidereus Nuncius*, a pamphlet published in 1610 (see figure 1.1), Galileo provided clear observational proof that the earth revolved around the sun, in contradiction to the church-sanctioned, earth-centric theories of Aristotle and Ptolemy. These new theories and the findings supporting them promised to revolutionize human understanding of the universe.

But these advances did not come without repercussions. By 1633, Galileo was under house arrest, the result of his ongoing conflicts with the Catholic Church. According to prevalent medieval theories from the time, the heavenly bodies such as the planets and stars were perfect, nearly godlike entities, composed of something called "quintessence," a hypothetical fifth element permeating all of nature. The term itself has lingered through our vocabulary as *quintessential*, "the essence of a thing in its purest and most concentrated form" (*Merriam-Webster's Dictionary*), but is obviously no longer used as a working, credible theory to explain the mysterious phenomena of our universe.

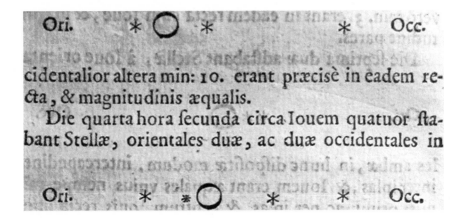

Figure 1.1. Detail of a page excerpted from *Sidereus Nuncius* (published in 1610), aka *The Starry Messenger,* showing Galileo's data created to visualize his planetary observations. Image courtesy of the History of Science Collections, University of Oklahoma Libraries.

Given that it is often difficult to change minds when power structures are involved, and the great risk it carries for those who aim to do so, how does one ultimately go about disproving such entrenched ways of thinking?

Thomas Kuhn's 1962 book *The Structure of Scientific Revolutions* provides us with a good framework for broaching this subject. He describes the adoption of Galileo's sun-centered theory as a prime example of the problems that one faces when attempting to change entrenched visions of reality. Yet, the importance of Kuhn's framework of "paradigms" is that it relies on evidence for its assertions, and thus the theories posited could eventually be disproved by others.

Kuhn essentially asserts that paradigmatic thinking and obsessive, unimaginative adherence to past models contributes to severe bottlenecks in science. As Kuhn notably points out, Galileo was often wrong and himself contributed to long-standing theories that in turn blocked change and progress. His own theory of the tides, for example, has long been discredited but held sway over other scientists for years. Although the act of science continually takes place, Kuhn further argues, within established theories—paradigms, as he termed them—experimentation often ends without the expected results appearing. Anomalies in these results spur scientists to disbelieve or ignore what they saw, despite evidence to the contrary. Eventually enough counterevidence is generated to allow breakthroughs and subsequent "paradigm shifts," a widespread and even clichéd term that later became trendy in the business world. In Galileo's case, he disproved an established but unscientific theory through observation and reasoning, with clear and repeatable methods, and with logic and evidence. This was a double-edged sword, as his own theories, in turn, are later disproven.

However, Galileo's impact on our current world cannot be overestimated. Many consider him to be the founder of modern science, the developer of the scientific method, and a major force in numerous scientific disciplines, including mathematics, geology, astronomy, and physics. But his development of using evidence to support his claims and hypotheses is perhaps what represents his longest-standing achievement and his greatest legacy to us in our modernized, data-driven world. As Galileo himself has said, "The universe . . . is written in the language of mathematics, and its characters are triangles, circles, and other geometric figures" (Drake, 1957). In other words, his revolution began not with perfectly realized theories that lasted for an eternity but with the evidence that needed first to be *found* and then explained to support new facts. In short, his impact lasts through his revolutionary use of data to support the theory.

Creating a New Quintessence: Digitization of the World, "Datalization of the Word"

The use of data has clearly impacted our modern notions of science and scientific method. One of the central components of the scientific method's experimental design involves gathering and sharing data. One online web page geared toward K–12 students describes this process as "values written down as the experiment progresses" (Science Stuff, 2007). As a rule of thumb, for most people performing quantitative experimentation, data is seen as equivalent to such empirically gathered numerical values. Indeed, that seems to be the case in the Galileo experiments as well: data represented the specific numerical values derived from his observation of the natural phenomena found in the night skies. And it is an incredibly powerful tool. As Christian Oestreicher writes, "This [mathematical] concordance between thinking and the environment is a gift quite specific to humanity" (Oestreicher, 2007, p. 279). It is a marvel, in other words, that we can predict and quantify what our notoriously fallible senses show us. The scientific method has absorbed the use of data, making it central to its process of theory, testing, analysis, and replication of results.

But jumping ahead three hundred years to the mid-twentieth century, we find that a new type of information, digital information, has begun to revise and expand our notions of what data can be. Whereas data would be part of a supporting hypothesis, the new uses of digital information begin to focus more on devising virtual models. Such models are used to predict the behavior of systems based on the gathering of data sets. The ease of this modeling is assisted by computers, graphic representations, and visualization of the data. To take it a step further, data is envisioned by many now as merely an extension of digitization itself. This digital designation or assignation turns items that were once "analog" physical objects—separated, somehow, from prior computational inquiry—and that are now quantifiable and therefore transformable, into numerical "data."

Consider the case of the "sinotype." One of the early computer science problems in the 1940s and 1950s attempted to solve how one might develop a digital typeset for a Chinese or Japanese-language computer. The solution to this issue wound up being a relatively simple application of element abstraction. As the Chinese characters are written following long-standing customs that have been systematized over millennia into easily constructed and remembered conceptual entities, researchers were able to break down the characters into their logically constructed constituent parts. Characters are written—as it is seen in figure 1.2—in simple steps and then combined to create larger characters. In order to convert these into a "type," each basic segment of the character was assigned a Roman letter (i.e., D, P, B, etc.). Complex segments joined together were then represented as strings of letters to be deciphered by a computer (Mullaney, 2016). As seen below, an analytical system is designed to build up characters from their essential nonalphabetic components. What was once generated by physical or analog methods (i.e., by handmade brushstrokes) became an automated process contributing to computable data (Caldwell, 1959).

Yet are these interpretations and implementations of information clear enough definitions of "data"? In many ways limiting this description of data as a value or a quantifiable thing is by itself incomplete. If it were complete, people would not also consider images to be data. Yet photographs have become essential evidence in environmental science for documenting climate

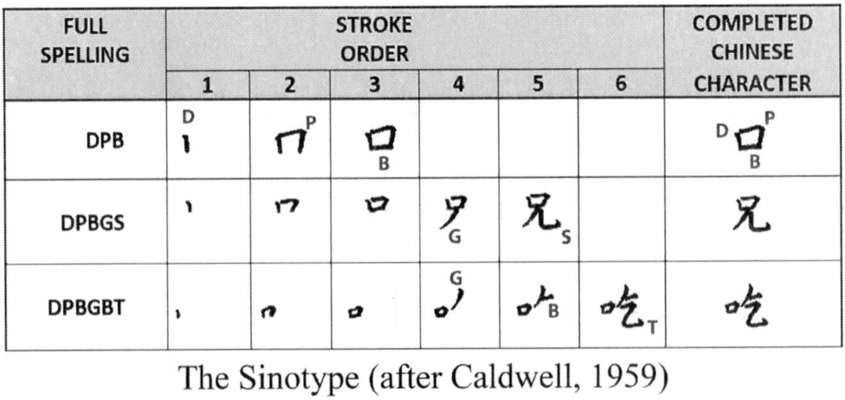

FULL SPELLING	STROKE ORDER						COMPLETED CHINESE CHARACTER
	1	2	3	4	5	6	
DPB	D 丨	冂 P	口 B				D 口 P B
DPBGS	丶	冂	冗	𠃌 G	尢 S		尢
DPBGBT	丶	冂	冖	G 𠃌	尣 B	尨 T	尨

The Sinotype (after Caldwell, 1959)

Figure 1.2.   Turning a Chinese character into a code (datalization) *Source:* Caldwell, 1959. Redrawn by author.

change, allowing researchers to see how past landscapes have morphed into current ones. Additionally, if this numerical definition of data were the complete story, people would not consider the drafts of scores or manuscripts from past composers and writers as worthy of analytical study. People would not examine print diaries or archived papers, hieroglyphics, or any old system of writing for evidence. These examples all fall outside the realm of "quantification" into qualitative thinking and reasoning. Furthermore, data itself is also considered to be of different types: qualitative for some disciplines such as the social sciences or humanities, and quantitative for others, such as physics and biology. Given the numerous exceptions to the rule, there must obviously be more to the concept than just numbers and computational analysis. The next sections will examine this protean term and bring us to a clearer and more universally applicable definition.

THE CONUNDRUM OF DATA: ARRIVING AT A WORKING DEFINITION

Original Sins, Unending Cycles, and Potential Hierarchies of Value

The term "data" that we use today originated in the 1500s. At first—and this is especially ironic in the case of Galileo—the term was used to denote a part of arguments used in theological arguments, referring to "something given or granted; something known or assumed as fact, and made the basis of reasoning; an assumption or premise from which inferences are drawn" (*Oxford English Dictionary* [*OED*]). The earliest use in the printed word occurred in 1646, yet simultaneously in the 1630s the word first begins to appear in its most common definition as "an item of (chiefly numerical) information, esp. one obtained by scientific work, a number of which are typically collected together for reference, analysis, or calculation" (*OED*).

But this does not quite fit as an apt definition in all situations. Some instead see data as part of a cycle, as in figure 1.3. If one does an online search for data cycle, one will find thousands of similar images. Data is generated as a thing, perhaps out of thin air even, and then incorporated as part of a wider circle of progression until it doubles back upon itself to generate even more data. Sometimes there are fewer steps, sometimes more. But what's common to these data cycle diagrams is that they see data often as discrete, concrete objects fitting neatly within a clearly defined process, capable of unlimited and unceasing use and reuse.

Taking it further, some envision data as existing within a hierarchy as in figure 1.4. At the bottom of the hierarchy resides data in its "raw" state, its existence supporting the creation of information itself. This, in turn, supports intelligence and knowledge, leading to the ultimate and most rarefied step of wisdom.

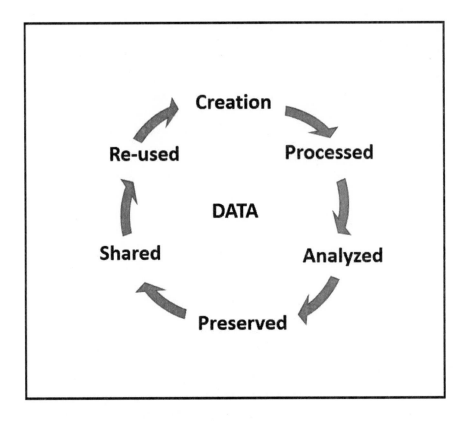

Figure 1.3.   A diagram of the data cycle, demonstrating data as discrete objects to be used and reused over an unspecified time period.

Yet when analyzed more closely, this too fails to fully explain "data." One of the main problems is that data is not always a clearly defined quantity. Indeed, the *OED*'s definition of data does not help clear up matters: "An item of information; a datum; a set of data." This does not satisfy since data could be considered a form of information, and information could be considered a form of data. Though they are not always interchangeable, the two terms are sometimes fused together and are occasionally inseparable. Intelligence is another matter. It can be described in numerous ways as well but not necessarily in terms of gathered data and information. Even examples of "raw data" can be considered primary sources in another field. This definition, for example, of "primary sources" used in the study of history is described as "direct, un-mediated information about the object of study" (Dalton and Charnigo, 2004). So confusion about terminology lingers.

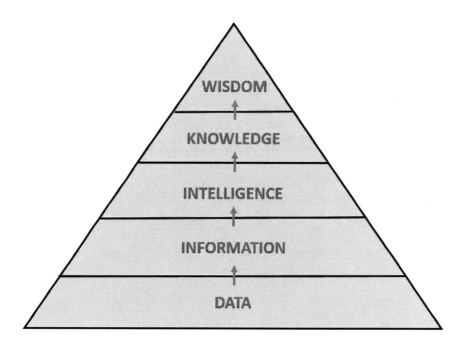

Figure 1.4. A sample information hierarchy (similar to Maslow's hierarchy), with data as the rawest form of information and moving upward to arrive at wisdom.

Hierarchies of Value and the Information Lifecycle

Data is also clearly tied up with and bound to the concept of information itself, but that only serves to confuse the situation even more. Anthony Liew (2007) sees data as a form of "unfiltered information." But unfortunately, the definition breaks down when he tries to define the term "information"; he defines it as "refined data . . . that has evolved to the point of being useful for some form of analysis." Again, he's interchanging the terms to define the other, and his circular logic fails to satisfy.

For several hundred years, libraries have been seen to fit within well-established information and scholarly production life cycles. As shown in figure 1.5, we can see that libraries provide the collection, preservation, and access aspects of information. This life cycle includes publishing as well, which until recently has not been part of the library's role. Yet since the 2000s, as a result of the development on online digital publishing platforms, libraries have been entering the publishing domain. The two cycles are now bridged, as seen above, by the overlapping of publishing and discovery steps in the two cycles. Libraries are now positioned to fill the gap between publication and discovery by creating open-access repositories, digital archives

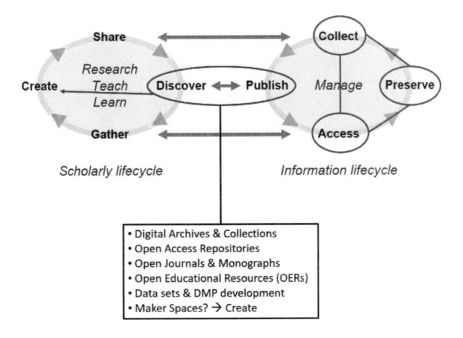

Figure 1.5.   The new model of library, research, and data development; parallel life cycles: scholarly and information life cycles. *Source:* California Digital Library, modified by author.

and collections, open journals, open educational resources (OERs), data set and data-management planning, and the like. It can be argued that the two models become joined once the library engages in the publication and dissemination of data, information, knowledge, and the ultimate goal of wisdom.

Conclusion

It should be clear from our brief analysis that data are not always part of a cyclical or hierarchical process. Some data are generated independently of scholarly activity. Data do not always result in new "information," since data can be considered a form of information itself in different contexts. It is certainly *not* the case that more data equals more intelligence. Knowledge, too, remains a woefully undefined concept, and "any attempt to locate its exact boundaries has nothing solid and reliable to go on" (Williamson, 2016). Yet the concept of data is definitely entwined within such fuzzy constructs and contexts. In fact, one might argue that data derive all meaning from their placement within a discipline and purpose. But if all of these definitions or characterizations and graphic explanations fail to fully explain data, then what is it really? The following section will explore this in more detail and provide us with a clear, working definition of data.

A WORKABLE DEFINITION:
DATA AS *ONTOLOGICAL ASSERTION*

First, going beyond those purely informatics, computational, and numeric definitions of data, we need to establish what data is trying to explain. As Christine Borgman (2015) argues, "Data are representations of observations, objects or other entities used as evidence of phenomena for the purposes of research or scholarship" (p. 28). In other words, there is an act of abstraction occurring in the creation of data itself. She takes it a step further and explains that "conceptualizing something as data is itself a scholarly act" (p. xviii). Data, is therefore a *rhetorical* term, in a sense, and not a discrete *object* or *thing* with an essence of its own (Rosenberg, 2013).

We might also argue that, beyond the physical and quantitative senses of the word, data is very much an *ontological assertion of existence* dependent upon physical, temporal, and cultural contexts, and buttressed by the assumption that something can be learned or derived from the universe. In contrast, one could argue that there would be no data possible in fundamentalism—only faith; there is furthermore no need for data to exist in a faith-based world either, since truth itself would be manifest only in the things that need not or cannot be measured. In essence, from a scientific-humanistic point of view, data is a rhetorical tool for proving our existence and fueling our capacity for reason based on objective observations.

Viewing data in this light, we can also anticipate that the understanding of what constitutes data itself will change dependent upon its context, its intended purpose, and its ultimate use. Therefore, each discipline will have different and even competing understandings of what data represents. But make no mistake, despite the various opinions on what constitutes data, it is still something that "has no essence of its own"; it is a malleable concept dependent upon one's chosen lens. Yet it is a fragile concept too, in the sense that any doubt of our own existence—an extreme position often held by radical skeptics or religious fanatics—can kill its usefulness. Therefore, to get at a clear understanding of data, we also need to examine the concept in wider contexts, especially with regard to purpose and type, general usage, and its overall growth as a tool for scientific inquiry.

Toward the Generation of Knowledge and Wisdom:
Misconceptions or Delusions of Grandeur?

The assertions put forth within the models presented above obviously place us within some untenable positions. We are forced to ask ourselves, Does data *actually* create information? Does knowledge *necessarily* come from information and contribute to our cultural wisdom?

The hierarchical models explored above do provide us with some basis for understanding, yet the development of models ultimately breaks down at the definitional level. Ultimately, if we look at data itself as a lens or a philosophy rather than as an actual thing—as an assertion of reality—then the hierarchy begins to make a little more sense. In some ways Liew's construction of data, information, and knowledge befuddles an already-befuddled approach. If data are merely "records" as he asserts, then how is it also not information and vice versa?

Ultimately any lasting definition of data needs to be seen as an assertion about reality; information is the physical or abstract vehicle of that data (possessed and parsed by human or nonhuman means); and knowledge is the human-readable possession that provides the framework for comparative analysis, prediction, and understanding of the wider world. Wisdom does not necessarily fit within a data paradigm since the assertion that evidence of the world exists need not be one of the tenets of wisdom.

Indeed, one might argue that wisdom exists far outside the realm of evidence as to be closer to enlightenment and personal self-understanding beyond the senses. It is unclear if data actually leads to anything beyond knowledge. Perhaps wisdom—as a concept allegedly extrapolated from the data-information-knowledge hierarchy—would be better relegated to the realms of metaphysics and faith. Perhaps the hierarchy itself needs to be scrapped in place of better, more realistic, and more accurate models.

DATA TYPES

Data Types and the Growth of Data

Now that we have established a workable concept of data, we can focus on some of the ways in which it is then implemented in research projects. The types of data generated and utilized generally fall into two broad types: quantitative, which specifically concerns numerical values; and qualitative, which concerns nonnumerical evidence. At the same time, the difference between quantitative and qualitative is also one of objectivity and subjectivity. Objective descriptions comprise the impartial measurement of items; subjective descriptions comprise things that might not be easily measured without using one's senses, such as smell, taste, touch, emotions, and the like. From a very basic standpoint, when one measures something and assigns numerical values to describe it, one is creating quantitative data; when one classifies or places a subjective judgment upon something, one is creating qualitative data.

When thinking of quantitative data, most people think of digital data as the prime example. It becomes easy to do so when the thing used to define it is itself a numerical value: either a (0) or a (1). This ease of creation and direct linkage to numbers likely contributes to the explosion of quantitative data. But numerical quantitative data need not be primarily digital. It could instead be a series of numbers written on paper and worked into equations or algorithms—computer or otherwise—to solve linear and nonlinear problems.

Quantitative data can be further broken down into discrete values and continuous values. Discrete values are basically countable entities comprised of finite limits, while continuous values comprise, technically speaking, a potentially infinite number of intermediary steps and are used to represent an ongoing, never-ending continuum of values. Values that are considered to be within a range would be continuous (i.e., temperatures), while discrete values may often be considered more binary in nature (i.e., yes/no; on/off; male/female).

Qualitative data can be harder to define at times. Often it has been characterized as whatever is not numerical. Though that is part of the story, it's not the full definition. Subjectively, using qualitative data allows one to provide judgments and orders to things that might not be found primarily in numbers. Although the subjective nature of qualitative data has also been one of its main points of criticism, not everything in the human world can be easily understood in terms of numerical and objective measurement. In that regard, qualitative data provides great insight into processes, ways of thinking, and experiences, as eyewitness accounts used for evidence, and so on. Qualitative data can also be broken down into further subsections dealing with the binomial, ordinal, and nominal aspects of something.

Binomials, for example, deal with dualisms, or binary constructs, such as true/false statements, right/wrong, accept/reject, or good/bad. They allow researchers to order evidence in such a way as to provide easy yes-no valuations of observed phenomena. Again, the simple two-way classification is dependent upon *human valuation* and not external measurements to make it useful and understandable. Ordinal qualitative data, on the other hand, extends this even further by providing a scale to rate and categorize things. A good example of this might be evaluating a film on a scale of zero to five stars. Given a large enough set of this data, one could perhaps extrapolate conclusions about what factors make for a successful and well-reviewed film. Finally, nominal qualitative data creates categories that are not implicitly or explicitly valued over another; the classification merely separates various values from other ones. Classifying the number of balloons in a bag based on color is a good example of this type of nominal data. Having more black balloons than blue balloons doesn't necessarily provide important information about the balloons themselves, or on how they are produced and distributed. It merely demonstrates how they can be identified uniquely (Martz, 2017).

SCHOLARLY COMMUNICATION, MASS DIGITIZATION, AND DATA IN LIBRARIES: GROWING AREAS

The focus of this book is also on how libraries fit within the realm of data, especially as it morphs into the era of "big data." The role that libraries have played in the development of modern data is understood only in part. It is well documented, though often forgotten, that libraries have continually contributed to and improved upon information and scholarly communication infrastructures since the nineteenth century. Libraries developed the foundations of information science with a series of innovations including classification systems (LC and Dewey), the development of controlled vocabularies and taxonomies (LCSH, MESH, etc.), and the resulting open stacks that allowed for the physical, firsthand browsing of library content. Libraries have kept pace with developments in the computer and information technology fields as well. AACR2, one of the first and perhaps the most comprehensive metadata schema ever devised, was developed by libraries for early resource description and then transferred to MARC (MAchine Readable Cataloging), which became a national standard for the digital dissemination of bibliographic data. Its impact lives on in contemporary libraries through the next-generation schema RDA (Resource Description and Access).

The development of online systems and the adoption of the Dublin Core schema, first developed to archive web pages, has allowed a standardized information infrastructure to expand even further. Online digital library collections and institutional repositories have helped to foster this online explosion. Since the 1990s, when the first Electronic Theses and Dissertations (ETDs) projects and online collections were developed in earnest by libraries, one of the central missions has been to archive and save the new digital information generated by new technologies. It took special foresight and understanding by these early pioneers to make the jump from print resources to digital. Some of the first projects, including several started by the Library of Congress, for example, helped to provide the framework for responsible, accountable, sustainable digital systems. Recognizing the malleability of digital content, early developers also sought to create trustworthy repository systems (i.e., Trusted Repositories Audit and Certification [TRAC]) that provide stable provenance for the new digitally available content.

The mid-2000s saw the development of social media and the mass book-digitization projects that gave rise to the massive digital libraries (MDLs) of Google Books, HathiTrust, Internet Archive, Digital Public Library of America, Europeana, and others. These also contribute to the amount of data out there. The mass digitization of books is essentially a new combination of the progression of big data with traditional print-based libraries. All of the written sentences of more than thirty million books have now been converted into one large searchable digital data set; all the information contained in all the digitized books now becomes potential data for researchers to use.

The copyright concerns raised by the Authors Guild in its two suits against Google and HathiTrust respectively may be alleviated by the rulings, but they still don't fully address the transformation of our literature into data. The implications of this change are still unknown. On one hand, Google and HathiTrust now provide these digital corpuses for researchers to explore and perhaps create new knowledge and inventions. But the control of our culture, as Jean-Noel Jeanneney presciently warned in 2005, is slowly being removed from our hands and placed into the interests of corporate entities that may or may not have our best interests at heart (Jeanneney, 2007). It remains to be seen if this is will have net-positive or net-negative effects. The Ngram viewer developed by Google, as seen in figure 1.6, for example, provides researchers with important data for historical information, but problems with the book scans, their metadata, their findability, and their representation of the culture at large still remain endemic to the service (Weiss and James, 2014).

Although MDLs are an extreme example of the "datalization of the word," data itself nevertheless continue to grow through research projects at all levels of society. Yet despite being willing to take on this challenge of

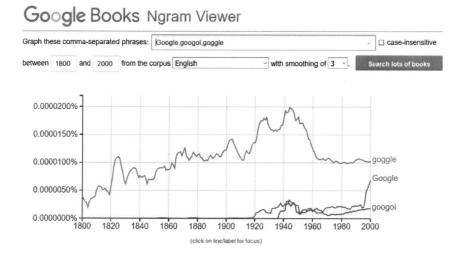

Figure 1.6.   Screenshot from Google's Ngram viewer showing the prevalence of the terms *goggle*, *google*, and *googol* from the years AD 1800 to 2000.

managing and archiving vast amounts of data, libraries are struggling with their new role as data steward. They are finding it difficult to determine the *extent* of the data that needs to be archived. In studies done by several researchers, there is a noticeable lack of understanding about the extent of the problem. Jeremy York and colleagues (2016) describe this as a "stewardship gap." In their own research they attempt to find out the amount of data that exists and how much needs to be preserved. Each academic and public institution may eventually need to consider how much data there really is and find methods to tackle this problem.

Unfortunately, the problem will only get worse until either simplified turnkey solutions are developed or the explosion of data becomes so self-evident that regional and national policies and procedures are developed to accommodate it. However, the solutions are not necessarily clearly laid out at this point.

REFERENCES

Borgman, C. (2015). *Big data, little data, no data: Scholarship in the networked world.* Cambridge, MA: MIT Press.

Caldwell, S. (1959). The sinotype—a machine for the composition of Chinese from a keyboard. *Journal of the Franklin Institute, 267*(6), 471–502. http://dx.doi.org/10.1016/0016-0032(59)90069-9.

Dalton, M., and Charnigo, L. (2004). Historians and their information sources. *College and Research Libraries , 65*(5), 400–425.

Drake, S. (1957). *Discoveries and opinions of Galileo.* New York: Doubleday.

Google. (2016). Google Books Ngram Viewer. https://books.google.com/ngrams.

Jeanneney, J-N. (2007). *Google and the myth of universal knowledge: A view from Europe.* Chicago: University of Chicago Press.

Kuhn, T. (1962). *The structure of scientific revolutions.* Chicago: University of Chicago Press.

Liew, A. (2007). Understanding data, information, knowledge and their inter-relationships. *Journal of Knowledge Management Practice, 8*(2). http://www.tlainc.com.

Martz, E. (2014). Understanding qualitative, quantitative, attribute, discrete and continuous data types. *Minitab Blog.* http://blog.minitab.com.

Mullaney, T. (2016). How Cold War rivalry helped launch the Chinese computer. Aeon. https://aeon.co/ideas/how-cold-war-rivalry-helped-launch-the-chinese-computer.

Oestreicher, C. (2007). A history of chaos theory. *Dialogues in Clinical Neuroscience, 9*(3), 279–289. https://www.ncbi.nlm.nih.gov.

Rosenberg, D. (2013). Data before the fact. In Lisa Gitelman (Ed.), *"Raw data" is an oxymoron* (pp. 15–40). Cambridge, MA: MIT Press.

Science Stuff. (2007). Science fair projects on the web. http://sciencestuff.com.

UC Curation Center and California Digital Library. (2010). UC3 Curation Foundations. https://www.google.com.

Weiss, A., and James, R. (2014). *Using massive digital libraries: A LITA guide.* Chicago: ALA TechSource, an imprint of the American Library Association.

Williamson, T. (2016). On vagueness, or, when is a heap of sand not a heap of sand? Aeon. https://aeon.co/ideas/on-vagueness-when-is-a-heap-of-sand-not-a-heap-of-sand.

York, J., Gutman M., and Berman, F. (2016). Will today's data be here tomorrow? Measuring the stewardship gap. iPRES Conference 2016 Proceedings, 102–111. http://www.ipres2016.ch.

Chapter Two

The Birth of Big Data

THE GROWTH OF DATA AND THE WEB: "DATALIZATION" OF THE WORLD, BUTTERFLIES, AND PERFECT STORMS

As seen in the previous chapter, data can be a rather slippery concept, and it would be better defined as a *concept* rather than as discrete numerical units. It should be noted that adding to the general confusion about defining data is the fact that in general parlance people seem to consider digitalized information as functionally equivalent to data. This transformation of the term from a generic concept to a discrete digital numerical "object"—insofar as a magnetic on/off switch numbered zero or one can actually "be" an object—has contributed to the misunderstandings about how to define data. Of course, now that anything can be "digitalized," the reasoning goes, anything can become data. We might call it the "datalization of the world," even at the expense of other forms of data.

How Did We Get to This Point?

Several factors have contributed to this increase in the amount of digital data generated. The most obvious of these has been the development of digital information systems. In library circles, the development of the personal computer is often seen as presaged by the thinker/scientist/bureaucrat Vannevar Bush. His vision for a "Memex" machine is often seen as a prescient prediction of the personalization of information—"an enlarged intimate supplement to one's memory," he called it—and the development of *hypertext* (Bush, 1945). The resulting developments of computer science during the 1950s and 1960s and afterward ushered in this new era of widespread digital information infrastructure.

In the same Bell Laboratory that Bush worked in the 1940s, Claude Shannon was also developing what became the foundations of modern digital information theory. His 1948 paper "A Mathematical Theory of Communication" outlined a new conception of information itself, abstracted from analog formats into digital ones (Shannon, 1948). Essentially, Shannon argued that one can code any message into bits, without knowing the destination; conversely, one can transmit and stream without knowing the source. Prior to this, there was little sense of information as an idea or as a measurable quantity. Subsequently, Shannon's conception helped information become stripped from its physical container, allowing for its ease of transmission, alteration, and separation from the physical world from which it was derived (Soni and Goodman, 2017). In retrospect, it seems obvious that once data and information were released from their contextual bindings and analog containers—which also served as their primary methods of conveyance—the proliferation of digital information through electronic means was a matter of time.

Complicating matters in tracing the development of the current data deluge, though, is the complementary and parallel development of the "information workforce"; as Edward Wolff (2005) observes, "We have moved from a society in which we work with our hands to one in which we work with our mind" (p. 38). Workers dealing with information and information technology of some form shifted from 36 percent of the workforce in 1950 to 59 percent by 2000. Noninformation workers, including manufacturing positions, declined by 22 percent during the same period (ibid.). Doubtless, the shift has accelerated over the past seventeen years. Though Wolff's statistics may be difficult to convert, and the term "information worker" may no longer be fashionable or applicable, statistics from a study in 2005 show rates of "knowledge workers" ranging from a low of 28 percent of the workforce (Davenport, 2005) to 45 percent (McKellar, 2005). Jump ahead five years to 2010, and a recent article by John Hagel and colleagues in the *Harvard Business Review* poses the question of whether by this point in time *all* workers shouldn't be considered "knowledge workers."

Though Bush suggested that all people might own their own Memex in the mid-1940s—complete with its own information-storage devices—he likely never envisioned the current state of affairs. Indeed, in contrast to the steadier growth and slow gravitation toward information or knowledge worker positions in the American workforce, the growth of digital data itself has grown at a far faster rate in the same period of time. In the early 1950s, the amount of digital data generated and stored was negligible, constrained by the low capacity of storage devices, slow calculation speeds, and immense expensive, and literally "buggy" hardware.

The improvements in capacity, speed, and hardware stability simultaneously increased and evolved as new technologies were developed to save, store, and transfer information. In the mid-1980s, with materials such as LP records, cassette and VHS tapes, and physical books in common usage, the amount of information in analog form represented about 2.6 exabytes (1 EB $= 10^{18}$ bytes of information), while digital information represented only about 0.02 exabytes of the whole. By 1993, the rate had remained mostly the same though, at approximately 3 percent of all information. By 2000, however, the amount of digital information had reached 25 percent of the total and then doubled to 50 percent by 2002. Martin Hilbert and Priscila López have dubbed this line of demarcation where digital information surpassed half of all information as the "beginning of the information age" (Hilbert and López, 2011). By 2007, 94 percent of the information saved, roughly 280 of 300 exabytes, was digital; the remaining 6 percent was comprised of analog materials.

The steady yet incessant growth of data has been documented by others as well in terms of the amount of information transferred or existing in the world. The information age was designated in various eras ranging from gigabyte to petabyte (2008–2015; Hilbert, 2016; *Nature*, 2008). Now, according to Cisco Systems estimates, we have reached the "Zettabyte Era" (1 ZB $= 10^{21}$ bytes). By 2016 it was estimated that annual global IP data transfer would equal 1 zettabyte of information, with 2.3 ZB transferred per year by 2020 (CISCO, 2016). Data projections suggest the deluge of total information will reach unimaginable proportions, growing tenfold from 4.4 ZB of data in 2014 to 44 ZB by 2020 (*Computer Weekly*, 2014; NJIT, 2016). The growth rate, as it can be seen in figure 2.1, seems to be supported by Hilbert's analysis as well (2016). Beyond that it's anyone's guess, though yottabyte (1 YB $= 10^{24}$ bytes), xenottabyte (10^{27} bytes), shilentnobyte (10^{30} bytes), and domegemegrottebyte (10^{33} bytes) are apparently the next steps in the numbering system—though this is unofficial and beyond the scope of the International Bureau of Weights and Measures (BIPM) standard prefixes of international units (Hoff, 2012).

Chaotic Butterflies: Emergent Systems and Modeling as a Data-Analysis Tool

However, the improved technology of data storage and information transfer alone does not sufficiently explain the current explosions in data growth, especially in the sciences and other research fields. For as the size of data has increased, so have the uses for data become more widespread. Important applicable and standardized uses for data have to exist for it to grow at this rate. One area that has been quick to adopt large-scale data usage is the physical sciences. Importantly, there have been specific advances in science and the scientific method that have helped researchers gather evidence in

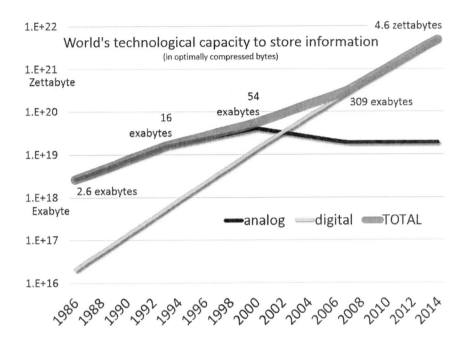

Figure 2.1.   Graph depicting the capacity of information storage and growth of telecom capacity. *Source:* **Hilbert, 2016.**

new ways, with new electronic monitoring systems and computer calculations providing the necessary tools to both generate and parse large data sets.

One of the great examples of the impact of computer science and information-technology developments on improving scientific inquiry can be seen in the establishment of emergent dynamic systems theory (also known as chaos theory). Emergent systems and complexity theory are interrelated and reliant upon the data and data sets that are the basis of computer simulations. The need for data sets and digital computing processes became essential for this branch of the sciences and now has become adopted in all branches of science, ranging from weather systems to medicine (i.e., heart rhythms, EKGs, etc.), economic theory, and the political sciences. As Christian Oestreicher writes, chaos theory "enables the description of a series of phenomena from the field of dynamics" (Oestreicher, 2007, p. 279). However, one can also argue that the processes to help demonstrate the importance of the field itself and provide the necessary visualization as proof and evidence of the phenomenon would not exist without the development of digital media, and large-scale data computations.

The most notable example of this new "description . . . of phenomena" in dynamics occurred in the early 1960s with Edward Lorenz and what he later called "strange attractors." Others have nicknamed this the "butterfly effect," where small minor variations in a localized area end up creating larger-scale anomalies and variations. These variations in the initial conditions "all land on the same object in the shape of a butterfly" (see figure 2.2) and wind up being predictable in their own right (Leys, Ghys, and Alvarez, n.d.). Stephen Wolfram on his website describes it as follows:

> In 1962 . . . Edward Lorenz did a computer simulation of a set of simplified differential equations for fluid convection . . . in which he saw complicated behavior that seemed to depend sensitively on initial conditions. . . . In the mid-1960s, notably through the work of Steve Smale, proofs were given that there could be differential equations in which such sensitivity is generic. In the late 1960s there began to be all sorts of simulations of differential equations with complicated behavior, first mainly on analog computers, and later on digital computers. (Wolfram, 2002)

This reliance on computation and modeling from previously unpatterned data sets has had an immense impact on the science that followed it. Ultimately, chaos theory is but one example of thousands in which data computation and data modeling become central to conducting science. Modeling is now standard operating procedure for numerous disciplines interested in replicating changes and demonstrating the power of computerized data. Other fields such as biology have taken up with data development, using servers to run their own modeling of the natural world (Mackelprang, 2016). Physicists, too, collect large data sets from their information-gathering processes. According to latest statistics, the European Organization for Nuclear Research (CERN) at the writing of this book generates approximately thirty petabytes of data annually (thirty times one million gigabytes; CERN, 2016; Warmbein, 2015). But it is important to keep in mind that the jump from analog computation to digital computers has allowed for the increase in both accuracy of the models created and the aggregation and analysis of extremely large data sets—especially as analysis begins to move from *ex-ante* to *postfactum* data interpretation. There is bound to be impact on the scientific method as well, especially as data in the aggregate begins to replace random sampling from smaller data sets (Hilbert, 2016). The impact of the digital in this deluge cannot be understated as it essentially has the power to alter, for better and for worse, the scientific method itself.

Coming Together: Perfect Storms

As suggested above, factors in the wider world contribute to the increase in the amount of data generated. Certainly, computers are now ubiquitous. The internet has become the de facto connective tool for the modern world. Cheaper data storage has allowed digital information to become the standard

Figure 2.2.   Strange attractors or the "butterfly effect" demonstrating a visualization of small factors aggregating to impact later developments but in clear, predictable ways. *Source:* **Wikipedia, Creative Commons 3.0 BY-SA.**

for all disciplines. Moore's law implies that the improvements of computers will continue at a rapid pace, doubling in capacity and speed every couple years.

However, missing from the discussion so far is the impact that "connections," or "connectivity," has had on the world of data exchange. For it is the connectivity from the various decentralized nodes—grassroots connections essentially—that have brought it all together to create the perfect conditions for exponential growth. The continual, iterative development of communications and wireless systems also provides the essential infrastructure for increased data sharing and transfer. Nova Spivack suggests that it is not just the connections between information but also the connections between people that have fueled the development of new web technologies and even new versions of the web (Spivack, 2007).

As seen in figure 2.3, we might currently position ourselves somewhere between Web 2.0 and Web 3.0 in terms of advancement beyond social media. Certainly Web 2.0 was a fundamental shift in the development of the internet and the way that humans connect. The current influence of Facebook, Google, Microsoft, Twitter, and so forth, cannot be denied. However, what lies beyond them? What lies beyond the viral videos of cats or babies eating chocolate cake? Some might say nothing. But certainly the web as an operating system for all types of software solutions is becoming a reality. Adobe no longer licenses standalone software; Google provides "Drive" for digital documents and spreadsheets; and primitive personal agents with proto-AI are beginning to tailor users' web-driven experiences. Ads targeting users based on their browsing and purchase behaviors have become the standard experience for all internet users. This suggests that the "semantic web," a term derived from the mid-2000s, is nevertheless in full swing. Yet beyond the semantic web awaits the so-called intelligent web, which is estimated to be in full force between 2020 and 2030, a mere half decade away. This would include unforeseen technologies that go beyond the screen and hint toward all-encompassing, immersive experiences of internet connectivity and the

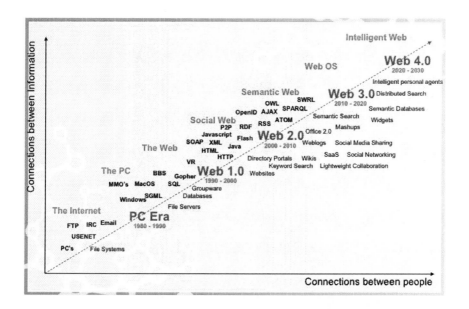

Figure 2.3. "Intelligence Is in the Connections" diagram; depicts the development of the web over time as a function of improved connections between information resources and between people. *Source:* Spivack, 2007.

tailoring of content to fit specific user needs at all times. The internet of things should be considered a step in this direction toward Web 3.0 and 4.0 and beyond.

Social Media

In terms of actual data generation, without getting too far into it, the social media explosion has also contributed greatly to this data explosion. It has been reported that Facebook, for example, in the third quarter of 2016 had roughly 1.75 billion active monthly users (Statista, 2016). Users uploaded three hundred million photos *daily*, 136,000 each *minute*. Users spend approximately twenty minutes on Facebook per visit. They generated or transferred 4.75 billion pieces of content daily in 2013 (Zephoria, 2016). We will examine these astounding statistics and their impact on people in subsequent chapters. But for now, these small examples of the amount of data generated, uploaded, and transferred clearly demonstrate that data has moved beyond our capacity to easily organize, understand, and analyze it.

IoT: The Internet of Things

This situation will only increase as other types of things besides computers and mobile devices (smartphones, iPads, etc.) come online. Once physical objects and tools become linked to the web and provide useful web analytics, the real explosion will occur. The nascent term "internet of things," or IoT, promises to fill in many of the gaps that prevent the full tracking of people's daily activities. Beyond the sedentary face time spent in front of a computer or phone screen, the IoT will provide data from numerous daily activities, including television watching, cooking, food consumption rates (based on contents of a refrigerator, for example), water and electrical usage rates, exercise regimens, and the like. But as Daniel Burrus writes in *Wired*, "When people talk about 'the next big thing,' they're never thinking big enough. It's not a lack of imagination; it's a lack of observation" (Burrus, 2014). The point is that we have underestimated the impact of things before, and the internet of things will be no different.

Indeed, what we're witnessing is the automation of communication and the insertion of quantified analysis into the rhythms and routines of daily life. It is essentially "machine-to-machine" communication, which outstrips and even makes irrelevant our basic human abilities to respond and analyze, that is used to examine our own interior and private lives. Consequently, estimates on the growth of the internet of things range from the low billions of connected items to the trillions (Howard, 2015). The potential for market growth is there. With 7.5 billion people in the world, such a data trail of marketable and monetized information would be immense.

Defining Big Data, or How Big Is Your Data Set?

What comes next, however, has certainly been impacted by the major factors outlined above. The ease of social media and the internet of things to situate and insinuate themselves into the daily lives of users has become a major growth factor. People's behaviors can be tracked based on how they interact with each other as well as how they interact with their devices, appliances, and assorted "things."

The term "big data" itself is quite generic, though telling, on par with the technophobic and somewhat derogatory terms such as big money, big government, big media, and so forth, which imply that their sizes amount to an abuse of power or indicate a sector that is out of the control of the "little" people. Francis Diebold (2012), who originally asserted he had coined the term, now suggests that "the term big data . . . probably originated in lunch-table conversations at Silicon Graphics Inc. (SGI) in the mid-1990s"; he also suggests that along with SGI lead scientist John Mashey, a few researchers in the field of computer science and economics—notably Sholom Weiss and Nitin Indurkhya (1998), Diebold (2000), and Douglass Laney (2001)—are ultimately the real pioneers of the term (Lohr, 2013). Very few, though, have had as much impact on the parameters of the term "big data" as Laney. Originally a data scientist at META group, Laney was the first to define big data as comprising of "three Vs" (volume, variety, and velocity) in an unpublished yet influential report (Laney, 2001). These vectors allowed one to define the scale, scope, and speed with which digital information could proliferate. It is still a compelling and useful method to help define "big data" and to help differentiate it from "normal" or "little" data.

Others have proposed further refinements to the original 3Vs by suggesting two more parameters, variability and veracity, to define the term. Both additions attempt to help define the quality of the data itself, that is, is it consistent as a data set? Is it reliable? Is it based on accurate measurements or readings? The proposed 5V criteria for big data and a clear explanation each are shown in table 2.1.

As useful as this set of criteria is, some are not convinced that the 5Vs accurately define all of what big data entails. Certainly the scope, speed, and scale of the data are important distinctions; consistency and accuracy are also essential—but that is important for all data sets, not just the "biggest of the big." The set of criteria also doesn't get at how data is used or what impact it might have on users and subjects compared with normal data.

Big Data: A "Pose" by Any Other Name?

In the absence of clear answers to these issues, others have attempted to define big data in ironically less quantifiable ways. Alex (Sandy) Pentland

Table 2.1.   "5V" criteria for defining and identifying big data.

Criteria	Description
Volume	The quantity of generated and stored data; large volumes of data provide a significant source of information for analysis.
Variety	The type and nature of the data; knowing this determines how it is to be used for analysis.
Velocity	The speed at which the data is generated and processed; speed of generation can provide insights as well as hindrances for accurate analysis.
Variability	The consistency or measure of sameness/uniformity of the data; inconsistency of the data can hamper processes to handle and manage it.
Veracity	The quality or accuracy of the captured data; quality can vary within a data set, affecting the analysis and impeding its usefulness.

(Edge, 2012), for example, defines big data as data about how people *behave* rather than their personally stated or proffered beliefs. He says, "I believe that the power of big data is that it is *information about people's behavior* instead of information about their beliefs. . . . It's the little data breadcrumbs that you leave behind you as you move around in the world" (Edge, 2012).

Hilbert takes this a step further and suggests that the "full name of big data should really be 'Big Data Analytics'" (Hilbert, 2016). One needs to consider, he argues, data independently from the "specific peta-, exa-, or zettabytes scale" and focus more on the process of making decisions based on the volume of information. He asserts that the ultimate goal is "analysis for intelligent decision-making," something that, as we see above with Nova Spivack's theories on intelligence and connections, is clearly progressing in time and providing the essential feedback loops and recursive thinking necessary to foster essential and intelligent solutions.

However, much as we saw in the previous chapter with "regular" data, despite the dominance of the 5Vs and the theories of Pentland, Spivack, and Hilbert, there is little consensus on the definition of big data. Other scholars and writers suggest variants on the characteristics of the term. For example, Peter Schilling and Kevin Bozic describe big data as a "*moving target . . .* [that] refers to the explosion of digitized data created by people, machines, sensors, tools and other mechanisms" (Schilling and Bozic, 2014, p. 3270). They continue by asserting that the most important aspect of big data is "not so much its size, but that it contains hidden as signal within noise some valuable predictive information" (p. 3270). Schilling and Bozic see it more as a code to be cracked—with something inherently valuable lurking within it, if only one can find it—and used for the sake of predicting future behaviors or conditions. The danger of this approach, of course, is that one can go looking for patterns in every corner and conveniently find one lurking there.

Additionally, Andrea De Mauro and colleagues (2014) assert that "big data represents the information assets characterized by such a High Volume, Velocity, and Variety to require specific technology and analytical methods *for its transformation into Value*." What's important to see is that the first three Vs are not as important as the striving toward some creation, or in their words, "transformation," into something with capital "v" Value. Yet Value itself is an incredibly abstract and loose term that is slippery at best and changes within the context it is placed. If the most important thing about big data is its "Value," what defines it will arguably change (for better or for worse) depending upon the values that define its current context. As a result, nothing universal could be determined by defining big data in this fashion.

Furthermore, some contend that one of the characteristics often touted about big data—its independence from hypothesis to derive conclusions as a result of its massive scale—is also one of its major flaws. This is a flaw that could be just as easily exploited as the variability of the contextual value placed upon it. Trevor Barnes suggests, "The past remains potent for big data and that proponents ignore it at their peril" (Barnes, 2013, p. 297); Danah Boyd and Kate Crawford assert, "Taken out of context, big data loses its meaning" (Boyd and Crawford, 2012, p. 670). This potential loss or compromising of the context in big data sets is a cause for major concern. As seen in previous chapter, data become meaningless when they are untethered to their origins or their reality. Without that connection, data become meaningless figures. Aside from the loss of information, the data could also be manipulated by compromised interests and used to draw unfounded or intentionally misleading conclusions—disinformation, in other words.

It is important to keep in mind, then, as definitions of big data are created and modified to meet new wrinkles as they appear, that many of the concepts are defined by the current prejudices of the definers. Many have a stake in suggesting, for example, that data has no connection to the past or is untethered to hypothesis, as it provides an easy justification for questionable or unregulated business practices. Furthermore, artificial intelligence aside, no one can currently replace the human side of the process: human analysis and interpretation of results are still necessary to draw wider, valid conclusions. Simply detecting patterns and correlations will not necessarily prove causation; indeed, the many false correlations that might arise without clearly examining logical fallacies should be considered a major misstep in the use of big data.

REFERENCES

Barnes, T. J. (2013). Big data, little history. *Dialogues in Human Geography, 3*(3), 297–302.

Boyd, D., and Crawford, K. (2012). Critical questions for big data. *Information, Communication and Society, 15*(5), 662–679. doi:10.1080/1369118X.2012.678878.

Burrus, D. (2014). The internet of things is far bigger than anyone realizes. *Wired.* https://www.wired.com.

Bush, V. (1945). As we may think. *Atlantic Monthly, 176*(1), 101–108.

CERN. (2016). Computing. https://home.cern.

CISCO. (2016). The zettabyte era: Trends and analysis. http://www.cisco.com.

Computer Weekly. (2014). Data set to grow 10-fold by 2020 as internet of things takes off. http://www.computerweekly.com.

Davenport, T. (2005). *Thinking for a living: How to get better performance and results from knowledge workers.* Boston: Harvard Business School Press.

De Mauro, A., Greco, M., and Grimaldi, M. (2014). What is big data? A consensual definition and a review of key research topics. Presented at the 4th International Conference on Integrated Information, Madrid. doi:10.13140/2.1.2341.5048.

Diebold, F. X. (2000). "Big Data Dynamic Factor Models for Macroeconomic Measurement and Forecasting." Discussion Read to the Eighth World Congress of the Econometric Society, Seattle, August. http://www.ssc.upenn.edu/~fdiebold/papers/paper40/temp-wc.PDF.

Diebold, F. X. (2012). A Personal perspective on the origin(s) and development of "big data": The phenomenon, the term, and the discipline. Penn Institute for Economic Research (PIER) Working Paper 13-003. https://papers.ssrn.com.

Edge. (2012). Reinventing society in the wake of big data, a conversation with Alex (Sandy) Pentland. http://www.edge.org.

Hagel, J., Brown, J. and Davison, L. (2010). Are all employees knowledge workers? *Harvard Business Review.* https://hbr.org.

Hilbert, M. (2016). Big data for development: A review of promises and challenges. *Development Policy Review, 34*(1), 135–174. http://www.martinhilbert.net.

Hilbert, M., and López, P. (2011). The world's technological capacity to store, communicate, and compute information. *Science, 332*(6025), 60–65. doi:10.1126/science.1200970.

Hoff, T. (2012). How big is a petabyte, exabyte, zettabyte, or a yottabyte? *High Scalability* (blog). http://highscalability.com.

Howard, P. (2015). Sketching out the internet of things trendline. Brookings. https://www.brookings.edu.

Laney, D. (2001). 3D data management: Controlling data volume, velocity and variety. *Gartner.* Unpublished white paper.

Leys, J., Ghys, E., and Alvarez, A. (n.d.). Chaos VII: Strange attractors; The butterfly effect. CHAOS: A Mathematical Adventure. http://www.chaos-math.org.

Lohr, S. (2013). The origins of "big data": An etymological detective story. *New York Times,* February 1, 2013. http://bits.blogs.nytimes.com.

Mackelprang, R. (2016). Mackelprang lab. http://www.csun.edu.

McKellar, H. (2005). The knowledge (worker) economy. *KM World.* http://www.kmworld.com.

Nature. (2008). Big data: Science in the petabyte era. Editor's summary. http://www.nature.com.

New Jersey Institute of Technology (NJIT). (2016). Big data and the IoT: The future of the smart city. http://graduatedegrees.online.njit.edu.

Oestreicher, C. (2007). A history of chaos theory. *Dialogues in Clinical Neuroscience, 9*(3), 279–289. https://www.ncbi.nlm.nih.gov.

Schilling, P., and Bozic, K. (2014). The big to do about "big data." *Clinical Orthopaedics and Related Research , 472*(11), 3270–3272.

Shannon, C. (1948). A mathematical theory of communication. *Bell System Technical Journal, 27,* 379–423. http://math.harvard.edu.

Soni, J., and Goodman, R. (2017). A man in a hurry: Claude Shannon's New York years. IEEE Spectrum. http://spectrum.ieee.org.

Spivack, N. (2007). Making sense of the semantic web. http://www.slideshare.net/syawal/nova-spivack-semantic-web-talk.

Statista. (2016). Statistics and facts about Facebook. https://www.statista.com.

Warmbein, B. (2015). Big data takes ROOT. CERN. https://home.cern.

Weiss, S. M., and Indurkhya, N. (1998). *Predictive Data Mining: A Practical Guide*. Burlington, MA: Morgan Kaufmann.

Wolff, E. (2005). The growth of information workers in the U.S. economy. Association for Computing Machinery. *Communications of the ACM, 48*(10), 37–42.

Wolfram, S. (2002). History of chaos theory. Wolfram Science. https://www.wolframscience.com.

Zephoria. (2016). The top 20 valuable Facebook statistics. Updated December 2016. https://zephoria.com.

Chapter Three

Approaches and Tools for Analyzing and Using Big Data

The Application of Data in Real-Life Situations

THE BASICS OF DATA-ANALYSIS TOOLS

Now that we have come to a basic framework to define big data, we now need to look at the approaches and tools that have been created to use it and the examples of how they are being implemented in the world at large. Data mining provides a good starting point for this discussion. Data mining is defined as "the process of analyzing data from different perspectives and summarizing it into useful information—information that can be used to increase revenue, cuts costs, or both" (Palace, 1996). Through this process, information is analyzed for the patterns it may possess within a particular database or data set. The data is then examined in order to find specific types of relationships among information stored within. These relationships include the following subdivisions: *classes*, which are specific groups of things or people that share characteristics; *clusters*, which are items grouped by logical relationship or preferences; *associations*, which are items or objects found linked together in some capacity, though not necessarily tied together, it should be noted, in direct *causal* relationships (since associations or correlations do not equate causation); and *sequences*, which are behavioral patterns and trends that suggest *direct cause-effect relationships*. Obviously, sequences are seen by many researchers as the most promising aspect of analyzing big data, and one of the most highly desired results of big data analysis, since determining a cause-effect relationship makes predicting the future (or future behaviors) a lot easier.

In this light, big data may really be nothing more than the implementation of previously developed data-mining techniques but on a much grander scale. Such techniques will be evident in the major elements employed in data mining, including extracting, transforming, and loading data onto a system; storing and managing data in a multidimensional database system; providing access to numerous analysts (on an open-access and proprietary basis); analyzing data by application software; and presenting data in useful formats, visualized in a graph, table, or interactive web-based widget. Additionally, there are multiple types of analysis performed on these data sets, including "artificial neural networks," which are nonlinear predictive models that learn through training, similar to biological neural networks; "genetic algorithms," defined as "a method for solving both constrained and unconstrained optimization problems based on a natural selection process that mimics biological evolution" (MathWorks, 2017); and "decision trees," which are tree-shaped structures representing sets of decisions. The decisions then generate rules for the classification of a data set; the "nearest neighbor method," which classifies each record in a data set based on a combination of the classes of the k record(s) most similar to it in a historical data set; the "rule induction," which is the extraction of if-then rules from data based on their statistical significance; and finally, "data visualization," which is the visual interpretation of complex relationships in multidimensional data (Palace, 1996). Along the lines of Martin Hilbert (2016), one of the leading information scientists currently working today, two distinct areas might be considered regarding the classification of big data: the first classification is *tracking* and the second is *mining*. I consider tracking to be a technique for the analysis and rendering of real-time data; mining would refer to previously created data, or "historical data sets," that may have been unlocked through digitization and the aggregation of digital content that might not have been possible to collect before.

A prime example showing the distinction between mining and tracking would be the Google, Internet Archive, and HathiTrust book-scanning projects, all of which have digitally scanned and aggregated online the digital metadata of millions of print books and their database records. Mining the data sets of previously published materials provides a snapshot into how and what people were thinking and writing in various eras, ranging from the earliest print books to the present day. The resulting analyses of these records and texts provides information of use to historians of the word and can provide useful tools for the examination of past events.

Twitter feeds, on the other hand, provide researchers with current, up-to-date and ongoing, real-time information on what people are thinking about as events unfold. The "tracking" aspect is then defined as something to help predict what *might* happen *next*, especially with regard to user behaviors, wants and needs, and desires and dislikes. By examining events as they unfold, researchers could anticipate how people might react to future events such as earthquakes or pandemics. They might also predict what they will purchase or watch depending on demographics or event conditions and parameters.

In this regard, big data should be seen as a two-pronged approach to examining human behavior that is equally concerned with the prediction of future actions as it is with the analytical inquiry of behaviors that have already occurred.

TRACKING

Hilbert (2016) examines tracking at length in his report "Big Data for Development: A Review of Promises and Challenges." Tracking encompasses recording and evaluating the words and thoughts that are written by online users, the locations indicating where they are, the self-reportage and automatic disclosures of what they are doing, and self-reportage and automatic disclosures of what they think and feel. Tracking can be applied to digital words created in social media, the locations broadcast by cell-phone technology, the human reactions to epidemics or natural disasters, and the records of financial transactions and personal behavior that happen to be captured by online digital technologies (Hilbert, 2016). He cautions that one needs to be careful of the things said in online environments as they have become susceptible to long-term examination and analysis. The ultimate goal of tracking, though, is not necessarily to surveil people in order to *curtail* their actions—though this is an essential aspect to spying and homeland security initiatives—but to tap into big data's predictive ability, allowing one to anticipate future actions for one's own profit on the one hand and for societal benefit on the other. This section will examine the various types of tracking currently used.

Word Tracking

This process involves tracking in real time—or in a set of limited time parameters—the frequency with which specific terms appear. These are subsequently mapped to hypotheses and predictions about future events or future behaviors. A representative work in the study of this area is Daniel Gruhl and colleagues' research regarding the "predictive power" of "online chatter" (2005). These days, real-world examples of word tracking abound. For example, various researchers have examined Google's search engine and how real-time searches for particular topics reflect events in the real world as they unfold, or as they had unfolded over a past period of time (Althouse, Ng, and Cummings, 2011).

Researchers, however, have noted limitations in the ability to correlate events with actual search behavior. Some of the limitations are due to the

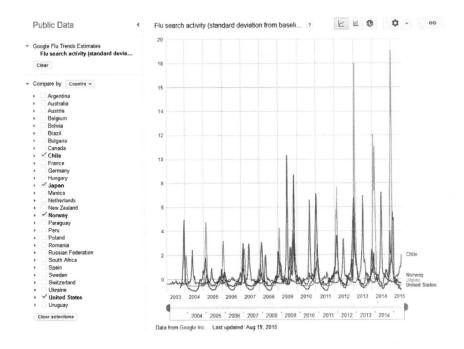

Figure 3.1.   Visualization of flu data showing four countries' variations in flu frequency. *Source:* Google, 2017.

questionable assumption that search actions are generally based on current, salient events. Indeed, there may be other motivations striking searchers at the time of inquiry that cannot be fully accounted for (Manovich, 2012). One perfect example of this is Google's flu trends (GFT), as seen in figure 3.1. At the time of its earliest implementation, the project was notoriously poor in predicting the outbreak during the 2013 flu season. As David Lazer and Ryan Kennedy (2015) state, "GFT failed—and failed spectacularly—missing at the peak of the 2013 flu season by 140 percent." The causes of this failure are unclear, though it seems likely, according to the authors, that the algorithm set up to track the words was applied incorrectly. This caused specific terms to be weighted more than they might actually have been worth. Furthermore, a correlation might have been assumed by the creators of the application, despite results possibly being based on chance alone. The conclusion one can draw from this example is that the data are only as good as the tools used to parse them. While word tracking may provide a representation of activities in the real world, gaps may exist between the intention and the reality.

Location Tracking

The ability to triangulate location based on mobile phones and mobile-device technology networks has allowed organizations to track where people are at specific moments in time. It furthermore provides a modicum of predictability in terms of determining where and when people might gather. Implementations are based on tracking how, why, and when people move from one location to another. Humans are subject to change, and the implementation of these studies allows researchers to understand better the motivations that literally "move" people.

Real-world examples of this type of tracking include examining migration patterns, especially as a result of catastrophic events and their impact upon people's behavior and movements. Also, the tracking of locations involves not just people but also appliances, machines, handheld portable devices, and automobiles. Location tracking can examine, for example, automobile traffic patterns in order to provide a real-time picture of traffic conditions, or to predict when traffic will be at its best or its worst at any given time. Monitoring crime and other police work is also an example of utilizing location tracking. This is used especially to estimate the potential for and probability of crime occurring based on people's movements and gatherings.

Obviously in the case of crime prevention, it is difficult to predict what people will do at any given moment. Getting a sense of how people might react on a large scale is certainly possible with macrochanges and macro-migration movements possible, but individuals are notoriously unpredictable. Is flock behavior accurate? What role does statistical error play in trying to examine human behavior? Is it justified to arrest a person with a 97 percent chance of committing a crime before it is committed? Predicting people's safety is certainly an important factor and motivation for tracking location and people's actions within certain situations, but it also raises the problem of one's sense of freedom and how that relates to crime, punishment, disaster, and personal agency. All of these important issues have yet to be fully addressed by people, governments, businesses, and nongovernmental organizations. It is hoped future laws and regulations will address them.

Nature Tracking

The natural world is notoriously difficult to predict. Earthquakes and tornadoes, weather and climate patterns, wildfires, mudslides, and the like, are all subject to drastic changes over time as parts of dynamic systems. As seen in the previous chapter, dynamic systems can nevertheless be predicted provided one has a sufficient amount of data to create models. Implementations of these models are based on monitoring condition changes in locales through the data gathered by devices or sensors. These devices include radio towers, cell phones and transmission stations, robotic sensors for land and water resources, weather satellites, and ubiquitous social media applications. Various real-world examples include observing "geographical area[s] covered by triangulation of mobile phone base transceiver stations" (Hilbert, 2016); examining the spread of the Zika virus through social media (Marr, 2016); tracking wildfires through satellite and ground sensors; and analyzing the potential for dengue fever outbreaks (Althouse, Ng, and Cummings, 2011). Each of these provides clear benefit to people, especially those on the fringes of civilization, living in poverty while subject to the diseases and isolation of the wild.

Obviously it is both difficult and expensive to set up sensors in remote areas. Some areas would also be difficult to implement sensors given the geopolitical parameters in play. Satellites are expensive. Weather systems are still difficult to predict, and the currently observed change in global climate only further complicates the matter. People and their societies rely heavily upon the analysis stemming from these existing communications technology infrastructures, yet they are not necessarily open systems given the proprietary nature of much of the technology. Furthermore, the encroachment of personal privacy, a topic we will examine in more detail in chapter 4, still exists.

Transactional Tracking

Perhaps one of the largest motivating factors behind big data is its promise to maximize profit. It can provide a real-time accounting of how money and currencies exchange hands. Ultimately it speaks to examining how corporations can maximize their efficiency and maximize profitability. In terms of real-world examples, Hilbert (2010) tracked the fluctuation in levels of mobile-phone recharging rates. If people are unable to recharge their phones—despite the necessity for having a functional cell phone—it may indicate deepening levels of poverty. Online vendors such as Amazon and eBay use transactional tracking to follow purchases and link them to personal accounts; banks and real-estate entities such as Zillow use this to track mortgages and home sales.

Implementations are based very much on examining human economic behavior, as well as human use of various devices. In particular, much of the information related to transactions is in the form of cell-phone information, especially as related to cell-phone charging, cell-phone usage, and billing. Changes in real estate would be observable through an examination of sales and tax records. But as with most of the abovementioned issues, predictive powers are still based on tenuous links between the use of a device and a person's internal motivations. Sometimes there's no way to truly understand another person's internal monologue. Tracking how financial transactions come and go, ebb and flow, will be important to corporations seeking an edge in the competitive markets.

Behavior Tracking

For some, big data boils down to examining how people behave. As Alex Pentland says, it is not about capturing people's spoken or written opinions on subjects but rather about their actions—their behavior, not internal thought (Edge, 2012). Hilbert discusses "abnormal" behaviors that become observable even as an "average collective behavior" becomes more clearly defined as a benchmark. Lessons gleaned from these studies become essential to the definition of big data itself. Implementations of behavior tracking range from observing real-time video and gaming use on one side of the activity spectrum to active tracking of people using various online applications. The examination of behavior is useful in the medical fields, gaming, and other physical activities. The tracking of behavior promises to increase as smart devices proliferate and the internet of things (IoT) becomes a more prevalent presence in people's lives. Smart appliances such as refrigerators or microwaves promise to provide insight into the actions of people that are seldom reported.

But again, privacy becomes one of the most important concerns for tracking behaviors. While it can certainly help sociologists to understand benchmark normal and abnormal behaviors among those in a certain group, it might also provide fodder for discrimination against specific subgroups within a dominant culture. Additionally, predictions of behavior can be fickle at best and subject to flawed analysis. In one notable example, Evangelos Kalampokis and colleagues "examined disease outbreaks, product sales, stock market volatility and elections outcome predictions" but found flaws in many other studies utilizing big data and conclude that "more than one-third of these studies infer predictive power without employing predictive analytics" (Kalampokis, Tambouris, and Tarabanis, 2013, p. 554). While it is important to know that a tool exists and what it can accomplish, it is often pointless to implement it if the tool is misused.

MINING (OF *HISTORICALLY* GENERATED DATASETS)

Word Mining

Somewhat related to data tracking is the mining of previously created, pre-digital-era data that has recently become available as digital information. One method of analyzing such information is the use of word mining, which is similar to word tracking but examines the frequency of terms or words or phrases mentioned in print/analog literature that has historically been bound by the limitations of the physical container. One method for word mining involves examining the frequency of terms as they appear in a digitized corpus of papers, books, archives, and so forth. In the library and museum world, researchers and librarians have for years examined the impact of digital media upon the findability, accessibility, and preservation of texts. The plethora of journals and scholarship about the theory and practice of digital librarianship attests to the near-universal adoption of digital collections in libraries. Additionally, many other parameters have been examined as well, including assessing returns on investments (ROI), the opening up of library space for student learning commons, and more.

Information science researchers use word-mining techniques to look at how languages have changed over time and to investigate the ways in which historical events have impacted the time periods they are examining. Digital humanities practitioners have developed techniques to make analog cultural materials more accessible in digital environments. One of the more striking examples of the potential for text mining stems from the Google Books and HathiTrust massive digital libraries. These digital corpuses comprise of tens of millions of books and provide a huge digital corpus for searching (Weiss and James, 2014). Both the process of Culturonomics and Ngram research in computer science provide strong examples of the power and reach of this research, especially in the realm of linguistics, history, and the social sciences (Jatowt et al., 2013; Michel et al., 2011).

As seen in figure 3.2, "computational history" scientists are able to examine how words come into and out of existence, providing clear overlap among the disciplines of linguistics, computer science, and STEM (science, technology, engineering, and mathematics) fields such as physics (Michel et al., 2011; Petersen et al., 2012; Shea, 2012). Others have developed similar approaches in the realm of history. *Historiometrics*, or *cliometrics* in some circles, for example, have been employed since the nineteenth century to examine individuals and their place within larger groups. Some questions that concerned them include "why . . . certain cultures thrived and others vanished; which societies are bellicose and why" (Gardner, 2017). The tools of big data analysis will likely fuel these academic areas in the coming years.

As this method is anchored in past actions and in nondigital formats, word mining is essentially similar to extracting resources from the ground: something is gained while something else—such as a meaning-laden container—is lost. However, just because the digital information becomes freed from context and thus more easily communicated with others, the impact of losing the physical container shouldn't be underemphasized. Indeed, meaning is conveyed through the book's cover and binding, the margins of the text itself, and even flimsy dust jackets. Newspapers that have been digitized have often had their accompanying advertisements and physical layouts erased in favor

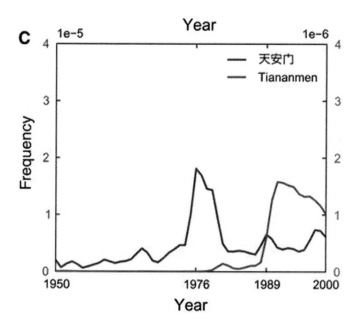

Figure 3.2. Frequency of the term "Tiananmen" in both Roman letters and 天安門 in Chinese characters from 1950 to 2000, showing the impact of the Tiananmen Square incident in 1989. *Source:* Michel et al., 2011.

of the digital text. Those studying graphic design would not be able to see these things as they were practiced at particular times.

APPLICATIONS IN VARIOUS INDUSTRIES AND DISCIPLINES

The applications of big data in the real world occur in numerous sectors of a robust economy and complex culture. Several of the real-world applications mentioned above straddle many of these sectors. The ability to track the health of patients and their eating habits is one such important example of this. One can view wider societal impacts of eating habits upon specific costs for health care. It might provide important insight into managing larger, universal, health-care systems.

GOVERNMENT AND POLITICS

Most world governments in first-world countries have developed initiatives and responses to the need for big data. The most notable example would be former US president Barack Obama's "Big Data Research and Development

Initiative" (Marzullo, 2016). This Obama administration initiative was launched in 2012 as a response to developments in the private sector regarding the use of publicly funded research data and an awareness that action needed to be taken on the government side to ensure that the public can actually access important information. The agencies impacted by the initiative include the National Science Foundation (NSF), the National Institutes of Health (NIH), the Department of Education (DOE), the Department of Defense (DOD), the Defense Advanced Research Projects Agency (DARPA), and the United States Geological Survey (USGS). The ultimate goal of the initiative is the development of "a vibrant big data innovation ecosystem" (ibid.). The federal Big Data Research and Development Strategic Plan is the most recent development of this earlier initiative and outlines ways in which the United States can utilize the results of big data analysis, especially in the areas of science, public health, education, defense, and the US geographical and geological surveys. These agencies each provide vital public goods, and focusing on the development of big data innovations, regardless of one's political convictions, is likely to provide distinct, tangible benefits to the common good.

Some drawbacks are notable though. The ultimate goals, like many government initiatives, appear to be somewhat unclear and defined in a partisan fashion, leading to misunderstandings on the one hand and political polarization on the other. Nevertheless, the changes have been important for strengthening public awareness of essential public-facing information. What is important to note, though, is that the greatest impact from the initiative has been seen more in the grant-funding procedures themselves than in the impact on general people. This is evident in the recent open-access movements and the mandates developed that require publicly funded research and data to be released directly to the public upon completion of the research. Researchers have made great efforts to meet the requirements of the new mandates upon threat of not receiving funding for their projects.

It is also notable to mention that political parties have begun to employ big data analysis techniques in an effort to improve election campaign results in recent years. The most well known of these in the United States is the Obama campaign's widely publicized use of big data analytics in the 2012 presidential election. This appears to be just the beginning of the phase, with subsequent elections likely using it more often. There is also the gathering of cell phone and other data from various agencies such as the NSA, the FBI, and the CIA. The drawbacks to these are limited privacy—the subject of the next chapter. It will only be nominally discussed here. But aside from that issue, the amount of data generated by these agencies and the scope of the data tracked and analyzed (including transactions, locations, metadata from phone use, and the like) is astounding.

EDUCATION

Big data's impact on education is complex. On one hand, national standardized testing has helped to quantify benchmarks of student success while also providing metrics for analyzing the efficacy of school instruction. Yet the issues of standardized testing are manifold. The role of metrics in education often impacts actual learning, since once a standardized test is implemented and mandated, education tends to "teach to the test," rather than introduce students to a broader curriculum. This often results in narrower avenues of inquiry and curiosity for students. Ensuring that funding levels remain secure, especially if funding is tied to test scores, means that more emphasis will be placed on tests than on determining whether learning has actually occurred. Although standardized tests can provide schools and accrediting bodies with large-scale assessments of groups of students for specific years, the tests nevertheless often fail to address specific student needs.

However, despite these limitations on aggregations of student data, what else could big data do to improve education, especially student learning? The holy grail of librarianship, for example, has been to tie frequency and quality of a student's use of library resources to their actual GPA. Knowing these things would yield tangible numbers on the value of a library especially when such a metric has been notoriously difficult to ascertain.

MEDIA, SOCIAL MEDIA, AND IT COMPANIES

Twitter, Facebook, LinkedIn, Google, and countless other social networking companies represent the vanguard of social media and are the primary managers of the vast amounts of data generated by their users. Despite their ubiquity, issues abound with these companies. To paraphrase a common trope: if you can't identify what the product is for the company, most likely the product is you. What this implies is that users, along with all of their self-supplied personal information and the data they have generated from their tracked online behaviors, are really the source of revenue for these companies. The profits these companies see are often generated by selling the information they have gathered about their users to vendors or retailers in return for placing ads targeted to these users. Private information becomes transformed into a monetized data stream.

RETAIL VENDORS

Along the same lines of the media/social media companies, online retailers such as Amazon, eBay, iTunes, and the like, employ similar strategies by inserting targeted ads to web users. When online, one is no longer surprised to find Amazon ads on third-party websites touting the very objects one was browsing just moments before. Such ad targeting has become essential to the social media world, providing a huge revenue engine to the online vendors that employ it.

STEM FIELDS

The sciences have been the quickest to adopt the use of big data techniques in their research. Part of this is the long-standing familiarity with using computers in research, but it's also due to the large amount of data generated by the experimentation itself. Certain disciplines are more likely to generate large amounts of data. As Christine Borgman (2015) rightly points out, there is a distinct "big science–little science dichotomy," which also dictates which research methods are employed and the amount of data generated by them. Particle physics, for example, generates significant amounts of data. A particle accelerator, for example, despite using just a tiny fraction of possible sensors to gather data, gathers multiple petabytes of information per year (Grossman and McKee, 2012). Other disciplines such as field ecology or biology of bird behavior, in contrast, eschew such large structures and collaborate in smaller, more localized circles. Yet, even as "small science" remains the most common approach in many areas, disciplines have begun developing "computational" versions of their studies. "Computational biology" analyzes the large data sets generated from observations and creates computer simulations to theorize causes and effects. The Mackelprang Laboratory at CSUN, for example, endeavors to integrate "next-generation tools such as high-throughput DNA sequencing with traditional microbiology approaches" (Mackelprang, 2016).

HUMANITIES FIELDS

The simplest way to describe the humanities might be as those academic disciplines that study human culture rather than the natural world. The term encompasses numerous fields utilizing conflicting research methods. Yet humanities has changed even as the digital age progresses, "borrowing techniques," as Borgman writes, and thinking "in terms of data, metadata, standards, interoperability, and sustainability" (Borgman, 2015, p. 162). The digital humanities are one newer outgrowth of the humanities that has embraced the working methods of big data. Researchers have moved away from the more traditional print text analysis to much larger sized data set samples made searchable through digitization. Ngrams, digitization, Culturonomics, and other methods have helped to increase the amount of data points available to humanities researchers (Petersen et al., 2012).

One of the exciting aspects of digital archive collections is the full-text searchability of large amounts of printed material that had been locked away in archives and special collections. The development of digital online finding aids over the past fifteen to twenty years has allowed researchers to search across numerous collections for mention of specific keywords. The transcription of oral histories into full-text searchable digital texts has also provided linguists with the ability to analyze the use and frequency of specific terms within speakers of dialects. Again, these inquiries are dependent upon the release of historical data rather than contemporary data developed in real-time scenarios.

LIBRARIES

Libraries certainly generate their own data related to the day-to-day operations, though often at a much smaller scale than other information-technology-intensive institutions. While there are specific benchmarks that librarians and administrators need to ensure they are gaining some return on their investments, libraries also try to use this information for assessing student and patron usage patterns. The main goal of most libraries in this era has been to find the link between student or patron success and library expenditures.

Yet libraries also have a role to play in the implementation of and access to big data, especially as it becomes generated by various entities without regard to its long-term preservation. Institutional repositories, institutional and grant-funder open-access mandates, and digital preservation have important roles to play in the development of big data. While not always directly creating and using data, the library nevertheless can act as an important infrastructure support for it. Big data is hurtling forward, sometimes without regard to its future accessibility. Libraries need to find ways to help store and preserve it for future generations.

But that is not to say that libraries cannot utilize big data for their own advantage. Boris Zetterlund (2016) asserts that "it's about moving from collection based to community orientated services." He outlines four important areas where libraries can utilize big data for themselves, including resources, benchmarking, community predictions and reactions, and service enrichment. All of these point toward enhancing the role of the library within a community by anticipating its needs in real time by tracking its own constituents. Library futures may depend on these important developments.

REFERENCES

Althouse, B. M., Ng, Y. Y., and Cummings, D. A. T. (2011). Prediction of dengue incidence using search query surveillance. *PLOS Neglected Tropical Diseases, 5*(8), e1258. doi:10.1371/journal.pntd.0001258.

Borgman, C. (2015). *Big data, little data, no data: Scholarship in the networked world.* Cambridge, MA: MIT Press.

Edge. (2012). Reinventing society in the wake of big data, a conversation with Alex (Sandy) Pentland. http://www.edge.org.

Gardner, H. (2017). Historiometrics. *Edge.* https://www.edge.org.

Google. (2017). Google Flu Trends. http://www.google.org.

Grossman L., and McKee, M. (2012). Is the LHC throwing away too much data? *New Scientist, 2856.* https://www.newscientist.com.

Gruhl, D., Guha, R., Kumar, R., Novak, J., and Tomkins, A. (2005). The predictive power of online chatter. In *Proceedings of the Eleventh ACM SIGKDD International Conference on Knowledge Discovery in Data Mining* (pp. 78–87). New York: ACM. doi:10.1145/1081870.1081883.

Hilbert, M. (2010). When is Cheap, Cheap Enough to Bridge the Digital Divide? Modeling Income Related Structural Challenges of Technology Diffusion in Latin America. *World Development, 38*(5), 756–770. doi:10.1016/j.worlddev.2009.11.019.

Hilbert, M. (2016). Big data for development: A review of promises and challenges. *Development Policy Review, 34*(1), 135–174. http://www.martinhilbert.net.

Jatowt, A., Kawai, H., Kanazawa, K., Tanaka, K., Kunieda, K., and Yamada, K. (2013). Multilingual, longitudinal analysis of future-related information on the web. Proceedings of the 4th International Conference on Culture and Computing (Culture and Computing 2013), IEEE Press, Kyoto, Japan, pp. 27–32.

Kalampokis, E., Tambouris, E., and Tarabanis, K. (2013). Understanding the predictive power of social media. *Internet Research, 23*(5), 544–559. doi:10.1108/IntR-06-2012-0114.

Lazer, D., and Kennedy, R. (2015). What we can learn from the epic failure of Google Flu Trends. *Wired.* https://www.wired.com.

Mackelprang, R. (2016). Mackelprang lab. http://www.csun.edu.

Manovich, L. (2012). Trending: The promises and the challenges of big social data. In M. Gold (Ed.), *Debates in the digital humanities* (pp. 460–476). Minneapolis: University of Minnesota Press. http://www.manovich.net.

Marr, B. (2016). Can big data help fight the Zika virus? *Forbes.* http://www.forbes.com.

Marzullo, K. (2016). Administrative issues strategic plan for big data research and development. White House blog. https://www.whitehouse.gov.

MathWorks. (2017). Find global minima for highly nonlinear problems. https://www.mathworks.com.

Michel, J., Shen, Y. K., Aiden, A. P., Veres, A., and Gray, M. K., Google Books team, Pickett, J., et al. (2011). Quantitative analysis of culture using millions of digitized books. *Science 331*(6014), 176–182.

Palace, B. (1996). Data mining: What is data mining? UCLA. http://www.anderson.ucla.edu.

Petersen, A., Tenenbaum, J., Havlin, S., and Stanley, H. (2012). Statistical laws governing fluctuations in word use from word birth to word death. *Scientific Reports, 2.*

Shea, C. (2012). The new science of the birth and death of words: Have physicists discovered the evolutionary laws of language in Google's library? *Wall Street Journal.* https://www.wsj.com.

Weiss, A., and James, R. (2014). *Using massive digital libraries: A LITA guide.* Chicago: ALA TechSource, an imprint of the American Library Association.

White House. (2012). Big data initiative. https://www.whitehouse.gov.

Zetterlund, B. (2016). Big data and libraries: Getting the most from your library data. Axiell. http://www.axiell.co.uk.

Part II

Reality Shocks

Chapter Four

Privacy, Libraries, and Big Data

The discussion surrounding internet privacy has become so polarized that it borders on hysteria and dystopian cliché on one side and optimistic denial on the other. It's rare to find balanced and fair objective discussions of privacy. Numerous online how-to guides demonstrate how people can erase their digital trails, often taking extreme measures at search obfuscation (Ohlheiser, 2017). Paranoia about government spying seems exacerbated by recent document releases from WikiLeaks, Edward Snowden, and other whistleblowers (Cameron, 2015; WikiLeaks, 2016). Meanwhile, proponents of the big data industry brazenly downplay the need for privacy and wonder whether it's needed at all (Ben-Shahar, 2016). And the US government's judicial responses to privacy concerns in the face of digital spying by the NSA, CIA, FBI, and other federal agencies appear contradictory at best and incompetent at worst (Cohen, 2013). Often involving reactionary rhetoric and overreaching assumptions of the "slippery-slope" sort, it is difficult at times to really understand what encompasses the true issues of privacy in the digital era.

This chapter will therefore try to sort through some of the more important theories of privacy and examine how they are tied to internet and digital technology. As seen in figure 4.1, the unintended consequences of moving from a print world to a digital one are widespread. An earnest attempt will be made to downplay paranoia and overreactions to the losses—either perceived or true—of privacy. The theories addressed in the chapter will help us to examine the impact of digital technology in a more rational light. This chapter will also review theories of privacy and draw conclusions based on their relevance to big data. I am especially interested in pursuing some of the following questions: How is privacy defined? What are the basic theories of privacy? Is there a dominant or appropriate theory of internet privacy? Who enforces such privacy? Who encroaches upon one's privacy and who doesn't? How has the internet changed people's conceptions of privacy? Finally, how has big data changed them further? Theory, reality, and future concerns will be addressed.

PRIVACY AND THE AMERICAN LIBRARY ASSOCIATION

To sufficiently parse the term "privacy," perhaps the first place to start should be the American Library Association (ALA), as that is the primary body governing the environments in which librarians work and provides much of the scope for this text. The ALA's policy manual clearly values privacy. It even includes "confidentiality/privacy" (their conflation, not mine) as one of the eleven core values of librarianship, which "reflect the history and ongoing development of the profession" (ALA, 2013). Additionally, the ALA further defines privacy in section B.2.1.17 of the manual as "the right to open inquiry without having the subject of one's interest exam-

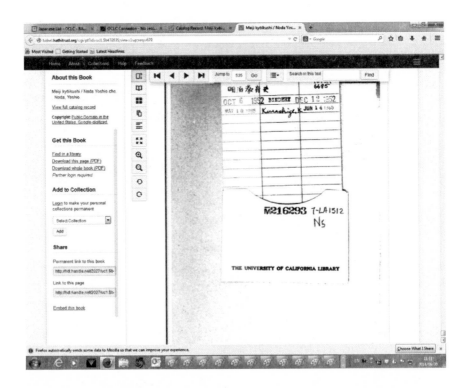

Figure 4.1. Digitized book, *Meiji Kyoikushi* by Yoshio Noda, showing card with patron's name and checkout date. From HathiTrust digital library (OCLC# OCL-551410546), https://babel.hathitrust.org.

ined or scrutinized by others." This appears to be solidly based on Samuel Warren and Louis Brandeis's (1890) foundational argument for a "right to privacy," written in 1890, which states that "the right to life has come to mean the right to enjoy life,—the right to be let alone."

One can see where the ALA's stance on "open inquiry" is rooted in this concept of the right to be left alone and away from the scrutiny of others in order to fulfill "information needs." Libraries as a result universally strive to provide nonintrusive spaces to patrons in accordance with these basic rights to privacy for all their inquiries without allowing third parties—or even the librarians and library staff themselves—access to sought-after topics. This instills patrons with confidence that their intentions would not be discovered by others without their consent; this policy also falls within the realm of intellectual freedom, another important pillar of librarianship. Such concepts of privacy and what constitutes a breach of privacy have changed over time, of course, adapting to meet current societal needs. Libraries no longer allow signatures to appear on a book's checkout slip, for example, in order to minimize scrutiny and promote that important sense of freedom; of course, as figure 4.1 demonstrates, there are unintended releases of information as a result of new technologies being adopted. Nevertheless, the concept of privacy remains an important ideal that forms the bedrock to many librarians' actions. Most library administrators subsequently find the ALA's currently adopted definition of privacy a useful guide for policy development and enforcement.

Interestingly, the ALA's definition of privacy includes examples of confidentiality within this definition as well (ALA, 2013). But this is where the clarity of their definition, with its very limited scope within the library world and its library-centered scenarios, begins to break down. As we will see, there is a problem with using confidentiality to define privacy. While it is true that the two terms surely overlap in some situations and that confidentiality has the ability to both contribute to and complement the concept of privacy, these terms are not addressing the same concerns. Indeed, Grant Campbell and Scott Cowan (2016), in their cogent analysis of the ALA's stance on privacy, suggest that the ALA's policy is "an ideal wrapped in a paradox" and wonder how to resolve what they see as conflicting concepts.

It should be noted that in the history of science, Thomas Kuhn (1962) suggests that inaccurate theories or "paradigms" often lead to strange contradictions and paradoxes within theories. While that may be beyond the scope of this book, Campbell and Cowan's criticism could be considered in light of this phenomenon. The fact that a paradox exists in their interpretation of the theory suggests that something may be amiss with the ALA's basic theory of privacy. Privacy, Campbell and Cowan argue, rests "at the intersection of behavior and identity," allowing users to "articulate a healthy relationship between what we are and what we do" (2016, p. 494). Pointing out where the policy fails to serve all its constituents—in this case members of the LGBTQ community and their own conflicting and sometimes simultaneous needs for *both* privacy *and* openness depending upon the audience—helps to show where the understanding of privacy in libraries needs a clearer and more nuanced approach.

In addition to the fundamental confusion about what constitutes privacy in libraries, big data has also changed the information landscape in terms of privacy concerns and magnified them by the changes to the scope, scale, speed, and potential value of personal information itself. There are implications to determining what is private—and what is confidential, for that matter—that need to be teased out more clearly. It is clear to me that the ALA position on privacy, despite its being updated as recently as 2013, may not be adequate in the big data era. This leads us to why it is important to further explore this issue in more detail and try to arrive at a much clearer and thus more applicable and *enforceable* concept of privacy.

FOUR CLASSIC THEORIES ON PRIVACY

In his important analysis on the subject of privacy, Herman Tavani (2007) outlines four classic theories of privacy: nonintrusion, seclusion, limitation, and control. Each theory, he argues, contains specific elements that serve to explain privacy but misses key components that might define the concept more completely and accurately. Perhaps most concerning of all is that each of these theories confuses or conflates privacy with other concepts, including "liberty, autonomy, secrecy, and solitude" (Tavani, 2007, p. 3).

The nonintrusion theory, for example, sees privacy as a person's ability to be left alone, or essentially "free from intrusion." Based on nineteenth-century legal scholarship, the theory unfortunately leads to the conflation of liberty with privacy. Though similar, the terms need to be parsed carefully. Privacy *allows for the exercise of liberty*, but liberty *does not inherently provide the power to conceal things* that might curtail privacy (Tavani, 2007). In other words, we may be free to do what we like, but we might not be able to prevent others from seeing what we are doing, something clearly at the heart of privacy.

In a real-world example of this, it seems that the ALA's position on privacy falls into this exact conundrum. We have the right to open inquiry, the ALA states—which is a form of liberty, not privacy—without that inquiry being observed—which would be an intrusion of one's privacy. Essentially, this is the classic nonintrusion interpretation of privacy. But the inherent conflation of the concepts of liberty and privacy, one could argue, contributes directly to the paradox that Campbell and Cowan so rightfully point out. It turns out that libraries *do* occasionally observe what patrons are doing.

Librarians *do* see that people are using computers, searching online, or browsing books. Libraries *will* sometimes monitor and restrict searches for things such as child pornography. Librarians sometimes even know the exact subjects that patrons are searching for. So if privacy means nonintrusion, does knowing what people are searching for in itself negate privacy in libraries? Of course not. There's more to it than that. But if we are going to truly advocate for privacy in libraries, we had better get our terms and conditions straight, or it will lead to confusions and paradoxes. In order to truly protect our patrons, librarians need to avoid confusing and conflating privacy with other concepts.

The *seclusion theory* of privacy, which differs in scope from nonintrusion theory, sees privacy as the sense of "being alone," which is another way of describing the condition of solitude. Yet solitude is not necessarily privacy either. At face value, one might assert that the more one is alone the more one has privacy. Yet a person can live privately among others; people can also live their lives exposed to others (as in the case of disgraced celebrities) but still hiding in seclusion. Furthermore, in the case of the ALA's policy, seclusion theory *would completely negate the possibility of ever attaining privacy at libraries*, since they are organizations comprised of dozens, if not hundreds, of information specialists, paraprofessionals, and trained assistants and volunteers. Too many people are involved in the process of providing library resources for seclusion theory to be fully applicable to libraries.

Interestingly the *control theory* of privacy is also hinted at in the ALA's policy, as the policy directs librarians and library staff to provide space so that users are not subject to the prying eyes of others without their consent (i.e., "scrutinized," which *suggests* unwarranted examination). What's not stated outright, but is implied, is the concept of autonomy. The implication, to put it in finer detail, is that the user should really be the one to control who has access to information users might consider privileged or confidential. Control theory considers self-determination to be the foundation of privacy; users should "determine for themselves when, how, and to what extent information about them is communicated to others" (Tavani, 2007, p. 7). But it is unclear how this is enforced and how much control one person should reasonably expect to hold. Tavani argues further that "one can have control over information without necessarily having privacy" (p. 8). Ultimately, the problem with utilizing this interpretation of privacy is the conflation of the terms of autonomy and privacy. Again, in the case of the ALA's policy, we are making assumptions about privacy that may not exist for all conditions. This lack of clarity is going to spell trouble if libraries wish to advocate for patron privacy but wind up advocating for patron *autonomy* instead.

Finally, the *limitation theory* of privacy asserts that privacy occurs when access to information about someone is "restricted in certain contexts." In other words, a person has privacy when third parties do not have knowledge of a person's personal information. This interpretation of privacy also appears to fit within the ALA's policy in that the library acts, to a certain degree, as a barrier to these third parties and prevents undesired elements from knowing what information (sometimes of a personal and revealing nature) a person is seeking. So in that sense, by refusing to allow others to see what patrons have checked out or accessed online, libraries contribute to the sense of privacy patrons may have about themselves.

But again, despite being a good working definition—and very useful for libraries and librarians too—it does not appear to hold up under analysis. In particular, the theory doesn't account for the autonomy people have in granting or limiting others' access to information. Instead, it seems to favor the external conditions of creating a sense of privacy rather than favoring an individual's actions. If followed closely, this line of reasoning would lead one to conclude, erroneously, that the more information is kept from others, the more privacy one has. Indeed, it may not necessarily be the case that patrons will be more private the more we prevent others from accessing information about our searching behaviors. One can argue that privacy also depends upon the type of information, the nature of those third-party entities observing, and whether the sharing of such information is actually legally required or defined as "private."

TOWARD A "UNIFIED THEORY" OF PRIVACY

It is clear then, from this analysis of the four main theories of privacy, that each seems to lack a vital component to fully define privacy and that the ALA's own concept of privacy is in turn insufficient to meet the needs of patrons. To address this problem, Tavani proposes a "grand unified theory" of restricted access/limited control (RALC). This might be a useful approach to take for librarians and information professionals to better serve library users.

RALC theory proposes that each of the four main theories of privacy is lacking something. RALC remedies this by focusing not purely on the problem of control; this control appeared to be a contradiction in the limitation theory of privacy—the one favored by the ALA. The more control the patron has, the argument goes, the more private he or she is. Yet as mentioned, it is somewhat paradoxical and remedied by the definition of "confidentiality," which promises to protect any information that did get used by the library or any other user. This seems to be why, at least to me, the ALA focuses so much on blurring those two concepts (along with liberty) as the one does seem to solve the inherent contradiction of the other. When patrons provide libraries with their private information, they are in effect losing their "perfect" privacy by relinquishing control of information about themselves. The library attempts to alleviate this problem by promising to be confidential with this information. But it still doesn't solve the inherent contradiction; it merely provides nonbinding assurances to users that despite losing your privacy you are safe because of confidentiality.

RALC theory attempts to solve this problem by introducing three important elements that are hinted at in the other definitions but are not spelled out as clearly they need to be: *choice*, *consent*, and *correction*. By using these three elements, library users can manage and set the limits of their privacy without being compromised by the gaps in privacy theory itself.

Choice

In order to preserve a sense of privacy, people above all else need to be able to implement control via choosing, in at least some minimal way, the situations that would allow others to access their personal information. Choice doesn't necessarily equate privacy so much as provide the mechanism for which people can develop a personal scale of privacy. This scale might range from complete privacy, where nothing is allowed to be shared, to complete publicity, where just about everything is shared.

The methods allowing one to do this would include being able to turn off a web cam at will, for example, in order to allow one's actions to go unobserved. One might also choose to keep it on for various reasons but still maintain one's own privacy. Or one might willingly allow others to see something about them, thus reducing one's own privacy for a specific set of conditions. But the key is an ability to choose the degrees to which the scale tips from complete restriction to complete openness and all the possible combinations between.

Libraries tend not to provide choice in this arena, however. Library privacy policies tend to assume that users will choose an interpretation of privacy that releases as little information as possible. This is, of course, the prudent approach, as it limits unforeseen liabilities on the side of the library and unnecessary (and sometimes irreparable) damage to patrons. But it should be noted that this approach falls far more within the library's own self-defined concept of disclosure and confidentiality rather than contributing automatically to a user's sense of privacy, which may in some cases be much looser than a library's.

Consent

Along with choice, consent must play an important role in the management of privacy. We often waive our control over the dissemination of information when agreeing to a bank's privacy policy, for example, or to the boilerplate user agreements found on social media websites. The consent is assumed when these agreements are signed, whether we have actually read the fine print or not. But consent, in essence, nevertheless represents a method by which people can manage their levels of privacy and information release.

Libraries utilize the information of patrons, addresses, phone numbers, and so forth, in order to run the basics of their services. It's possible to provide a circulation service without identification of the user, but surely it's a lot more difficult without this information, especially if the library is worried about losing valuable books or media to theft. Consent is often traded for using the library's statement of confidentiality, which in essence binds the user and library together, forcing the library to protect the information it has requested in exchange for the basic services it provides. Libraries need, of course, to consider whether using the information they have gathered about patrons is worth the potential risk of breaking the original consent agreement. Many believe it is not and conclude that the consent agreement should never be altered in any manner for any purpose.

Correction

Finally, the third important piece of the privacy management puzzle involves the ability for users to *alter* or *amend* previous decisions on the release of their personal information. Ultimately, like the previous elements, correction relates to people's ability to control information about them. If we are truly in command of our own information, instead of a third party like Facebook being in control, then the correction of that released information should be an easy, straightforward solution.

Unfortunately, in the digital age, this is often the most difficult issue to resolve. As Kevin Kelly has famously said, "The internet is the world's largest copy machine" (Groeger, 2011). Once an item is online, it is backed up, cached, and indexed by various tech companies—including Google for its search engine. It becomes very challenging to remove it completely. As Kelly (2016) also asserts, "If something can be copied and it touches the internet, it will be copied." While copyrighted works can be subject to the Digital Millennium Copyright Act (DMCA) and thus removed within the strict confines of the law, in the case of personal information that might have been given or released to third parties, it may be less easily removed.

Google's own online removal policy, for example, leaves a lot of room for the company to maneuver when it comes to removing certain types of information. Google's policy states that it will remove personal information, unless they "believe that a removal request is being used to try and remove other, non-personal information from search results" (Google, 2017). Google also reserves the right to refuse the removal of personal information if it "can be found on official government websites," since they now deem that to be public information. This is hardly reassuring for those wishing to correct what they believe to be mistakes in the release of their personal information.

Legislation does exist for people, though, to help protect their privacy and to provide guidelines for organizations handling personal information. The Family Educational Rights and Privacy Act (FERPA), the Health Insurance Portability and Accountability Act (HIPAA), the Fair Credit Reporting Act (FCRA), and the Electronic Communications Privacy Act (ECPA), to name just a few, all provide protections for people within very specific guidelines. FERPA oversees regulations pertaining to student education records, restricting the use of personal information held by educational institutions. HIPAA protects medical information; FCRA regulates the use of consumer information and its application to credit and loan; ECPA restricts wiretapping and other surveillance activities, though this has been amended and has subsequently been widened in scope by the USA PATRIOT Act and FISA (Foreign Intelligence Surveillance Act) Amendments Act.

But ultimately, the issue remains whether one can correct mistakes or change one's mind about released information. Libraries need to be cognizant of their role in releasing information and how they might help their patrons correct data breaches, or help them with addressing second thoughts about what they have shared. One online service called StopDataMining.me provides information to people on what data brokers exist and what type of information they are currently tracking. The site also includes methods for people to "exercise their opt-out choices," helping people correct breaches of privacy (StopDataMining.me, 2017). They have a master list of approximately fifty data broker companies. Libraries would be well advised to consider ways of assisting such services, especially as this list likely represents the tip of the iceberg in terms of the number of companies tracking people.

PRIVACY IN THE AGE OF BIG DATA

Now that we have examined the issues of privacy and the obvious challenges associated with defining and enforcing it, we need to review how big data further impacts the current philosophy of privacy beyond the typical concerns. As Cynthia Dwork and Deirdre Mulligan (2013) write, "If privacy and transparency are not the panacea to the risks posed by big data, what is?" A number of scholars and researchers see big data as an imminent threat to the concept of privacy itself, and even possibly as an existential threat removing personal autonomy (Boyd and Crawford, 2012; *Choice Reviews Online*, 2014; Janes, 2012; Kerr and Earle, 2013; Rubinstein, 2012). Some of this analysis contains heated rhetoric or succumbs to panic based on worst-case scenarios. Some of it, like Omri Ben-Shahar's (2016) analysis, downplays the issue; he instead sees privacy as a tradable commodity, where "consumers are happy to use their privacy as the New Money."

However, a lot of ground needs to be covered between these two extremes. If personal data is the building block of one's privacy, then anything blocking the identifiability of the user to his or her data will reduce potential profit. In other words, private *identifiable* information is worth far more in the eyes of an information technology or social media company than partially visible information. If anonymous data is worth less to a corporation, will a company go to the extent of breaking privacy policies in order to turn a bigger profit? Big data reflects the technological changes in how information is gathered, shared, and utilized. But without proper privacy policies developed in answer to these technological and sociological changes, we may be damaging ourselves and our institutions by allowing "pre-emptive social decision-making" to control us (Kerr and Earle, 2013).

To help answer some of these issues, Daniel O'Leary (2015) provides a useful framework to examine the main concerns for privacy and the areas of "encroachment" where a reduction in privacy may be occurring within big data. He provides a helpful framework by examining the so-called 5Vs of big data in relationship to privacy. It should be noted, though, that in his analysis he finds the main source of problems in big data attributable to the "unevenness" of the data. I would argue, though, that this is not the only problem with big data and privacy.

Volume

While the amount of data generated by "big data" is one of its important characteristics, it is also one that changes the nature of dealing with that data. The generation of vast amounts of data about individuals as well as about groups of people can improve the analysis of trends in behavior, attitude, ideas, and so on, on a large scale. But issues related to privacy arise with this "piling up" of information. A number of questions come to mind. What are the limits of acceptable data gathering on an individual? How much data is too much for a person or group? How much is just enough? Does this increase in volume change our own relationship to the data as well?

One of the important parameters to consider is what should be the *minimum* amount of information required for a particular use? This is a problem researchers often encounter when collecting data on their own subjects, and it is a bone of contention for institutional review boards when analyzing the necessity of how much data is collected and the rationale expressed for that collection. The minimum standard, as it applies to the federal regulation HIPAA, states that "protected health information should not be used or disclosed when it is not necessary to satisfy a particular purpose or carry out a function" (US HHS, 2003). In this case we have clear boundaries defining what should be a minimal amount of data necessary for doing a specific job or fulfilling a specific purpose, though HIPAA itself is limited in scope.

Unfortunately, such boundaries do not appear to be enforced in the era of big data, where not only do minimal standards not exist but also they are seen as hindrances to the development of commerce, industry, research, and other complex aspects of a global economy. Privacy policies will nevertheless need to deal with and enforce minimal data standards in order to protect privacy. One problem with this, too, is how organizations will assess whether they or others have exceeded specific minimal guidelines on data collection.

The question also remains whether volume by itself compromises the basic concept of privacy. This is unclear as more information is gathered as well as shared. Yet the key is still determining how much data is being used and why. If the purpose of using so much data does not match the original intention, then one's consent is obviously breached. Furthermore, if the amount of data gathered on a particular subject vastly outstrips the actual return value of a particular project, there might be greater temptation to reuse or redistribute that data for different purposes just to improve returns on investment.

Velocity

The speed at which information passes between hands is a major factor for the proliferation of data. Viral videos are one such phenomenon of digital information being passed between people at astounding speed. Information-transfer rates are dependent, of course, upon information infrastructures such as Ethernet, and so forth. But importantly, digital information is now transferrable to others at near-instant rates. Information is gathered and collected more quickly as well. One scholar has indicated that "90 percent of the world's data has been generated in the past two years" (O'Leary, 2015, p. 93). The speed of this aggregation is staggering.

The essential question that this rapid transfer and aggregation of information raises then is How does velocity impact privacy? The situation that most impacts privacy involves information that is released or gathered without consent and then utilized by others so quickly that it becomes universally available even before the affected parties can notice the breach. Speed represents a major concession on the control of that information. Along the same lines, if information is gathered at a quick pace and the consumer or target is not aware of this, it may be too late to prevent third parties from using it before the gathering is stopped.

Currently, some organizations, such as those in social media and advertising, push for rapid data dissemination, but others exist, especially regulatory agencies related to health fields and education, to ensure that it is not unduly released. This tension between organizations might cause problems for the people whose information is at the center of such disputes or tensions. Speed is often valued in the information economy to the detriment of the safety or well-being of others. Privacy policies will need to be developed that fully address this problem and mitigate the effects of unauthorized rapid transfers of information.

Variety

Another important aspect of big data is its variety. There are many types of data about people ranging from biometric, financial, demographic, economic, public-facing, and personal information. More variables are possible as more technology becomes linked to the internet of things. Television-watching habits, for example, can be monitored by smart televisions. Refrigerators can track when and how often their owners use them. But how many types of data should reasonably exist about a person? Do policies and the philosophical definitions of privacy bound them or account for them in reasonable ways?

Obviously more information will exist about some people than others. It was not imaginable fifty years ago that people's behavior could be analyzed by their fridge, but now that it is a reality. It is important, then, to anticipate new developments and new technologies. The essential issue becomes whether privacy policies can combat the widening varieties of data, anticipating the impact of data that has yet to be widely created, or doesn't even yet exist. In other words, what preventative measures can be taken as new technologies begin to track behaviors?

In scripting a policy, we need to ask ourselves, does the ALA or any institution for that matter consider the variety of information being generated by big data? We certainly know enough to keep patron library use records private. But what about videos posted online of library users? One viral video in 2012 depicted a student at a university library throwing a temper tantrum during finals. The student was filmed without her knowledge, and the video was uploaded for all to see. Does a library's privacy policy extend into this realm as well? As wearable technologies such as Google Glass become more prevalent, will a library's privacy policy need to mention or even go so far as to *proscribe* the use of such devices? It is unclear at this point, but given the potential for such devices to proliferate, it needs to be considered carefully.

Veracity/Reliability

Finally, the veracity and reliability of information needs to be called into question. Of course this is important for all data sets, but even more so as the volume, variety, and velocity increase. At such rapidly increasing scales, how can data remain reliable? This is an essential question, of course, for all librarians, especially as we try to preserve information in the long term and respect an object's original provenance. One of the obvious problems with tracking reliability is the ability to falsify records. This is the stuff of dystopian novels. At the same time it's possible that digital objects lose their tether to reality, that is, they become stripped of their metadata, leaving just images or digital files without context. In this regard, information loses its reliability, and in the words of O'Leary, "the quality of the inferences that can be drawn may be limited" and as a result "damaging and possibly incorrect inferences" may be created and propagated further (2015, p. 94).

But is veracity really part of the issue of privacy? In the sense that information is released and then "maladapted" or manipulated to meet the needs of others, then it may speak to potential damage, especially if compromising information, or *Kompromat* in Russian, is released and proliferates. That potential for manufactured damaging content stresses the need for safeguards regarding information itself. Security remains an integral part of privacy. It has been said that only those with something to hide will resist information transparency, but in this situation, if anyone can release and then manipulate information, no one is truly safe.

Ultimately, the concept of privacy and privacy policies will need to incorporate the need to be able to check the veracity and reliability of the information being gathered. If there are errors in the gathering process or errors in the dissemination process, users should have a right to recall or to amend the information. It is unclear whether many privacy policies provide this kind of action.

Value

Finally, where does privacy fit within the concept of "value" in big data? Certainly data becomes valuable for the corporations and companies that aggregate and use it, especially as they are willing to sometimes provide nominal payment or an exchange of services for this information. But data is also important for the workings and trappings of governments and politics. The desire to predict the future is rooted in the fear of being caught in unsolvable future problems as well as the fear of missing out on something. We all want to foresee troubles ahead and avoid things like the stock market crash of 2008–2009; alternatively, we all wish we had invested in Apple in the early 1980s. If only we had known or had the power to interpret the signs! The value of data also depends very much on how it might be utilized to draw important conclusions about group or individual behaviors and preferences.

On the opposite side, the push for privacy is also a push sometimes for the need to remain anonymous. But what happens when privacy is turned into a commodity where one would pay to avoid a certain level of intrusion? Ben-

Shahar (2016) argues that this "grand bargain" in which "free services [are given] in return for personal information" is the heart and soul of the information economy, a "New Currency" for our brave new world. He laments that privacy policies and lawsuits ensuring their enforcement will only derail this economy. He insists that people are getting quite a good deal from companies in this grand bargain.

What is more interesting from his assertions, though, is what was *not* noted in the original text. In the comments section of the online magazine *Forbes*, visible in figure 4.2, where Ben-Shahar's article was originally published, a reader identifies the "big data paradox." The commenter argues that the greater the potential for data to be valuable to corporations, the greater the risk to the privacy of the individuals whose data was used. Yet Ben-Shahar sees this as a problem for big data and companies working with it losing value! In his words, "it only sharpens the unintended cost of privacy protection." Anonymized data, he claims, would likely be worth less than identifiable data.

Through this example, the conflict between personal privacy as a public good and the bottom line of private corporations becomes a lot clearer. It could be argued that the value of data collected by social media companies is inversely proportional to the privacy limitations imposed upon that data. Laissez-faire capitalists would see this as a reason for "deregulation" or "relaxation" of privacy laws and policies. Privacy is seen as cutting directly into maximal profit. Ben-Shahar, for his part, sees "no proven need for protective regulation" and colors the privacy lawsuits against Google or Facebook as a "pretense" fabricated by lawyers more interested in scoring a settlement than looking out for their clients' best interests. But this is clearly untrue to anyone who can see past free-market ideology. It is obvious in his mind that complete digital sharing would be the ideal default human condition and that privacy would be the service one pays to attain it.

To reasonable people, this type of rhetoric viewing personal data as the "New Currency" should appear to be incredibly counterproductive. Commonsense notions of the value of long-standing societal norms such as privacy are systematically inverted in the name of reaping all-important short-term profit. Privacy policies, though, must find ways to deal with this line of psychopathological thinking. Not everything can or should be commodified. Some things are better utilized as part of a commons for all of a society to benefit, including water, air, electrical utilities, nationalized parks, roads, and of course personal privacy. Not everything magically improves when it is subject to deregulation; the problems seen with Enron in the late 1990s are a good cautionary tale against the privatization of electrical utilities. Contrary to what Ben-Shahar asserts, there *are* proven needs for privacy, *especially* in the age of big data, and they need to be protected. Not everyone is happy

Figure 4.2. **Screenshots showing the comments section in *Forbes* magazine online for the article "Privacy Is the New Money, Thanks to Big Data." *Source:* Ben-Shahar, 2016.**

with or gaining much from these so-called grand bargains, and the potential for the misuse and abuse of personal information is immense.

Combining Data Sources

Though the 5Vs of big data have an important role in helping us to assess privacy concerns and the potential impact of big data on privacy policies, another aspect needs to be addressed that hasn't been fully explored. Big data, it has been noted, has the ability to pull data from various, decentralized sources. But does the sum of these parts, so to speak, become something greater when seen as a whole? In many ways the recombination of various data sets—the mashups, the aggregations of data on a mass scale, and the combined data points—contributes to a larger whole that creates something entirely new. Elements or bits and pieces of data that in small isolated numbers may not violate privacy or reveal sensitive information about a person have the potential to do so when combined.

Much like a mosaic, the individual parts become less important than their contribution to the whole picture. Ultimately, privacy policy would need to be aware of the potential for disparate elements to be combined in unexpected but very revealing ways. This may be where privacy itself breaks irreparably. On the one hand, it is still possible for one to control small batches of data within smaller contexts, but it is unclear what will happen when one set of data is combined with another. Are privacy theories equipped to deal with recombined data? Can reconstruction and recombination techniques circumvent privacy policies? Such loopholes among the many current privacy policies may exist. It is up to information professionals to identify and close these loopholes to avoid breaches and damage to people's reputations and sense of privacy.

Expanding Contexts and Cultural-Specific Privacy

Finally, when information is generated and aggregated, does the context in which it is placed impact its ability to remain private? The question may seem to have an obvious answer, but as we have seen with the definitions of privacy itself, context doesn't always dictate whether something is private or not. Some situations and contexts *require* the disclosure of information. However, what happens when data is released or shared with wider audiences beyond what was originally intended? Does that necessarily represent a reduction of privacy? Furthermore, when data is contained in smaller pools, does it follow that it also enjoys a "safer" existence? Does wider distribution automatically represent a lessening of one's privacy?

What if that information is shared on an international stage? Khairulliza Salleh and Lech Janczewski (2016) rightly point out that "privacy regulations that are country specific may seriously hinder big data initiatives" (p. 24). Although varying regulations allow different types of information to be released, the application of laws remains nation based. International agreements still require local enforcements. Additionally, people in different countries and cultures will find some information more embarrassing or compromising than others and will demand the enforcement of privacy in different ways.

But other questions remain. How specifically does the concept of privacy change depending upon which country it is viewed in? Do cultures value certain types of information over others? Do certain cultures prefer more or less information shared about them? Are concepts of privacy and current privacy polices equipped to deal with the international nature of big data and the often multinational companies that create and analyze it? US law is not able to enforce its citizens' privacy if it is breached in or by another country. As a result, what frameworks or best practices need to be developed on an international scale to address problems of privacy for all people of the world?

These questions are quite difficult to answer definitively. Obviously, new privacy policies will need to address this issue of wider audiences that were not originally existing when the information was created. The expanding context in which data finds itself stored, shared, and recombined becomes an important consideration. Privacy policies will need to explore all of the potential conditions—whether national or international, within a main culture or a subculture—to which the data is subjected.

CONCLUSION: PERFECT STORMS ALIGNED AGAINST PRIVACY

It becomes clear once we get past some of the heated or biased rhetoric on both sides of the issue that the combination of an ill-defined philosophy of privacy, the somewhat weak or ineffective policies based upon it, and the technological innovations that have arisen through big data will have a profound impact, for better and for worse, upon our personal lives and institutions. The big worry for most reasonable people is that the combination of big data's speed and variety, the malleable nature of digital data itself, and the ability for information to be recombined from various sources, along with expanding audiences and the belief that anonymized data is less valuable "in the marketplace" could together form a new definition of privacy that meets only the needs of businesses and information technology markets and not the needs of regular people looking "for the right to enjoy life" (Warren and Brandeis, 1890).

As Salleh and Janczewski (2016) write, "Security and privacy issues of big data not only originate from technological deficiencies, but . . . may also be the outcome of organizational culture and environmental influences" (p. 19). Unless better and more robust privacy policies are developed, privacy might be easily circumvented by such obvious and widespread "deficiencies" and "influences." The ALA policies, for example, show weakness in their theoretical underpinnings as well as in the face of wider technological impacts brought on by big data. Furthermore, since the ALA deals mostly with North American concerns and US law, how would privacy policies be applied to situations related to China, Japan, or Russia? What needs to be done to make sure that privacy does not become a target of politicized calls for "deregulation"? The next chapter will look into some of these negative aspects that have occurred with the major developers of big data—the big data overreach of certain corporations.

REFERENCES

American Library Association (ALA). (2013). ALA policy manual, section B: Positions and public policy statements. http://www.ala.org.

Ben-Shahar, O. (2016). Privacy is the new money, thanks to big data. *Forbes*. http://www.forbes.com.

Boyd, D., and Crawford, K. (2012). Critical questions for big data. *Information, Communication and Society, 15*(5), 662–679. doi:10.1080/1369118X.2012.678878.

Cameron, D. (2015). Edward Snowden tells you what encrypted messaging apps you should use. *Daily Dot*. http://www.dailydot.com.

Campbell, G. D., and Cowan, S. R. (2016). The paradox of privacy: Revisiting a core library value in an age of big data and linked data. *Library Trends, 64*(3), 492–511.

Choice Reviews Online. (2014). Privacy in the age of big data: Recognizing threats, defending your rights, and protecting your family. *52*(2). https://www.choicereviews.org.

Cohen, A. (2013). Is the NSA's spying constitutional? It depends which judge you ask. *Atlantic*. https://www.theatlantic.com.

Dwork, C., and Mulligan, D. (2013). It's not privacy and it's not fair. *Stanford Law Review, 35*. https://www.stanfordlawreview.org.

Google. (2017). Privacy policy, terms of service: Removal policies. https://support.google.com.

Groeger, L. (2011). Kevin Kelly's 6 words for the modern internet. *Wired*. https://www.wired.com.

Janes, J. (2012). Data, data, everywhere: As the big data beast fattens, will privacy and ethics get gobbled up? *American Libraries*. https://americanlibrariesmagazine.org.

Kelly, K. (@kevin2kelly). (2016). The internet is the world's largest copy machine. Twitter, April 24, 2016, 1:00 p.m. https://twitter.com/kevin2kelly/status/724327067865612289.

Kerr, I., and Earle, J. (2013). Prediction, preemption, presumption: How big data threatens big picture privacy. *Stanford Law Review*. https://www.stanfordlawreview.org.

Kuhn, T. (1962). *The structure of scientific revolutions*. Chicago: University of Chicago Press.

Ohlheiser, A. (2017). Erasing yourself from the internet is nearly impossible. But here's how you can try. *Washington Post*. https://www.washingtonpost.com.

O'Leary, D. (2015). Big data and privacy: Emerging issues. *Intelligent Systems, IEEE, 30*(6), 92–96.

Rubinstein, I. (2012). Big data: The end of privacy or a new beginning? NYU Public Law and Legal Theory Working Papers 357. http://lsr.nellco.org.

Salleh, K., and Janczewski, L. (2016). Technological, organizational and environmental security and privacy issues of big data: A literature review. *Procedia Computer Science , 100*, 19–28.

StopDataMining.me. (2017). Master list of data broker opt-out links. https://www.stopdatamining.me.

Tavani, H. T. (2007). Philosophical theories of privacy: Implications for an adequate online privacy policy. *Metaphilosophy, 38*(1), 1–22.

US Department of Health and Human Services (HHS). (2003). HIPAA health information privacy minimum necessary requirement. https://www.hhs.gov.

Warren, S., and Brandeis, L. (1890). The right to privacy. *Harvard Law Review, 14*(5), 193–220. Online version at http://groups.csail.mit.edu.

WikiLeaks. (2016). German BND-NSA inquiry exhibits. https://wikileaks.org.

Chapter Five

Big Data and Corporate Overreach

The bare facts of surveillance capitalism necessarily arouse my indignation because they demean human dignity.

— Shoshana Zuboff

"WITH FRIENDS LIKE THESE": ISSUES OF PRIVACY, PERSONAL FREEDOM, AND THE "NEW PROPAGANDA"

In *What Would Google Do?* Jeff Jarvis's enthusiastic "techsplanation" of the reasons for Google's ascendancy in the internet economy, the author asserts that in the future *all* people—regardless of their place in society, or their chosen career and industry, or their desire to retain whatever elements of privacy still exist—will need some *Googlejuice*, his term for that certain "magical" essence that drives up notoriety and, since it is central to the new information *economy*, one's personal profit. People will benefit, he argues, with an increased exposure to the outside world of their daily life, their goals, and their achievements. Jarvis dubs this the "New Publicness," insisting that we "all want to be found on Google. We all want 'Googlejuice'" (Jarvis, 2009, p. 43). Individuals, therefore, need a "search presence" and should release onto the web not only such things as a public-facing resume or CV but also information about our houses, our cars, or even our golf clubs, should we ever want to *sell* them. Both convenience *and* opportunity abound in this online world of enlightened self-interest—and by the way, those who cannot be found in Google "might as well not exist" (p. 43).

Sounds like a rather harsh assessment, doesn't it? Aside from the obvious pandering to Google as the *current* dominant player in the information technology field, Jarvis's apologia also downplays the problems of privacy and overplays the benevolent and rational self-interest that seems to be so much

65

at the heart of pro-business analysis and rhetoric. The choice in his mind is a stark one: either appear in Google or be left behind. This applies not just to businessmen or MBAs, his obvious audience for the book, but also to regular individuals. There is, of course, some germ of truth to his argument. There are measurable social, economic, and educational improvements stemming from internet access; one estimate suggests that "expanding internet access to an additional 2.2 billion people can increase GDP in developing countries by $2.2 trillion, create 140 million new jobs, and lift 160 million people out of extreme poverty" (Deloitte, 2014). So, yes, online access is important both socially and economically. It can be life changing, and LinkedIn, Facebook, or any other personal and professional website profiles provide exposure to an audience potentially interested in someone's marketable skills. In an era where eight men own *half* of humanity's accrued wealth, the digital divide starkly separates the haves from the have-nots (Mullany, 2017).

As a result, those unable or unwilling to use the internet are placed at significant social, economic, and educational disadvantages. Even now a digital divide persists in the United States between the ones able to access the internet and those unable to. Pew Research Center finds that 13 percent of the US population still does not use the internet. As seen in figure 5.1, the breakdown of this digital divide is disproportionate among age groups (41 percent people over sixty-five do not use the internet), race and ethnicity (Hispanics and black Americans are slightly less likely to use the internet), and class (middle and upper-middle class use the internet more; Perrin and Duggan, 2015). This is still markedly better, though, than the worldwide averages of internet use. In fact, 4.2 billion (approximately 57 percent) of the world's population, primarily people living in extreme poverty in undeveloped countries, do not have access to the internet (United Nations Broadband Commission, 2015).

But despite the obvious economic and social benefits to being online, the push by Jarvis—and he represents just *one* of many proponents of this "New Publicness," or "New Currency" (Ben-Shahar, 2016), which could just as easily slide into "New Propaganda"—to abandon privacy concerns for the sake of a little "Googlejuice" seems incredibly short-sighted. What happens, for instance, if Google decides to sell the data it has collected about its users? What happens if certain types of information or opinion become more valued and thus incentivized? In light of the demonstrated advantages to be online, what benefit might Google gain by actively leveraging its position as the preeminent holder of data about people? What if Ben-Shahar's so-called Grand Bargain turns out to be a Grand Con instead, as the University of Oxford's Computational Propaganda Research Project might indicate (Oxford Internet Institute, 2017)?

It's not that far-fetched. Bill Davidow finds that the internet itself has evolved over the years from an egalitarian, free-form information commons

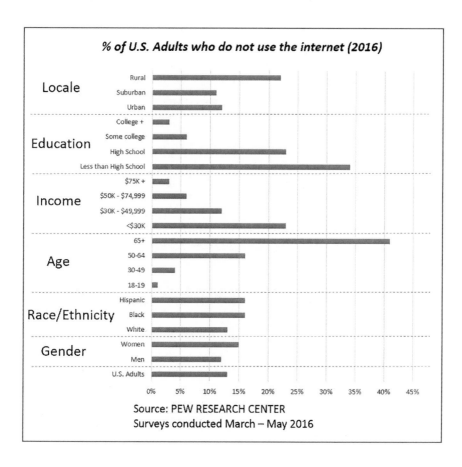

Figure 5.1. Chart showing the differences in internet use among various groups in the United States broken down by gender, race/ethnicity, age, economic class/ income, education, and locale. *Source:* Anderson and Perrin, 2016. Redrawn by author.

to a latter-day "skinner box," "integrated with operant conditioning techniques to motivate us" into lingering longer online and purchasing things, or at the very least clicking advertisements from now-ubiquitous "click bait" (Davidow, 2013). Taking this concept further, Shoshana Zuboff finds that the internet, in combination with big data analysis and tracking, is the force behind a new conception of free-market ideology called "surveillance capitalism," which aims to monetize the tracking of human behaviors on a large scale and conduct ongoing experimentation using the internet's infrastructure to better extract predictions of future behavior. The result of this, she believes, will be to "demean human dignity" (Zuboff, 2016) to benefit a few at the expense of everyone else (Taplin, 2017).

This chapter will attempt to look at some of the negative sides of this rush toward "New Publicity" and "New Currency." While it is tempting to fall into the enthusiastic and unquestioning camp of the Jarvises and Ben-Shahars of the world, consistently downplaying the negative side of tech giants poses some significant risks to individuals and societies. Ultimately, reality will need to win out over the hype, fantasy, and propaganda for the New Publicity and New Currency to be anything but attempts at corporate dominance in personal information markets. This chapter will therefore examine such problems related to data gathering and the overreach of corporations in their zeal to gather as much unmediated and nonanonymized data as possible. Unfortunately, this identity-tagged information is the very data that appears to be the most valuable to companies, and thus the most vulnerable to abuse. As a framework we will continue using Herman Tavani's approach to privacy, which defines the concept in terms of *consent*, *choice*, and *correction*. We will examine a number of cases in each where it seems apparent that overreach has occurred.

CORPORATE PRIVACY OVERREACH REGARDING CONSENT

Consent, as we saw in the previous chapter, should be considered one of the three important pillars of any concept of privacy and a foundation for a viable privacy policy. As a basic right in the concept of privacy, people should be allowed to decide whether or not information about their behavior is (a) recorded and (b) shared with others. An article appearing in the *Washington Post* in February 2017 outlines a case where the television manufacturer, Vizio, settled out of court with the Federal Trade Commission (FTC) and the State of New Jersey's attorney general for "secretly collecting—and selling—data about its customers' locations, demographics, and viewing habits" (Tsukayama, 2017). More troubling was that the company appears to have been recording "second-by-second information" of more than eleven million users of these televisions. Not only did they conduct a real-time examination of the behaviors of their users without their consent, but also they sold the information to third parties specializing in ad targeting.

If that weren't bad enough, the company also linked that information to demographic information such as gender, age, and income, providing more structured data about its users than just raw data. That shows a clear intent to manipulate the data in ways that would drive up the value of that information. The inclusion of that demographic information is tempting to corporations who gather the data to expand their profitability. In their defense, Vizio claims that individual users could not have been identified in the data they aggregated. However, this case shows that the line dividing personal privacy and corporate selling of that data is an extremely thin one. Vizio is but one step away from providing the most valuable information of all: personalized, individually recognizable data.

Some good things come out of the settlement though. According to Kevin Moriarty (2017), counsel for the Federal Trade Commission, "From now on, VIZIO is required to prominently disclose their data collection and sharing practices and get permission from the TV owners. The company also has to delete most of the data it already collected and put in place a privacy program that also checks their partners' privacy practices." Consent of the user will be required from now on for Vizio to collect this information.

Importantly, the retention of the data Vizio collects will also be monitored. This has long been an essential pillar of records management. Clear policies and best practices regarding data retention have been in full effect for print archives and other information-intensive organizations. Companies and organizations with long histories of records management—such as libraries, archives, hospitals, insurance companies, and so forth—are well aware of the laws and restrictions that surround information use, reuse, and release. However, in the sudden shift from companies moving from typical manufacturing functions (i.e., television manufacture) to the internet of things (IoT), which moves these manufacturers clearly into the sphere of information management, these types of missteps are bound to occur more frequently without clear oversight of their practices.

In the end, Vizio was penalized for collecting data without the consent of the users. No one had any idea that their behaviors were being monitored; they were never notified or given a chance to opt out of it. Vizio also never spelled out what would be done with this data, or how long it would be retained. Unfortunately, this likely represents only the tip of the iceberg. As the case was settled out of court, Vizio avoided any acknowledgment of wrongdoing. In the appearance of contrition, Vizio general counsel Jerry Huang stated, "Today, the FTC has made clear that all smart-TV makers should get people's consent before collecting and sharing television viewing information" (Tsukayama, 2017). Though the company seems chastised, the truth is that the regulations already exist to make these things clear. Vizio chose not to obey these guidelines and was caught. It is not unreasonable to suspect that many other companies have tried the same things and just haven't been caught.

Indeed, new technologies are being devised that will make it easier to track people while being ever-more intrusive and surreptitious enough to circumvent the notion of consent. One company, TVision, created a tracking system based on a body identification technology similar to the Xbox Kinect that can monitor a person's body language to determine whether or not viewers are actually looking at the television. At some point, facial recognition might be adopted to help determine your level of interest in the program or commercial being broadcast (Maheshwari, 2017). Current privacy policies do not necessarily consider privacy beyond whether someone is monitoring or not. But we also need to be able to provide clear limits. If not, it might be possible for companies to glean information about us without being aware of its importance—such as knowing exactly what mood we are in at a specific point in time just by monitoring our faces and body language.

Innocuous-looking toys, such as the Cayla talking doll or a CloudPet stuffed animal, that are linked to the internet have easily been hacked and the information sold to third parties, possibly organized crime (Franceschi-Bicchierai, 2017; Freytas-Tamura, 2017). The Disney Corporation has been accused of spying on children through dozens of its smartphone/iPad apps, in a likely violation of Federal Trade Commission rules, as well as COPPA, the Children's Online Privacy Protection Act, which is a federal act intended to protect the privacy of children (Fung and Shaban, 2017). The problem is ultimately one of both overreaching ambition to profit from the internet of things and the failure to competently consider the rights of consumers. In all cases, consumers and users of these products had no say in how the data was gathered, stored, and protected. Worse, in the case of children, there was no ability for the users to give legal consent given their ages; it is unconscionable to prey upon those who lack the ability to distinguish between levels for privacy or even the concept itself.

CORPORATE PRIVACY OVERREACH REGARDING CORRECTION

The second major component for any philosophy of privacy and subsequently any enforceable policy is the ability of individuals to correct and alter the status of information that has been gathered or shared with others. The more our data is collected, aggregated, and shared, the more chances exist for errors and unwanted releases to appear in the system. This problem was found to exist in a few different ways in the Google Books digitization project when metadata was gathered across numerous partnering institutions, resulting in a large number of errors. The problem was exacerbated by the combination of the sheer numbers of the texts involved in the project, the scant oversight on the quality of the metadata gathered, and the poor quality control of the scans themselves (James and Weiss, 2012). The problem stemmed from the automated aspects of the process as the subject heading metadata was imported not from libraries or cultural institutions—whose purview has developed robust and highly accurate metadata schema—but from Book Industry Standards and Communications (BISAC) Subject Codes (James and Weiss, 2012). This set was designed by the Book Industry Study Group to provide headings for booksellers and publishers to facilitate sales and merchandise distribution, not to aid memory institutions in collection development or organization, and is a poor choice for a large-scale digital library (BISG, 2016). Fortunately, such errors are merely a nuisance; they don't compromise human beings' safety and privacy in any real way, and they are easily amendable, once identified, as long as the institution responsible is willing to carry out the requisite changes.

The greater danger of big data, however, stems not *only* in the automated amplification of such errors but also from the widespread distribution of these errors at an extremely rapid pace. It doesn't take long on the internet for errors to be shared and reshared until they can be taken in some quarters as literal fact. Fiction can become "alternate facts" when cited in enough places that have the veneer of respectability. Veracity is one of the defining components of big data, yet this aspect is the most easily compromised in absence of digital safeguards that allow users to see how and when data was altered and by whom. The ability to account for and correct errors, therefore, becomes fundamentally important to preserving necessary ties to reality and factual information. This is the responsibility of not only the individuals affected but also the organizations that gather and handle their information. Yet, all too often, the drivers of these errors are not people—who can be held accountable for their actions—but *automata*, machines incorporating algorithmic functions in their decision-making processes operating without specific regard to law or custom.

A recent article shines light on the problems that Uber drivers are having with this automated, algorithmic approach to the evaluation of employee job performance (Pasquale, 2015). Drivers for the company are assessed based upon a rating system that relies in part on customer satisfaction. Drivers who fall below a certain threshold of "star ratings" are fired; ultimately the company has "no real appeal recourse or other due process in play for a rating system that can instantly put a driver out of work—it simply crunches the numbers" (Pasquale, 2015). Given the right (or wrong) combination of data, a driver's livelihood and actions are impacted in profound ways. However, the data collected about drivers is not merely customer ratings. The company also collects "Telematics," a branch of information technology concerned with the long-distance transmission of computerized information, which sends the driver's smartphone GPS location as well as the car accelerometer and gyroscope information to a central computer for data collection and processing (Hines, 2016). Not surprisingly, the company gathers information on Uber users as well, tracking their locations through their "Uber App" downloaded onto user cell phones. Recently, the company began collecting data about its users *even when they were not using the service* (Hawkins, 2016).

Tracking customers while using the app is not necessarily a major violation of privacy, though it is unclear if the privacy policy or user agreement makes such actions clear. However, Uber blurs the line on privacy by also tracking users outside of the specific uses of that app. This speaks directly to the previous section on consent yet also provides us with an issue on whether such behaviors can be rolled back. Can the information gathered even be retrieved and then deleted? But even worse for the Uber drivers—who are presumably protected by labor rights—there appears to be no recourse for them in a process that has become automated and abstracted by an algorithm-based decision-making process. If faulty information is gathered and perpetuated by an automated system, who is held responsible for the faulty decisions that result? An algorithm would not be liable. Would the company be liable for this? It's not clear.

At the same time, algorithms determining outcomes and making decisions are becoming more and more common and are assumed to be "incorruptible" because the automaton creating it is, ipso facto, incorruptible. Yet, as E. J. Spode (2017) reveals in his analysis of the algorithm-based, digital-ledger-technology blockchain, the "automation of trust is illusory." Even the best, supposedly invulnerable systems that espouse a "trustless" operation, where fallible humans are replaced by infallible numbers and coding, can still be hacked. Blockchain was no exception. Ethereum, a blockchain-based crypto-currency platform touted as a replacement for "self-executing contracts," and a potential replacement for corporation CEOs (as corporate decision making could be theoretically coded into the blockchain's ledgers), was hacked in 2016, resulting in the siphoning off of nearly fifty million dollars from its books (Spode, 2017).

Credit scores are a much more prosaic example of this problem of placing trust in *seemingly* objective systems. Many of us are dependent upon good credit scores to secure loans, get credit cards, or even obtain jobs. The score itself, though, is merely an abstraction of human behavior used to validate future trustworthy (or untrustworthy) behavior. FICO, the main credit scorer in the United States, has "found that words someone uses in his Facebook status could help predict his creditworthiness" (*Economist*, 2017). There are several problems with this. First, what happens if the algorithm determining one's credit score is compromised or hacked? The number itself would be misleading. Second, what happens if the score is further based upon faulty information from social media or subject to hacking and disinformation? In the case of a CV-sorting software application, for example, the analyzing algorithm was incorrect in its analysis and disqualified all twenty-nine thousand applicants to a position. It may be time-saving to employ these systems, but the accuracy in the decision making may be lost. As these types of "algorithmically driven decisions" increase and become more sophisticated—though not necessarily accurate—an "errant or discriminatory piece of information can wreck someone's employment or credit prospects" (Pasquale, 2015). And that remains to this day incredibly difficult to correct in even the most forgiving of circumstances.

CORPORATE PRIVACY OVERREACH REGARDING CHOICE

One of the essential questions examined in the previous chapter was How much data is *enough* data and who gets to decide the limits? As people have a lot to lose when privacy is violated, it is essential that they know when and where they can draw the line demarking their desire to remain private. People need to know when they can shut off data collection or monitoring. This points specifically to the need for *choice* as an essential component of a modern philosophy of privacy. The best rule of thumb, at least to me, originates from the Health Insurance Portability and Accountability Act (HIPAA) regulations privacy and confidentiality explanatory pages: "Protected health information should not be used or disclosed when it is not necessary to satisfy a particular purpose or carry out a function" (US HHS, 2003).

In one example, an employee at a company named Intermex was subjected to constant monitoring both on the job and off, raising the issue of where the work-life boundaries should exist. The employee claims to have been fired for complaining about and disabling an app that had been monitoring her behavior round the clock. The problem with this situation is that the employee had a complete lack of choice in what, when, and how data about her was collected. In the end, she was punished with job termination for choosing not to be monitored at all times. The company claims that it needs to ensure against corporate espionage and hacking; as a result, it feels the monitoring is justified. It also appears to be interested in predicting whether employees are showing signs of future problems. Utilizing "predictive analysis" will assist companies like Intermex in avoiding surprises from their employees. But that requires, at least for them, constant surveillance to create a usable baseline for comparison (Picchi, 2015).

In another notable example, a couple of Los Angeles–based companies are selling software that develops a profile of employees with the help of an algorithm. The profile attempts to create a baseline of a person's "normal behavior" in order to better identify an employee's potentially suspicious behavior (Lawrence, 2015). Taking things even further, companies have also developed radio-frequency identification (RFID) chips to embed under people's skin, to provide both security for chip-reading checkpoints and convenience for chip-reading vending machines or other amenities. Yet again, the issue remains problematic, for as they say, "trackable data is hackable data" (Paquette, 2017), and the choice to remove compromising technology becomes even more difficult when it has been inserted into one's body.

The central issue remains, too, that people should be allowed to set the conditions that track their behaviors, but employees in these companies are not really afforded this basic right as fear of reprisals or punishment could really be the motivating factor to comply. It appears that regulations similar to those enforced by HIPAA will need to be established universally in the era of big data. Currently only California, Minnesota, Tennessee, and Texas "have laws preventing the use of mobile tracking devices in order to track other individuals" (Moon, 2014). Federal regulations, though, might need to be in place so that if someone is constantly monitored, ideally by their consent—through wearable technology, implants, or mobile phones—the choice to limit data still remains in their power.

HANDS CAUGHT IN THE COOKIE JAR: ONLINE WEB TRACKING AND WEBSITE PRIVACY POLICIES

Finally, it is important to make note of the ubiquitous *cookie*, messages that web servers pass to web browsers when users visit internet sites. The cookies track information given by a user's computer as well as self-supplied information. They are mostly used for identifying users and allow for convenient browsing. Yet despite the ease of use they afford to web users, this aspect of privacy remains somewhat unexamined. Figure 5.2 shows a fairly common cookie and privacy agreement. Cookies were subject to some early web age controversy and have been fairly well regulated since the early 2000s in the United States (see "US Government Privacy, Security, and Accessibility Policies," https://www.usa.gov/policies) and in the European Union (see Directive 2002/58/EC on Privacy and Electronic Communications).

At bottom, cookies are essentially small nonexecutable text files placed on a web user's computer hard drive; this allows a website's web server to identify the online user visiting its site. In other words, it's an "internet user's identification card" (AboutCookies.org, n.d.). Although the purpose of the

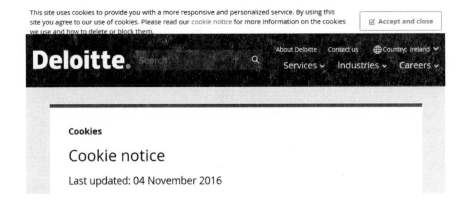

Figure 5.2.   Screenshot of a cookie notice appearing in the header of a web page; clear information is provided about the use of cookies and the rationale for it; people are also allowed to opt out or accept. *Source:* Deloitte, 2017.

cookie is generally to facilitate the communication between the user's computer and the website, they are also used "to monitor their users' web surfing habits and profile them for marketing purposes (for example, to find out which products or services they are interested in and send them targeted advertisements)" (ibid.). Overall, on a small scale or on familiar websites, cookies appear to be fairly benign.

But the interesting thing regarding the AboutCookies.org website is that even as they admit to the monitoring that takes place as users browse the web, they also claim that cookies are not dangerous and do not threaten internet user privacy. Despite their attempts to reassure users or to provide business-oriented justification for companies such as Deloitte, the contradictions as well as the history of their implementation are telling. They admit that "users' information is passed to third party web sites without the users' knowledge or consent, such as information on surfing habits" (ibid.). Privacy is being encroached upon specifically in the areas of consent, choice, and correction, especially when users are unaware of the monitoring being done. Their position also ignores the easily identifiable security holes that have also been known to occur in the implementation of web cookies, including network eavesdropping, DNS cache poisoning, cookie theft, proxy request security holes, and cross-site request forgeries. This is concerning since their website seems well established in terms of the number of backlinks to the site (nearly 33.4 million) and is cited by other well-established IT websites like Deloitte (Woorank, 2017).

While seemingly innocuous, targeted ads from such vendors as Amazon, Wayfair, and the like, represent the power that cookies have in *nudging* our behaviors (Symons, 2011). It may be true that cookies are merely small text files incapable of searching and collecting information from your hard drive, and that there is ultimately nothing to fear from them, but that is beside the point. It's like saying that a videotape in the surveillance camera is not a threat because it is merely composed of magnetic impulses on reels of thin plastic incapable of acting on their own without an agent. The problem isn't what they *merely are*; it's how they are *used*. When organizations—business or governmental, legitimate or otherwise—have the power to alter or impact our behaviors without our knowledge or consent, no matter how small the mechanism used to do so, it nevertheless represents a breach. A person's power to choose, alter, or amend these messages is compromised or taken away, resulting in lost privacy and diminished autonomy.

Furthermore, seemingly private, privileged, and confidential activities such as writing an email are now subjected to third-party monitoring as well. While these third parties are not necessarily scanning content in order to censor or curtail what people are saying, companies such as Google, Yahoo, and Microsoft are nevertheless blurring the distinction between what should be a private conversation between individuals and an attempt to sell merchandise or services. However, the distinction ought to remain clear and not subject to these nudging forces. Unfortunately, Gmail, Yahoo! Mail, and Microsoft's Hotmail, three of the most popular web-based email applications, scan users' messages either to provide them with targeted ads in exchange for free usage of the service or to ostensibly block spam (Brustein, 2013; Mitchell, 2013). Zuboff's (2016) concept of surveillance capitalism best explains this intrusive monetization of what used to be simple correspondence between people. Of course, the agreements users accept (and often do not completely read) for these services allow for such scanning of messages, leaving users without much choice but to accept and give up privacy, or to refuse and use a different email application. From this perspective, the Grand Bargain of the big data era is not looking like such a great deal for regular users who want to assert their privacy.

It becomes clear when looking at the various examples and seeing the number of cases coming out about the disclosure and use of data that a clear framework of privacy needs to be in place to prevent this type of overreach in the digital world and in the era of big data. Whether this is based in US national law as universally recognized and enforceable regulations or in smaller party-to-party privacy agreements remains to be seen. Nevertheless, clear frameworks must exist and must be fought over. As algorithms dominate decision making and we begin to move into the field of "predictive" data analysis—which will preempt the behaviors of people based on predetermined warning signs—it is even more important to have clear practices in place that demonstrate not only what lines can or cannot be crossed but also under what circumstances. This chapter, of course, has only covered the business world and its forays into big data and user monitoring. The next chapter, however, will examine the role that big data analytics plays in the realm of government oversight, monitoring, and political surveillance.

REFERENCES

AboutCookies.org. (n.d.). Cookies: Frequently asked questions. http://www.aboutcookies.org.

Anderson, M., and Perrin, A. (2016). 13% of Americans don't use the internet. Who are they? Pew Research Center. http://www.pewresearch.org.

Ben-Shahar, O. (2016). Privacy is the new money, thanks to big data. *Forbes*. http://www.forbes.com.

Book Industry Study Group. (BISG). (2016). BISAC subject codes. http://bisg.org.

Brustein, J. (2013). Yahoo Mail users, prepare for creepy, Gmail-style ads. Bloomberg. https://www.bloomberg.com.

Davidow, B. (2013). "Skinnerian marketing": Skinner marketing; We're the rats, and Facebook likes are the reward. *Atlantic*. https://www.theatlantic.com.

Deloitte. (2014). Value of connectivity: Economic and social benefits of expanding internet access. https://www2.deloitte.com.

Deloitte. (2017). Cookie notice. https://www2.deloitte.com.

Economist. (2017). Big data, financial services and privacy. https://www.economist.com.

Franceschi-Bicchierai, L. (2017). Internet of things teddy bear leaked 2 million parent and kids message recordings. Motherboard. https://motherboard.vice.com.

Freytas-Tamura, K. (2017). The bright-eyed talking doll that just might be a spy. *New York Times*. https://www.nytimes.com.

Fung, B., and Shaban, H. (2017). These 42 Disney apps are allegedly spying on your kids. *Washington Post*. https://www.washingtonpost.com.

Hawkins, A. J. (2016). Uber wants to track your location even when you're not using the app. Verge. http://www.theverge.com.

Hines, N. (2016). How does Uber track drivers? Telematics. Inverse. https://www.inverse.com.

James, R., and Weiss, A. (2012). An Assessment of Google Books' Metadata. *Journal of Library Metadata*, *12*(1): 15–22.

Jarvis, J. (2009). *What Would Google Do?* New York: Collins Business.

Lawrence, D. (2015). Companies are tracking employees to nab traitors. Bloomberg. https://www.bloomberg.com.

Maheshwari, S. (2017). For marketers, TV sets are an invaluable pair of eyes. *New York Times*. https://www.nytimes.com.

Mitchell, D. (2013). Much like Google, Microsoft also scans your email. *Fortune*. http://fortune.com.

Moon, L. (2014). Key considerations when monitoring employees using GPS tracking devices. *National Law Review*. http://www.natlawreview.com.

Moriarty, K. (2017). VIZIO settlement: Smart TVs should not track your shows without your O.K. Federal Trade Commission Consumer Information Blog. https://www.consumer.ftc.gov.

Mullany, G. (2017). World's 8 richest have as much wealth as bottom half of global population. *New York Times*. https://www.nytimes.com.

Oxford Internet Institute, University of Oxford. (2017). The computational propaganda research project. http://comprop.oii.ox.ac.uk.

Paquette, D. (2017). Her dilemma: Do I let my employer microchip me? *Washington Post*. https://www.washingtonpost.com.

Pasquale, F. (2015). Digital star chamber. Aeon. https://aeon.co.

Perrin, A., and Duggan, M. (2015). Americans' internet access: 2000–2015. Pew Research Center. http://www.pewinternet.org.

Picchi, A. (2015). Do companies have a right to watch employees 24/7? *CBS News Money-Watch*. http://www.cbsnews.com.

Spode, E. J. (2017). The great cryptocurrency heist. Aeon. https://aeon.co.

Symons, J. (2011). Marketing: Are you being nudged in the right direction? Attercopia. https://www.attercopia.co.uk.

Taplin, J. (2017). Google doesn't want what's best for us. *New York Times*. https://www.nytimes.com.

Tsukayama, H. (2017). These smart TVs were apparently spying on their owners. *Washington Post*. https://www.washingtonpost.com.

United Nations Broadband Commission. (2015). The state of broadband 2015. UNESCO Open Access Repository. http://www.broadbandcommission.org.

US Department of Health and Human Services (HHS). (2003). HIPAA health information privacy minimum necessary requirement. https://www.hhs.gov.

Woorank. (2017). Aboutcookies.org. https://www.woorank.com.

Zuboff, Shoshana. (2016). Google as a fortune teller: The secrets of surveillance capitalism. Frankfurter Allgemeine Zeitung. http://www.faz.net.

Chapter Six

Liberty and Justice for All

The Surveillance State in the Age of Big Data

Whenever you hear a man speak of his love for his country, it is a sign that he expects to be paid for it.

—H. L. Mencken

I've been in a place where what was said was not real, and what was real was not allowed, where people disappeared behind doors and were never heard from again, or were smuggled into other realms.

—Anna Funder

IN A "DEEP STATE" OF MIND

Surveillance is the ugly side of the big data; imagine all aspects of one's digital footprint—both voluntary and involuntary—recorded and analyzed for threats and then saved for possible use against you later. Surveillance itself is a mechanism of power, and to examine the roots of surveillance is to get at the sources of this power: political, physical, spiritual, and otherwise. The prospect of examining in detail the secrecy, disinformation, and fringy aspects surrounding the topic of government surveillance and the recent widespread term "deep state" fills me with trepidation. I am well aware just how unhinged it looks to zero in on the phantasms of paranoid and unsubstantiated conspiracy theories. From lizard people and flat-earthers to faked moon landings, anti-vaxxers, and the aliens of Area 51, conspiracy theories have sucked in otherwise-intelligent people willing to believe the absurd despite the existence of convincing counterevidence (Osberg, 2015; Shermer, 2013, 2014). Additionally, when confronted by evidence that contradicts such beliefs, people have a tendency to dig in and bolster their originally held beliefs. This "backfire effect" means that corrections to information held as factual can "increase the strength of the participants' misconceptions if those corrections contradicted their ideologies" (McRaney, 2011). It is just too far outside perspective for comfort, and so people will reject everything that doesn't affirm their prior beliefs.

But recent observations by numerous *mainstream* thinkers, authors, and democracy watchdogs suggest that regardless of the political representatives in place, or which parties control the Congress or the presidency, other powers may actually have more control over the United States' national agenda and the direction in which the country is going. Add to this the surprising number of news stories occurring in early 2017, and the evidence appears to be piling up and pointing toward a series of large-scale surveillance operations. This apparatus, dubbed the "deep state," is suggested by some to be enforced by the so-called military-industrial complex, designed to benefit various plutocratic business leaders in the country, and is enforced by the numerous agencies that exist with large bureaucratic powers beyond the two- and four-year cycles of national elections (Bunch, 2017; Moyers, 2015). These "permanent power factions" exist beyond the country's democratic conventions and exercise power in secret (Greenwald, 2017). Spelled out in this manner, it *still* reads like paranoia. With cycles of fake news and political administrations citing their own "alternate facts," it is hard to take much of anything at face value, let alone vast conspiracies hiding in plain sight or buried deep within intricate, perpetually funded bureaucratic structures. Others, such as Doyle McManus or Max Fisher (2017), remain voices of reason and suggest, rather than a deep, secretive state, there is a "broad state" of resistance at work in the current political climate (McManus, 2017), or that the term itself is merely a meaningless and distorted interpretation of the Turkish concept derin devlet (R.J.E., 2017).

At the risk of alienating readers who may favor one side of the political spectrum above another, the fact remains that the US government *has* shown ample evidence of tipping the scales in favor of the billionaire class at the expense of all others—including those in need of health care, a usable infrastructure, social welfare, livable minimum wages, justice against the abuses of Wall Street greed, environmental safety, and so on. It has been relatively easy for funding to go toward the destruction of countries (Iraq and Afghanistan), toward bailing out those who caused the Great Recession of 2008–2010, or toward creating corporate welfare policies, but incredibly difficult to get adequate funding to repair roads and bridges, fix inequalities in the educational system, or even provide pipes for clean water as Flint, Michigan, has shown. Defunding agencies is not uncommon (Dennis, 2017). Income and wealth inequality has increased steadily in the United States since the 1970s (Piketty and Goldhammer, 2014). Quality-of-life concerns have become secondary to the discredited but seemingly undead faith-based ideology of supply-side economics and deregulated markets in which the purported "creators of jobs" are the ones most deserving of a release on their tax burdens. Governor Sam Brownback's failed voodoo economics tax experiment in Kansas since 2011 should have put the final nail in the Laffer curve coffin. Yet the idea persists, based as it is on a *tiny* kernel of truth that must be implemented under the *right* set of conditions (Ritholtz, 2017).

Ultimately, the closest thing the United States has to an official religion is capitalism, and laissez-faire capitalism is its ideological, though increasingly unsustainable, stab at fundamentalism (Jouet, 2012). Solving the problems caused by these systemic inequalities requires centered pragmatists, not ideologues (Collier, 2017). Of course, this digression into the propaganda of capitalism only takes us so far. There are plenty of other factors involved contributing to the current state of affairs in the United States, not just strange conspiracies or questionable decisions being made by the government, or policies built upon discredited economic theories. It is not the purpose of this book to delve too deeply into them either, as numerous commentaries and discussions by highly credentialed political theoreticians exist (Collier, 2017; Fukuyama, 1989; Zuboff, 2016).

Instead, the real issue at stake for this book is the perpetuation of the type of targeted propaganda, or "fake news" in the current parlance, that arguably nudges whole groups of people into voting against their own interests (Jan, 2017) and the chilling effect that surveillance has had on whole populations and their ability to hold or investigate unpopular opinions and topics (Cushing, 2016; Penney, 2016). Some of the propaganda is the result of manipulative "bots," online executable program codes that function like real people by posting texts onto social media platforms (i.e., Twitter, Facebook, online news forums, etc.) to shape public opinion or discredit rival viewpoints and ideas, creating "a swamp of unreality, a world where you don't know whether the emotions you are feeling are manipulated by men or machines" (Applebaum, 2017). The recent investigations by the FBI during the presidential election cycle of 2016 didn't solely demonstrate that our politicians are careless or corrupt; instead, they served to reveal the vast and unmatched surveillance and manipulative technological powers that exist within their reach as well as the reach of hackers external to the United States (Bunch, 2017). Other scandals in recent years regarding the CIA, the NSA, and even local/regional police suggest that the technologies capable of gathering massive amounts of data are widespread and can be implemented at multiple levels of government.

It remains to be seen whether all this hints at a true "deep state," as some assert, or is merely a reflection of the unease people have with ever-changing power structures, as most conspiracy theories seem to reveal of their believers. The issues are nevertheless valid; the feeling of distrust is palpable *and* legitimate, and represents a problem far greater than political factions. The causes of such distress still bear investigation as well as the role that libraries might take in helping to mitigate some of the distrust that has built up recently.

This chapter will examine these issues of big data collection through the lenses of privacy, liberty, and intellectual freedom as they relate to the public sphere and the ideals of democracy. Conversely, the issues of encroachment of civil liberties and the prediction of behaviors (though mostly those deemed *antisocial* behaviors) will be addressed as well. Extreme effort will be made to avoid sweeping generalizations or statements without documented reference to well-respected scholars, concrete factual evidence, or reasonable argumentation.

THE MODERN SURVEILLANCE APPARATUS: A QUICK OVERVIEW OF ITS DEVELOPMENT

Before getting into what types of data or the extent of data collection occurring in the United States, we will spend a little time examining the structure of the modern surveillance apparatus. Reginald Whitaker (1999) calls the twentieth century "the century of Intelligence," which he characterizes as a systematic acquisition and sorting of information. Systematic is the key concept as despite being old, the adage is that spying is the second oldest profession in the world "and just as honorable as the first" (p. 15).

Indeed, spying has been around as long as humanity itself, but it is mainly in the twentieth century that spying became an incredibly "organized bureaucratic activity" (ibid., p. 2). The most notorious of this is probably the example of East Germany from the immediate postwar period until the fall of the Berlin Wall and the collapse of communism in 1989. Whitaker traces the development of the East German Stasi as a combination of "both Gestapo and Cheka [Soviet Union's Commission to Combat Counterrevolution and Sabotage—an early precursor to the KGB] traditions in the Stasi with a surveillance apparatus that penetrated every nook and cranny of civil society, turning friends into informers against friends, even spouses against spouses" (ibid., p. 26). Anna Funder recounts that "the only mass medium the government couldn't control was the signal from western television stations" (2002, p. 17). In terms of raw numbers, the Stasi reached an incredible surveillance ratio of one agent for every two hundred citizens, but some estimates that include part-time informers have estimated one agent for every six and a half people (Koehler, 1999). In light of these figures, it is no wonder that East Germany is often considered the most surveilled state in history (Annie, 2015; Rosenberg, 2007), especially as various Western agencies simultaneously engaged in espionage activities against their East German counterparts.

By the fall of the Berlin Wall and the reunification of Germany, surveillance had undergone significant changes from previous decades, relying much more on electronic video and audio recording devices than on traditional cloak-and-dagger approaches. But despite being the most surveilled state utilizing current devices, East German authorities nevertheless relied primarily on analog technologies: tape recordings, film, and paper files, along with physical harassment, gaslighting techniques known as *Zersetzung*, and the like. In the months after the collapse of East Germany, former Stasi agents shredded, burned, and destroyed as much paper as they could until protests and legislation prevented further destruction. Afterward, however, six hundred million scraps of paper were nevertheless recovered and the information contained in them retained. One East German woman learned from this document recovery that over eighty informants had been spying on her (Rosenberg, 2007). Yet, despite the scope and the exhaustive collection activities, the materials thankfully remained bound to their analog materials, limiting the extent to which that information could be shared.

However, the world has changed significantly since the days of the Cold War. Digital technologies have evolved to the point that what seemed impossible a few years ago, such as face recognition and artificial intelligence (AI) algorithmic decision making, are now easily implemented in specific contexts. Digital technology has the power to eliminate the "ephemeral" from day-to-day conversation, correspondence, or discussion, allowing conversations that used to be lost to time and experience to be recorded, stored, and accessed again.

"COLLECT IT ALL": SURVEILLANCE IN THE UNITED STATES

The story of organized surveillance activities in the United States starts with the FBI, which was founded in the late nineteenth century, and continues with more surveillance agencies established during and after World War II. The NSA, the CIA, and the FBI all increased their surveillance activities through the 1950s and 1960s at the height of the Cold War and have never ceased. Though difficult for obvious reasons to recount the activities of multiple organizations carrying out clandestine operations, there have nevertheless been reports by fearless journalists, historians, political appointees, and whistleblowers over the years who have revealed their secrets. Several of these will be recounted here, including the 1976 Church report and the Snowden files, released through WikiLeaks, the main source of recent primary information on espionage activities.

In the wake of the 9/11 terrorist attacks, much has been ceded to the intelligence community in order to wage the war on terror. The famous adage attributed to Benjamin Franklin, "Those who would give up Essential Liberty to purchase a little Temporary Safety, deserve neither Liberty nor Safety," is often used as a counterargument to the encroachment occurring under the surveillance state. There is some kernel of truth to this, but it is hardly axiomatic. It doesn't follow that giving up a little liberty for the sake of safety means we don't deserve either. That's a little too pat. At heart, though, is a conflict in worldviews. It seems that each generation must confront the tradeoffs that exist between "liberty" on the one hand and "security" on the other. I urge readers to judge this on their own as they read through the ample evidence of surveillance activities that exists. Readers should determine for themselves how much security they need and how much liberty they are willing to give up in return for it.

The Church Committee: "There Are No Rules in Such a Game"

The Church Committee, or in formal parlance, the "Senate Select Committee to study governmental operations with respect to intelligence activities (1975–1976)," was one of several investigations in the mid-1970s, following the Watergate hearings, the Rockefeller Report (aka the US President's Commission on CIA Activities within the United States), and the Pike Committee (aka US House Permanent Select Committee on Intelligence) into the abuses of surveillance and covert operations by America's secretive intelligence organizations. Essentially starting with surveillance activities in the 1940s and ranging through to the early 1970s, the Church Committee examined the state of the surveillance community and found rampant abuses at the hands of the United States' intelligence-gathering organizations, including the FBI, the CIA, and the NSA (United States Congress, Senate, 1976). It found fault with what it perceived to be rampant abuses, exacerbated by little oversight and a lack of regard for the rule of law. In a telling quotation from the Hoover Commission Report from 1954, the report states, "There are no rules in such a game. Hitherto accepted norms of human conduct do not apply. If the U.S. is to survive, long-standing American concepts of 'fair play' must be reconsidered" (ibid.).

The Church report also pinpoints the main issue: the dilemma of secrecy while attempting to maintain an open constitutional government. The Church Committee believed the following issues needed to be resolved:

- Lack of clear legislation defining the authority for permissible intelligence activities.
- Secrecy shields these groups from full accountability.
- Covert action allows a "secret shortcut around the democratic process."
- The line between public and private action has been blurred, undermining sense of integrity.

- Waste and redundancy are rampant among the organizations because of secrecy and lack of Congressional oversight.
- Secrecy is a "tragic conceit"; any policies based on it damage America's reputation not only internationally but among its own citizens as well. (United States Congress, Senate, 1976)

The impact of the committee, though, has been long-standing. One of the main pieces of legislation to stem, in part, from the Church Committee was the Foreign Intelligence Surveillance Act of 1978 (FISA). This legislation outlined clear limitations for the intelligence community, including electronic surveillance activities, physical searching, pen registers (i.e., number tracing), and access to business records.

Ironically, as Russell Miller (2008) asserts, "the reaction against the Church Committee . . . appears to have had greater influence than the committee itself" (p. xvi). In the post-9/11-era political realignment, Vice President Dick Cheney appears to have done much to dismantle the protections FISA had created. Subsequent amendments, including the Terrorist Surveillance Act of 2006, the Protect America Act of 2007, the Foreign Intelligence Surveillance Act of 1978, the Amendments Act of 2008, and the 2015 USA Freedom Act, have served to broaden the powers of the intelligence community while diminishing the original FISA provisions.

9/11 Surveillance: The PATRIOT Act; "History Was Repeating Itself"

The aftermath of the terrorist attacks on September 11, 2001, brought about immediate "Church bashing" (Miller, 2008). Within days Senator Kit Bond (R-Missouri) and other conservative commentators, including the well-known novelist Tom Clancy, asserted that the attacks were a direct result of the regulations and prohibitions put in place as a result of the Church Committee's report from 1976 and its related legislation, FISA. Others believed the Church Committee "maimed the American intelligence community, turning the CIA into 'the functional equivalent of the Department of Agriculture'" (Miller, 2009, p. 2).

As a result, the most comprehensive loosening of FISA occurred a mere six weeks after the September 11 attack with the USAPATRIOT Act of 2001, an acronym for "Uniting and Strengthening America by Providing Appropriate Tools Required to Intercept and Obstruct Terrorism Act of 2001," described as "an Act to deter and punish terrorist acts in the United States and around the world, to enhance law enforcement investigatory tools, and for other purposes." All of this is merely doublespeak describing the loosening of the basic protections afforded by the FISA act. The ten titles of the USAPATRIOT Act covered various aspects of homeland security, including domestic security, surveillance, anti–money-laundering, border security, information sharing, terrorism and criminal law, and improved intelligence.

What is particularly germane to this discussion is what appears in Title II: Surveillance Procedures. Title II expanded the ability to surveil both *noncitizens and citizens* alike and removed the necessity to justify doing so. Wiretapping permissions were also widened to allow access to email and websites. Warrants were expanded to include voicemails. Later amendments to the FISA act, the 2007 amendments in particular, served to expand the limits initially imposed upon espionage activities. Ultimately the legacy of these amendments to the original act provided more room for interpretation and leeway for intelligence organizations to spy on a growing number of people.

Edward Snowden and the Post-9/11 NSA Spying Programs

The scope of the NSA's spying program is immense; as quoted in Glenn Greenwald's book (2014), an NSA operative states "collection is outpacing our ability to ingest, process and store to the 'norms' to which we have become accustomed" (p. 151). In 2006, the NSA predicted metadata collection would grow by 600 billion records each year, with roughly 1 to 2 billion new telephone calls collected every day. Greenwald determined from his analysis of the Snowden documents released on WikiLeaks that the NSA could record 20 billion communications per day, 1.7 billion of which were generated by American citizens. Overall in 2012, 20 trillion transactions of US citizens were successfully tracked. Ultimately, *75 percent of all internet traffic was monitored and recorded* in some fashion by the NSA and 1 trillion pieces of metadata were processed. The Snowden papers led Greenwald to conclude "the US government had built a system that has as its goal the complete elimination of electronic privacy worldwide" (Greenwald, 2014, p. 94).

Ultimately, the NSA justifies its program as a protection of American interests in all areas of life, including security, economics, diplomacy, and as a safeguard for government programs. They also justify the scope by fixating on the differences between content and metadata. In their minds, the scope of gathering one trillion phone metadata records is irrelevant since they are not gathering the content, just the *description* of the calls. But this is quite disingenuous. Just noting who, how long, and when one person calls another person can tell a lot about a person's state of mind, their situation, and even their political inclinations. As Edward Felten states, metadata can act as "a proxy for content"; it is easily analyzed, is precise, and creates more complete pictures of scenarios, contacts, and overall personal networks (Greenwald, 2014, p. 134).

As of writing this book in 2017, a number of explosive revelations on the scope and scale of the surveillance apparatus in the United States occurred in quick succession and help to shed further light on these assertions. On March 7, 2017, as reported in the *Washington Post* and many other reputable news organizations, WikiLeaks released what it calls "Vault 7" (WikiLeaks, 2017c), a collection of documents that reveal some of the CIA's covert activities and contain the "hacking methods that many experts already assumed the agency had developed" (Miller and Nakashima, 2017). This "trove" of hacking tools allowed the CIA to compromise ordinary, commonly used consumer devices (Miller and Nakashima, 2017). Adding to the general feeling of unease, the current US president then accused, without any evidence it must be noted, the previous administration of wiretapping his offices. Speculation on the motives or purposes of such an accusation is manifold. However, the general climate of paranoia that fuels these speculations must be understood from the wider context of the surveillance state that some call a modern-day panopticon. The day of big brother is, indeed, here (Cunningham, 2017).

INTERSECTION OF BIG BROTHER AND BIG DATA CORPORATIONS

Despite the revelations found in Vault 7 that seem to suggest corporations are in part the unwitting victims of the intelligence community's rapacious need to surveil, the overall scope of surveillance could not have been accomplished by itself or through entirely homegrown inventions; indeed, the government has had to cooperate with telecommunication companies in order to extend its reach "to prevent the slightest piece of electronic communication from evading its systemic grasp" (Greenwald, 2014, p. 94).

What may not be widely known is the US government and its intelligence organizations spend 70 percent of their budgets on contractors, many of which are private-sector corporations (ibid.). There are numerous companies filling the need that the government agencies have to meet their surveillance operations. This is also born out, ironically, in the Vault 7 revelations, as it was an *unnamed third-party contractor* who apparently leaked the codes they used under the direction of the CIA.

Government agencies are also partnering with seemingly legitimate companies. Stratfor (2017), which is listed in WikiLeaks as a well-known government "collaborator," calls itself a "geopolitical intelligence platform and publisher." The partnership between Stratfor and the CIA shows another example of how the corporate world and government work together to gather data on others. WikiLeaks explains more on their website: the emails extracted from the Snowden files reveal the inner workings of *a company that fronts as an intelligence publisher*, but provides confidential intelligence services to large corporations, such as Bhopal's Dow Chemical Co., Lockheed Martin, Northrop Grumman, Raytheon and government agencies, including the US Department of Homeland Security, the US Marines and the US Defense Intelligence Agency. The emails show Stratfor's web of informers, pay-off structure, payment laundering techniques and psychological methods. (WikiLeaks, 2017a)

Additionally, the government works with so-called Special Source Operations (SSOs), which is a series of strategic partnerships with more than eighty global companies. The government data-collecting initiative PRISM gathers data from the servers of the nine largest internet companies (Greenwald, 2014). The NSA also works closely with Microsoft, despite its public outcries against other tech rivals for allowing backdoor access. Microsoft (2017) publicly asserts that emails in Outlook can be kept private: "Only the recipient who has the private key that matches the public key used to encrypt the message can decipher the message for reading." But Outlook, as evidenced in the Snowden papers, is not a secure software program, and backdoor access exists that will allow government agencies to circumvent the program's encryption key (Greenwald, 2014).

In the recent revelations stemming from the release of Vault 7, it has also come to light that numerous companies work as contractors for the federal government, providing "zero day" services. Zero day refers to the types of security flaws found in devices that have not been disclosed to the public (or to companies) and are immediately exploitable since no one else has been made aware of them. The Rand Corporation report entitled "Zero Days, Thousands of Nights" suggests more than two dozen contractors each pull in between $1 million to $2.5 million per year for such services (Ablon and Bogart, 2017). According to David Ignatius of the *Washington Post*, "More than 200 zero-day exploits studied by Rand went undetected for an average of 6.9 years, with only 5.8 percent discovered by competitors within a year" (Ignatius, 2017). In that regard, the problem is exacerbated when the government itself is choosing to exploit vulnerable technologies in order to gain an edge in surveillance. In the end, once a vulnerability is noticed by someone, it only takes about three weeks for a fully functioning exploit to be developed (Ablon and Bogart, 2017). This demonstrates there is a clear motivation by the government to keep tech vulnerabilities secret from companies despite the potentially negative effects on users.

COUNTERSURVEILLANCE GROUPS, THEIR MEASURES, AND THEIR STRATEGIES

After reading about this international apparatus of spying and mass data collection, one wonders if there is anything anyone can do, or if there are measures anyone can take to counteract such large-scale intrusions. With the law not entirely on our side, government agencies hiding their actions, and numerous multinational corporations being two-faced about their involvement, it is looking bleak for the protection of privacy.

As the Church Committee stated *forty years ago*, the only way to fight the erosion of privacy and the abuses from surveillance is through transparency. Even if we can't assume that our emails or other electronic communications are entirely free from surveillance, we can attempt to keep it in the light. For better and for worse, WikiLeaks has provided some of that transparency. Democracy nongovernment organization (NGO) watchdogs also provide some of this transparency but need to have stronger teeth. Additionally, there are countertechnologies being developed and implemented, but it is unclear whether these are effective in any capacity. Many have assumed that encryption can safeguard privacy, but it appears this is not the case, especially with so many "back doors" built into the technology. This section will examine some of these antisurveillance groups and measures in more detail.

WikiLeaks

Currently the single most important and most widely accessed source of information for spying, intelligence, corporate malfeasance, and so on, is WikiLeaks. Founded in 2006 by Julian Assange, the freely available website provides the most comprehensive source of classified, private, and hacked information in the world (WikiLeaks, 2017d). It has been cited by more than twenty-eight thousand scholarly articles, academic papers, and court filings. Its partners include the top newspapers and news organizations in the world, ranging from the *New York Times* and the *Washington Post* in the United States to *Der Spiegel* in Germany, *El Pais* in Spain, *Le Monde* in France, and more (WikiLeaks, 2017b). Much of what we generally know about the scope of spying in the digital age stems from this invaluable but controversial resource.

Controversy does seem to follow the organization. Regarding the March 2017 release of the "CIA hacking toolkit," for example, WikiLeaks has recently come out to state that it will release the code gleaned from the CIA to corporations in order to help them prevent the future hacking of such devices (Nakashima, Dwoskin, and Barrett, 2017). This might be seen as an admirable public position to take for some, on the one hand, since it makes a clear statement on the importance of personal privacy and cybersecurity in the face of clear government overreach. The position also allows corporations to save face by pretending to be the victims of a vast intelligence community conspiracy working against them. Of course, in truth, it also gives them a chance to right a wrong that they likely had a significant part in. Some of the companies affected by this leak were *already* working very closely with the CIA or other government spy agencies to provide access to information through either back doors or the wholesale sharing of information. The offer to share the CIA's code with them strikes me as more like a self-serving stunt and a convenient forgetting of the complicity of corporations in the development of the surveillance state (and, even worse, surveillance capitalism) than a true long-term solution to the problem. Providing this code still doesn't change the fact that IT corporations routinely cooperate with spy agencies. Releasing the hacking code won't solve that fundamental problem.

However, prior to releasing the code, WikiLeaks apparently has required the companies affected—which include Google, Apple, and Microsoft (all companies with known relationships with the NSA and intelligence community already)—to meet a set of as-of-yet-undisclosed demands. The speculation is that part of the demands would include at least a shortened timeline (likely within ninety days) to secure the devices affected (Francheschi-Bicchierai, 2017).

Unsurprisingly, the WikiLeaks decision has been met with significant backlash in the public discourse in the United States. Fareed Zakaria, to name just one of the many high-profile authors writing about WikiLeaks, has come out against the leaks as well as the plan to provide the code to affected corporations. Unfortunately, his argument boils down to a simplistic appeal to American exceptionalism. American institutions, he argues, are far more transparent and subject to far more oversight than their counterparts in China, Russia, North Korea, and the like. Yet WikiLeaks has yet to release anything by them, whom Zakaria sees as far more dangerous. He believes this to be inherently unfair. While that may be the case from an "objective" perspective, in arguing that America should be held to a higher standard, *he can't fairly criticize WikiLeaks for doing just that.*

Zakaria also claims that Assange's actions are the result of a malicious obsession, suggesting the United States is "its obsessive target" (Zakaria, 2017). He may have a point. But it also seems just as likely that WikiLeaks is suggesting that if America is going to consider itself exceptional, then it should act that way. It is far more dangerous to have a wolf in sheep's clothing escaping detection than it is to have wolves freely roaming about. Furthermore, while WikiLeaks' motives may not always be transparent—and it is often unclear to me why they do what they do—their leaks revealing American covert activities expose much of the hypocrisy in the country's use of military force and the justifications provided for it.

Another contradiction to Zakaria's assertion is the revelation that Wiki-Leaks has been able to release American intelligence primarily because the United States has created its own leaky boat easily hacked by using out-sourced, private contractors in place of government workers to handle the most confidential information. Indeed, Edward Snowden himself was an employee of Booz-Allen, a corporate contractor for the NSA (Shorrock, 2017). The fact that it was a lot easier to get this information from these contractors than other foreign governments that do not engage in outsourcing might explain why there's a whole lot more of this information being released. Vault 7 is but another example of a third-party contractor mishandling federal government information; it is not primarily the result of obsessive behavior.

Democracy and Human Rights Watchdog Organizations

Aside from WikiLeaks there are a number of watchdogs and pro-democracy groups that are attempting to combat the surveillance state apparatus. One of the most important ones in the United States is the American Civil Liberties Union (ACLU), whose mission is "to safeguard everyone's rights" (ACLU, 2017a). Their strategies involve litigation, advocacy of rights, and providing a clear delineation of what constitutes encroachment of the liberties and freedoms set aside for all people in the United States. Their historical involvement advocating for human rights is long and illustrious, being on the right side of history for civil rights, gay rights, antiracism legislation, and more. Many of their concerns have been unpopular or controversial at the time they took their stances, including their defense of free speech among hate groups such as the Ku Klux Klan, or siding against the 1942 Presidential Executive Order 9066, which forced the internment of 110,000 Japanese Americans. Unsurprisingly, they have come out against the NSA and other agencies in their surveillance activities (ACLU, 2017b). Indeed, taking a note from previous events in history, they assert "powerful, secret surveillance tools will almost certainly be abused for political ends and turned dispropor-tionately on disfavored minorities" (ibid.). Their priorities are clearly for preserving the democratic pillars of American society.

Other groups of note that are attempting to curtail surveillance are Priva-cy International (PI), the Privacy Rights Clearinghouse (PRC), and the Elec-tronic Frontier Foundation (EFF). Each of these groups attempts, in various ways, to provide avenues for people to protect themselves against surveil-lance. The EFF, for example, focuses on online privacy and legal matters related to online culture and information science (EFF, 2017; McCandlish, 2002). Privacy International investigates "the secret world of government surveillance and expose the companies enabling it" (Privacy International, 2017a). Several of their initiatives involve fostering a global privacy movement, standing up to what they call "data exploitation," and challenging "unprecedented state surveillance capabilities" (Privacy International, 2017b).

The Privacy Rights Clearinghouse is a nonprofit organization advocating consumer privacy and is especially active in the state of California (PRC, 2017a). Of especial interest is their listing of data breaches that have occurred since 2005. According to their tally, 5,356 data breaches have occurred, which released more than 908 million documents (PRC, 2017b). They account for the various types of data breaches that happen as well, including payment card fraud, hacking and malware, insider leaks, lost physical documents, losses of portable and stationary devices, unintended disclosures, and more. Examining their database of card fraud instances, one can search through the publicly disclosed instances that occurred in various locations across the United States. A lot of the instances involve the skimming of credit card information from gas stations in several states including Nevada, Utah, and California.

IMPACT OF SURVEILLANCE ON THE ROLE OF LIBRARIES AND LIBRARIANS

But what of the impact from this pervasive surveillance culture on libraries and librarians? What role or responsibility does a library have in the age of mass surveillance? Are libraries complicit in the surveillance state by the fact that they are online and largely unable to prevent such widespread and intrusive spying activities? Of course, if libraries are complicit in this manner, then any online organization becomes a partner, even if unwitting, in surveillance too.

Many in librarianship would argue that the concept of privacy is essential to building the trust of library users. Libraries provide information and in turn generate their own information about their users. Some of this information is necessary for running a library, including authentication for database access, user information to lend and keep track of books, and so on. Generally this doesn't elicit much interest beyond the need to assess the return on investment of purchased resources, or the occasional forays into measuring student success. But sometimes the type of subject matter that patrons use has fallen under the microscope of government agencies. Libraries in certain eras have been compelled by warranted searches or by law to give up access to private patron records. It is not unreasonable to assume that if 75 percent of internet traffic is capable of being observed by the NSA that libraries and library usage falls within this.

Even if one has nothing to hide, the mere knowledge of being watched complicates the trust-based relationship that libraries have with their users.

Keeping that trust requires standing up for the rights of users. In the period of time immediately following the passage of the USA PATRIOT Act, for example, libraries and librarians forcefully pushed back against what they saw as intrusive violations of patron privacy. This was an admirable stand against what is still seen as an overreach into the freedoms of American citizens to pursue knowledge wherever it might lead—even ideas and concepts could that appear dangerous to the state. But the USA PATRIOT Act has largely given way to other FISA amendments, allowing further encroachments to occur. How do libraries fit within the WikiLeaks era? Do they tout its ability to release information? Do they link to it, or try to ignore it? These decisions need to be made en masse as a profession to ensure users that libraries are on their side as private individuals regardless of political, religious, or ideological inclinations.

Of course the ultimate danger of surveillance is the possibility that a mistrust of all institutions will become widespread, much like the poisoned rhetoric that currently attempts to invalidate news organizations as "fake news" has permeated discussion of the media. Jon Penney has shown with statistically significant evidence that people are less likely to search for controversial subjects on Wikipedia given knowledge of the NSA/PRISM spying program (Penney, 2016). Not only was there a visible and immediate decline in searching for specific salient terms or ideas in Wikipedia, but also Penney's evidence clearly showed effects that lingered for the weeks and months to follow. Wikipedia is merely one source, but one can imagine similar scenarios playing out across various online catalogs in the nation. Zygmunt Bauman and colleagues (2014) argue that the scale of the spying is so vast and far reaching that it has become "impossible to be certain about the difference between nationals and foreigners" (p. 125). One can argue that the opposite could hold true as well: people will begin to question the legitimacy of any and all institutions, however tenuously linked to surveillance organizations they actually are, further eroding any sense of trust in the institutions designed to help them.

Admirably, the American Library Association (ALA) has held firm on its stance against surveillance for the past sixteen years. When the Bush administration began its post-9/11 strengthening of the legality of surveillance and effectively widened its scope, the ALA provided clear written responses to this, especially in its development of privacy guidelines and an ALA policy on government intimidation (ALA, 2017). In a series of articles published between 2001 and 2004, the ALA advanced clear counterpolicy against the encroachment of the FBI and warned about the chilling effects on people, privacy, and the fragility of the right to free speech (ibid.). Of course in the years since the scaling back of the USA PATRIOT Act, libraries are no longer at the front lines of the battle.

But the Snowden papers and the release of Vault 7 demonstrate that the problem of surveillance has not gone away; in fact, scaling back the controversial aspects of the law's amendments did not result in the library "winning" the war. In fact, what's happened is that the fight over surveillance has gone underground somewhat, fought in secrecy without the awareness of librarians, information professionals, and privacy watchdogs. Librarians need to remain wary of this, because the ultimate impact that mass surveillance will have on libraries is that the trust built up over centuries will erode. People will begin to associate libraries with the types of institutions that regularly misuse information and abuse their trust. The first data leaks of library information that lead to convictions of users, whenever they occur, will be damning. Before this happens, libraries will need to distance themselves from the fray; they will need to provide clear strategies for minimizing surveillance and preserving patron privacy at whatever extent still possible under the law. These strategies need to be clearly stated publicly and enforced as much as possible. The goodwill generated by the librarians opposing the USA PATRIOT Act and standing up for their patrons still lingers. Let us hope it can persist in the light of further advances in the surveillance state. Let us hope librarians are never seen as pieces of the spy apparatus. Though, given the scale and scope of surveillance in the United States in 2017, it could possibly occur unless we have a clear vision and strategy for ongoing vigilance.

COMING UP FOR AIR

In the end, it remains to be seen whether the "deep state" exists or is merely an aggregation of all the fears we've ever had about loss of power due to recent unceasing technological advances. Truly respectable people and organizations have gone out of their way to shed light on the problems of big data, big information, and Big Brother. There is hope, though, that organizations such as WikiLeaks, the ACLU, and even the ALA will remain ever vigilant and keep check on overreach whenever and wherever it occurs. As long as there are courageous reporters, journalists, politicians, whistleblowers—and, yes, even courageous librarians—there remains the hope that privacy can remain an actual "thing."

But we'll end here with a chilling thought, as Whitaker suggests, that "the totalitarian vision is so compelling because it represents the architectural skeleton of modern power" (1999, p. 28). In other words, the roots of our problems stem from allowing power to remain unchecked and hidden in the shadows. When organizations are allowed to act in secrecy, as the Church Committee proved forty years ago, abuses will invariably occur. The good news is that organizations such as the ACLU, the EFF, the PI, and others—

including the ALA, libraries, and most of all, librarians—still exist with broad support for their activities from a majority of Americans. It remains to be seen if oversight will help to curtail some of the worst abuses of the past ten years.

REFERENCES

Ablon, L., and Bogart, T. (2017). Zero days, thousands of nights: The life and times of zero-day vulnerabilities and their exploits. RAND Corporation. http://www.rand.org.

American Civil Liberties Union (ACLU). (2017a). About the ACLU. https://www.aclu.org.

American Civil Liberties Union (ACLU). (2017b). National security: Privacy and surveillance. https://www.aclu.org.

American Library Association (ALA). (2017). The FBI in your library. http://www.ala.org.

Annie. (2015). *Stasiland*, by Anna Funder. *Bookish Type* (blog). https://abookish-type.wordpress.com.

Applebaum, A. (2017). Maybe the A.I. dystopia is already here. *Washington Post*. https://www.washingtonpost.com.

Bauman, Z., Bigo, D., Esteves, P., Guild, E., Jabri, V., et al. (2014). After Snowden: Rethinking the impact of surveillance. *International Political Sociology*, 8(2), 121–144.

Bunch, W. (2017). The people need to take down Trump. Not the deep state. *Philadelphia Daily News*. http://www.philly.com.

Collier. P. (2017). How to save capitalism from itself. *Times Literary Supplement*. http://www.the-tls.co.uk.

Cunningham, P. (2017). Vault 7 and the electronic panopticon. *Japan Times*. http://www.japantimes.co.jp.

Cushing, T. (2016). The chilling effect of mass surveillance quantified. Techdirt. https://www.techdirt.com.

Dennis, B. (2017). Scott Pruitt, longtime adversary of EPA, confirmed to lead the agency. *Washington Post*. https://www.washingtonpost.com.

Electronic Frontier Foundation (EFF). (2017). Home page. https://www.eff.org.

Fisher, M. (2017). What happens when you fight a "deep state" that doesn't exist. *New York Times*. https://www.nytimes.com.

Francheschi-Bicchierai, L. (2017). WikiLeaks won't tell tech companies how to patch CIA zero-days until its demands are met. Motherboard. https://motherboard.vice.com.

Fukuyama, F. (1989). The end of history? *National Interest* (16), 3–18.

Funder, A. (2002). *Stasiland: Stories from behind the Berlin Wall*. New York: HarperCollins.

Greenwald, G. (2014). *No place to hide: Edward Snowden, the NSA, and the US surveillance state*. New York: Henry Holt.

Greenwald, G. (2017). Greenwald: Empowering the "deep state" to undermine Trump is prescription for destroying democracy. Democracy Now! Interview with Democracy Now. https://www.democracynow.org.

Ignatius, D. (2017). The real shocker in the WikiLeaks scoop. *Washington Post*. https://www.washingtonpost.com.

Jan, T. (2017). The biggest beneficiaries of the government safety net: Working-class whites. *Washington Post Wonkblog*. https://www.washingtonpost.com.

Jouet, M. (2012). Religious and free-market fundamentalism have more in common than their fans in the Tea Party. Truthout. http://www.truth-out.org.

Koehler, J. O. (1999). Revenge versus the rule of law. In *Stasi: The untold story of the East German secret police*. Boulder, CO: Westview. http://www.nytimes.com/books.

McCandlish, S. (2002). EFF's top 12 ways to protect your online privacy. Electronic Frontier Foundation. https://www.eff.org.

McManus, D. (2017). Is the "deep state" out to get Trump? We're not there yet. *Los Angeles Times*. http://www.latimes.com.

McRaney, D. (2011). The backfire effect. *You Are Not So Smart: A Celebration of Self-Delusion* (blog). https://youarenotsosmart.com.

Microsoft. (2017). Encrypt email messages: Outlook. Support Office. https://support.office.com.

Miller, G., and Nakashima, E. (2017). WikiLeaks says it has obtained trove of CIA hacking tools. *Washington Post.* https://www.washingtonpost.com.

Miller, R. (2008). *US national security, intelligence and democracy: From the Church Committee to the war on terror.* London: Routledge.

Moyers, B. (2015). The plutocrats are winning: Don't let them! *Huffington Post.* http://www.huffingtonpost.com.

Nakashima, E., Dwoskin, E., and Barrett, D. (2017). WikiLeaks pledges to release software code of CIA hacking tools to tech firms. *Washington Post.* https://www.washingtonpost.com.

Osberg, M. (2015). The psychology behind why we believe in conspiracy theories. Atlas Obscura. http://www.atlasobscura.com.

Penney, J. (2016). Chilling effects: Online surveillance and Wikipedia use. *Berkeley Technology Law Journal, 31*(1), 117–182. https://ssrn.com/abstract=2769645.

Piketty, T., and Goldhammer, A. (2014). *Capital in the twenty-first century.* Cambridge, MA: Belknap.

Privacy International. (2017a). About us. https://www.privacyinternational.org.

Privacy International. (2017b). What we do. https://www.privacyinternational.org.

Privacy Rights Clearinghouse (PRC). (2017a). About the Privacy Rights Clearinghouse. https://www.privacyrights.org.

Privacy Rights Clearinghouse (PRC). (2017b). Data breaches. PRC. https://www.privacyrights.org.

R.J.E. (2017). What is the "deep state"? *Economist Explains* (blog). http://www.economist.com.

Ritholtz, B. (2017). How much can you cut taxes? Don't ask Kansas. Bloomberg. https://www.bloomberg.com.

Rosenberg, S. (2007). Computers to solve Stasi puzzle. *BBC News.* http://news.bbc.co.uk.

Shermer, M. (2013). Conspiracy theories: Why we believe the unbelievable. *Los Angeles Times.* http://articles.latimes.com.

Shermer, M. (2014). Why do people believe in conspiracy theories? *Scientific American.* https://www.scientificamerican.com.

Shorrock, T. (2017). Why does WikiLeaks keep publishing US state secrets? Private contractors. *Washington Post.* https://www.washingtonpost.com.

Stratfor. (2017). About Stratfor. https://www.stratfor.com.

United States of America. UNITING AND STRENGTHENING AMERICA BY PROVIDING APPROPRIATE TOOLS REQUIRED TO INTERCEPT AND OBSTRUCT TERRORISM (USAPATRIOT ACT) ACT OF 2001. Government Publishing Office. https://www.gpo.gov/fdsys/pkg/PLAW-107publ56/html/PLAW-107publ56.htm.

United States Congress, Senate. (1976). Select Committee to Study Governmental Operations with Respect to Intelligence Activities. Final report of the Select Committee to Study Governmental Operations with Respect to Intelligence Activities, United States Senate, together with additional, supplemental, and separate views. Book 1. Library of Congress, Congressional Research Service. https://archive.org.

Whitaker, R. (1999). *The end of privacy: How total surveillance is becoming a reality.* New York: New Press.

WikiLeaks. (2017a). The global intelligence files. https://wikileaks.org.

WikiLeaks. (2017b). Partners. https://wikileaks.org.

WikiLeaks. (2017c). Vault 7: CIA hacking tools revealed. https://wikileaks.org.

WikiLeaks. (2017d). What is WikiLeaks. https://wikileaks.org.

Zakaria, F. (2017). America must defend itself against the real national security menace. *Washington Post.* https://www.washingtonpost.com.

Zuboff, Shoshana. (2016). Google as a fortune teller: The secrets of surveillance capitalism. Frankfurter Allgemeine Zeitung. http://www.faz.net.

Chapter Seven

The Shock of Information Overload and Big Data

And further, by these, my son, be admonished: of making many books there is
no end; and much study is a weariness of the flesh.

—Ecclesiastes 12:12

DEPTH AND BREADTH: OMNISCIENCE AND OMNIPRESENCE

The era of big data, for all of its controversial issues with eroding privacy,
compromised autonomy, and overreliance on predictive behavior analysis,
still finds its fundamental roots in the desire to accumulate information. This
desire has appeared in the development of online massive digital libraries
such as the HathiTrust, Google Books, or the Internet Archive, each of which
attempts to organize and accumulate the full extent of human creation as
printed in book form. We are reminded, too, that such ambitious desires for
bounding the infinite are ancient ones. The library at Alexandria remains one
of the most visible symbols of this desire to encapsulate within finite walls
the world's broadest reaches of knowledge. It also remains one of the great
symbols of loss and represents, as Alberto Manguel (2006) describes it, "a
shadow of the world" currently existing now. Alexandria is a symbol of not
only what we have kept and lost but also what we have *excluded* and lost—
the universal mind of remembering *and* forgetting. In contrast, Jorge
Borges's "Library of Babel" speaks to the impossibility of collecting and
managing the infinite, which, as Umberto Eco notes, is a fantasy "where
mathematics verges on metaphysics" (Eco, 2009, p. 369). The desire for the
vertiginous heights of knowledge in the Library of Babel combined with the
breadth and width of the Library of Alexandria bring us two glimpses of the

infinite: *infinite knowledge* versus *infinite information*. Add into this mixture the internet, which promises not only *omniscience* but also *omnipresence*, and we find ourselves in strikingly new territory where past, present, and future (in the form of futurism and instantaneous dissemination) mingles with the depth and breadth of *all* human experience.

But we are also finding that the striving for these utopian dreams of complete awareness and universal coverage of the human condition ultimately does little more than expose the limitations of the human mind. Despite studies suggesting that the upper bounds of the human mind are possibly underutilized by huge orders of magnitude (Bartol et al., 2015), in every desire to "accumulate it all" there is an attendant feeling of being overwhelmed by it. This sensation of information overload is not new, as Anne Blair has shown in her examination of the historical record. It is a concept that has persisted for centuries, if not millennia. Importantly, she sees information overload not as a negative reaction to any specific technology, or even as a form of technophobia, but instead as a general response to our own desires to preserve information. She argues that "overload was born from a drive to accumulate and save which became particularly visible in the Renaissance as individuals and institutions collected copies of ancient texts, exotic natural specimens and artifacts, forming the kernel of libraries and museums that have sometimes endured to the present" (Blair, 2011).

Hers is an important distinction since it suggests that—despite the advances in technology occurring since the Middle Ages, or even classical antiquity—our information tools are not necessarily the direct causes of our anxieties about information. Instead, it is a visceral reaction to the personal realization of the potential loss of information that drives this anxiety. The greater the amount of information compiled, Blair would argue, the greater the amount of anxiety and awareness of risk about its demise and about its future usefulness will occur. Certainly, Borges's despairing librarians in the endless Library of Babel hint at this overwhelming loss of meaning in the face of infinite incomprehensibility.

Leaving metaphysics aside for a moment, coping with the practical impact on our decisions to collect and preserve all of our information also drives our own anxieties in the information age. Sometimes it seems as if information has a mind of its own, growing independently of our own free will. Our own real-world solutions to these questions of simple organization become a challenge. Current warnings among librarians about a looming "digital dark age" may be yet another manifestation of these anxieties. This chapter will look at the impact that information overload has on the library and library users, especially as the era of big data exponentially drives up the amount of information available.

THEORIES OF INFORMATION OVERLOAD

In chapter 2, which examined the growth of data as it morphs into the concept of big data, we discovered through Martin Hilbert and Priscila López (2011) that the amount of information being generated and exchanged exceeds human ability to comprehend it. Yet the capabilities of preserving and storing this information evolve and have been able to generally handle the amount that gets generated. Though Blair argues that feelings of anxiety stemming from data growth are fueled less by technology or "new discovery" and more by desires to "seeking out and stockpiling information," I believe that the technology variable cannot be ruled out entirely (Blair, 2010, p. 12). Luz Quiroga and colleagues (2004) have argued that "one of the consequences of the internet is that anyone with access can become an author and a publisher. As a result, the quality of the information is diverse and the quantity of information is daunting. . . . This problem is not new but it is certainly aggravated with the advent of computerization, and more recently, the Internet" (9).

The one variable that Blair does not examine in her hypothesis is the construction of the concept of quality. While we may have an urge to seek and stockpile information, we also have a natural urge in the face of increased information to valuate and organize it. Without hierarchy, it could be argued, there would be far less selectivity. As an example, there are thirty-six billion bottles of wine produced worldwide yearly; *Wine Spectator*'s number ranking system, as employed and filtered by the vendor Total Wine and More (see figure 7.1), helps people to more easily choose what they want. People will not try thousands of bottles of wine, let alone a billion, before settling on a favorite. Instead, they'll try wine based on others' recommendations; there is no other way to make sense of it all without some ranking, classification, and astute selection. The same efforts can be seen in the music industry as well. There were seventy-five thousand albums released in the United States in 2010 (*Billboard*, 2011). To cope with this glut, Pitchfork or other raters provide services about specific genres of music to let us know which is worth our time listening to and which isn't. Most people wind up mostly satisfied with these strategies of separating the bad from the good. Only the paid professionals, industry stakeholders, or obsessive fans and enthusiasts will ever go to the trouble of sampling everything they possibly can. Even then there are limits; music critics such as Robert Christgau, who has reviewed thousands of albums in his career, are unable or unwilling to listen to specific genres (Christgau, 2008). Publications on the internet are, of course, part of this valuation urge as well; the popularity of lists on the internet speaks to some of this desire for order in the information. Obviously, libraries and librarians fulfill similar roles of valuation and collection.

But the ephemeral quality of digital media and technology exacerbates the current problem of excessive scale. Wine, despite the large amount of production, is nevertheless a perishable commodity, subject to limitations in resources and market forces; physical music is subject to the limitations of one's pocketbook and the manufacturing of the physical container; and print books are limited by their paper stock and binding materials. Information on the internet, however, is ruled less by these forces of economic scarcity. Digital media has the ability to proliferate through copies independent of available resources. As long as the electricity is there to power it, digital information can be replicated, changed, shared, and remade ad infinitum, or until the upper limits of the system have been met. It is not infinite but close enough sometimes for practical purposes to be infinite. As a result, the ability to stockpile and seek out information can grow easily beyond the typical human capacity to do so.

It is also more difficult for people—even experts and professionals like librarians—to vet the quality of the information being generated without regard to demand or limited resources. While it is often the case that quality books and CDs are often judged by the quality of their containers' physical characteristics (the aphorism is *not* always right!), digital media are much harder to evaluate in terms even of their own physicality. Pulp dime-store novels have historically and quite literally been ignored by merit of the cheap materials making them, for sometimes the cheapness of the container mirrors the cheapness of the literary contents, though not always. In this light, the internet is absolutely a game changer when it comes to democratizing infor-

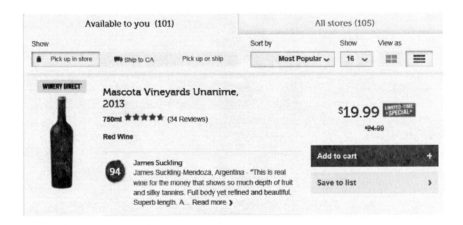

Figure 7.1.   Ranking system of wine, by letting users evaluate information in meaningful ways, reducing stress and anxiety about too many choices. *Source: Total Wine and More, 2017.*

mation while also contributing to our own cognitive overload. Of course, by minimizing technology in her argument, Blair weakens her own point that human nature doesn't change over time; such anxieties have a way of seeming new and unique when they are in fact deep-seated human behaviors responding to very similar stimuli.

Although Blair doesn't see technology as a primary vehicle for the phenomenon of information overload, the technology driving big data has grossly increased the amount, speed, and ease with which data and information are aggregated. Add to that the ephemeral, but recordable qualities of the internet and the digital realm, and we are in an age of peak information overload, especially as we are currently unable to manage the expectations of social media along with the volume of the data generated, the velocity at which it's created, and the realization that the long-term solutions to storing that data are questionable at best.

How Is Information Overload Defined?

Before we can examine the extent to which big data impacts people's feelings of anxiety and information overload, we need to examine how the term "information overload" has been defined by numerous practitioners and scholars over the years. Multiple definitions have been proposed by Martin Eppler and Jeanne Mengis (2004) in their excellent and comprehensive review of information overload research. One long-used framework of information-overload studies examines how much information can be potentially integrated into the decision-making process before one's ability to make an accurate decision begins to decline (Chewning and Harrell, 1990; Cook, 1993; Griffeth, Carson, and Marin, 1988). At some point, the theory suggests, there occurs a breakdown in decision-making efficacy. People reach a state of "lesser utilization" of all available information, as demonstrated in the U-curve in figure 7.2, and their accuracy in making a rational decision declines. For these researchers, information overload is a matter of measuring a person's ability to make rational decisions against a theoretical peak or optimal set of conditions.

But the actual limit may be hard to determine. As a result, another avenue of inquiry in information overload is concerned less with the U-curve of decision-making accuracies and more with the problem of *when* the volume of the information exceeds the person's ability to process it (Jacoby, Speller, and Berning, 1974; Malhotra, Jain, and Lagakos, 1982; Meyer, 1998). While this is similar to the previous theory, the experimentation focuses more on human cognitive limitations than on the actual amount of information a person may have encountered or the types of decisions that have to be made. They are more interested in seeing how long it takes for individuals to reach states of stress and confusion. This approach ultimately sees humans less as

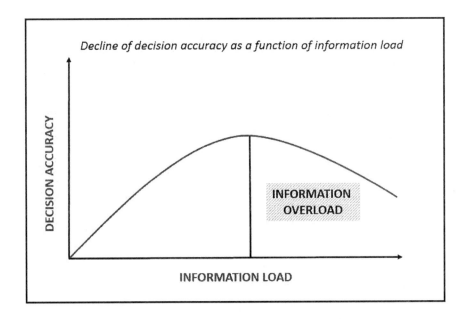

Figure 7.2.   Decline of decision accuracy as a function of information load.
Source: **Eppler and Mengis, 2004.**

rational individuals making decisions with clear-cut answers—accurate, or otherwise—and more as a species limited in cognitive abilities, subject to irrational emotions and physical interference, and grappling with those limitations.

Taking this further, some researchers see information overload primarily in terms of mental and physical capacities, as if people were metaphorical buckets, reaching their limits when too much information filled up the container (Shenk, 1997; Wurman, 1989). For these researchers, information overload occurs when a person tries to incorporate information far beyond the *energy* that person has available for it. When the amount of information a person encounters surpasses their physical and mental energies to process it, information overload occurs. The theory implies that a state of information overload, therefore, could occur in *any person* at *any time*, not because their mental container for information has been filled, but because one happens to be mentally or physically tired, and as a result the container has shrunk. On any given day or time, then, depending on the levels of energy one has, the conditions defined as information overload could be met.

But information overload is not always triggered by merely a theoretical amount of information encountered or a predetermined physical boundary surpassed by people. Other researchers have considered how time constraints also impact a person's sense of cognitive overload (Schick, Gorden, and Haka, 1990; Tuttle and Burton, 1999). The less time someone has to perform certain tasks, it is argued, the more acute the sensations of information overload will seem. The concept can therefore also be seen as an intersection of the information-processing demands of the task and the time available to complete or process the tasks. This is a notable distinction as many other concepts focus primarily on a quantified but theoretical amount of information and the physical cognitive limits of the human mind, but not necessarily the environmental and situational constraints that contribute to feelings of anxiety and stress.

Additionally, researchers have found that distinctions need to be made on not only the amount of information and time constraints but also the *nature and type* of information a person is being asked to handle (Iselin, 1988, 1993; Keller and Staelin, 1987; Owen, 1992; Schneider, 1987). Simple tasks and objective (i.e., emotionally neutral) information contribute less to a person's feeling of information overload. Instead, emotionally laden or deep, complex information would be far more difficult for people to process than simple ideas or information of a factual nature. Information overload is determined, therefore, not merely by the quantity of information or a person's inherent human cognitive and physical limitations but also by the qualities and connotations of the information that a person encounters. Complicating this further is the realization that some people are triggered from past traumatic experiences by information that others might consider neutral. As a result, researchers have come to realize that a person's internal sense of control and agency impact information overload more so than perhaps any objective quantified benchmark (Abdel-Khalik, 1973; Galbraith, 1974; Iselin, 1993; O'Reilly, 1980). Externally derived measurements of the amount of information a person encounters, these researchers believe, cannot explain all the variations in human capacity to process it. Instead, information overload is a result of a person's subjective feelings. When decision makers *believe* that they have to handle more information than they can efficiently use, they have reached a state of information overload. Rather than objective external observation, information overload is more a self-reported "state of being."

Ultimately, what all these variations on the theory of information overload have as a common element is the belief that any amount of information—be it structured data, knowledge, factual information, quantities or qualities, and the like—will have an impact on a person's ability to "parse" it. While some researchers see hard and fast limits, others are willing to entertain more variables in their analyses. Some will see the limitations as individual and context specific, while others will see it purely as a numeric value impacted by the amount of time allowed to perform specific tasks within specific parameters. Ultimately, whether the advent of information overload is triggered by volume, variety, or personal emotional states, it is nevertheless important to reveal what the limitations are of human cognitive abilities and the impact that new technology has upon it. Ways to alleviate these conditions can also only be devised once the causes and the symptoms of it are clearly demarcated.

MITIGATING THE EFFECTS OF BIG DATA AND INFORMATION OVERLOAD IN LIBRARIES

Information Overload and Libraries: A Quick Primer

Libraries are often imagined as intermediaries between the unfettered production and sharing of information and the necessity of imposing a system of organization upon it. Blair (2003, 2010, 2011) sees libraries as both a manifestation of and a contributor to the urge to collect and preserve that ultimately leads to information overload. The organizational systems imposed upon information and data ironically facilitate the generation of more information. One might argue, though, that libraries are not merely entities existing between and subject to opposing forces, nor are they the unwitting and symbolic contributors to the deluge of information and information structures. They are, instead, the fault lines of information exchange itself, providing limited structure and stability on the one hand while functioning as conduits that release built-up tension along predetermined lines. Energies flow through them in the form of staff and users, money, information, and policy, yet they also adapt as external and internal forces influence them. They channel the disparate forces related to information management, the burdens of economic digital scarcity and copyright, and user desires for open-access to information and the principles of free and unfettered inquiry.

It should come as no surprise, then, that library and information science researchers are exploring the ways in which libraries mitigate, contribute to, or expose the problems of information overload. Carol Tenopir as early as 1990 found that the move toward online databases in the late 1980s contributed to feelings of information overload in library patrons. Quiroga and colleagues researched the roles libraries play in *improving* how information is accessed and thus reducing cognitive load on library users through the use of personal information finders and filters. David Bawden and Lyn Robinson (2009) examine the "dark side of information" and point out the problem raised by Randy Reichardt of "reference overload," which is "caused when a library inadvertently offers too many relevant resources to users" (p. 183). Amrita Dhawan (2013) examines libraries' online catalogs and compares them to Google Books in terms of how they handle information overload and promote "mindfulness."

Solutions for these noted problems span the gamut from improving information architecture, reducing irrelevant choices, improving retrieval through search filters, and focusing on information literacy skills, especially through improved communication between librarians and patrons. Ultimately the research points to the contradictory roles of libraries as alleviators and facilitators of information overload at the fault lines of information exchange and the cycle of knowledge generation.

Countermeasures and Coping Mechanisms

How libraries first began is always an interesting discussion. There are numerous theories on the reasons that libraries exist in the first place. Libraries can be seen as mirrors of their communities or the ambitions of their constituents, such as a national library or a public library serving a Hispanic population. Some see libraries as ambitions toward universal comprehension, where all knowledge is somehow bounded and contained within their walls, such as the famed universal library at Alexandria, or the Google Books Project (Weiss and James, 2014). Some see them as monuments to their creators or donors, such as the Carnegie Libraries, or the ancient libraries of some emperors and kings, or tyrants and despots. Some see them as repositories of hope and future dreams, where universal knowledge and understanding can be given to all mankind. As Manguel eloquently states, "Any library . . . offers to whoever explores it a reflection of what he or she seeks, a tantalizing wisp of intuition of who we are as readers, a glimpse into the secret aspects of the self" (Manguel, 2006, p. 305), though, to be honest, most people have come to see them merely as warehouses serving a certain population.

Regardless of the impetus for their development, libraries through the centuries have attempted to act as bulwarks against the rising tide of available information, keeping time and ephemera at bay by organizing life and information through rational categorizations. Libraries have adopted numerous ways to categorize and classify that information. Early classification schemes helped to alleviate the problems of information overload as book collections got larger and publication became more prevalent. Digital MARC records helped patrons find information more quickly and with less hassle than analog card-catalog counterparts. Libraries attempt to organize databases, for example, by clearly demarcated academic subjects, allowing users to search in more directed ways through indexes of millions of records. The use of controlled vocabulary and keyword search helps users find their way through the morass. Libraries have adapted in the past to meet the changes in the world, and they are capable of doing so again in this era, but current measures may not yet be sufficient to meet the challenges of big data.

When data has reached beyond human capability to reasonably read through even the most representative parts of a discipline, as is happening now, then the whole enterprise has a possibility of truly failing. Bawden and

Robinson (2009) have dubbed this situation as "infobesity," which they describe as "a situation of personal information overload," akin to a fast-food diet heavy on empty calories but light on actual substance (p. 185). Though it is a problematic definition, it does help to describe, through this metaphor, the anxiety and base technophobia of the big data era. Some of the coping mechanisms that spring from infobesity include *information withdrawal*, when people minimize their sources of information to levels they find comforting, and information avoidance, where people ignore all information whether relevant or irrelevant because there is just too much of it. These conditions have given way to the practice of "satisficing," which is a rationalization people describe as taking in just enough information to meet a need and no more. *Just enough is good enough* becomes the mantra of the big data era since it has become impossible to read and analyze everything. As a result some define this as a kind of "bounded rationality" where the limits of one's capacity to comprehend everything are tacitly understood, and the limits this represents are accepted as an unavoidable reality. Wider contexts and holistic approaches are thus ignored in favor of a more limited analysis that leads to understanding within narrower scopes.

But satisficing leads to some extreme and even outrageous positions, where people choose to ignore *everything*. Too many books are being published for an individual to read, the reasoning goes, so the only way to cope is to not read them (Good, 2017). Many readers have therefore begun to abandon, as a coping mechanism, the rat race of reading itself! Indeed, some scholars have actually suggested that the only way to stay up on the field is to avoid reading itself. "To understand literature . . . we must stop reading books," asserts one scholar who examines eighteenth- and nineteenth-century British literature by text mining the digitized corpus of these books (Good, 2017). This is obviously an extreme position that works for a specific approach to scholarship, but it is one that finds its roots in information overload. Taking satisficing a step further, these professional readers and scholars have consciously abandoned the act of reading altogether and instead rely on the digital "tools of the trade" to mine and sift through the extraordinary amount of information for patterns to make sense of the world. Yet such positions are so extreme that they contradict the point of information and information literacy. But perhaps this is the future.

Or perhaps not. Not all people advocate throwing the baby out with the bathwater. In fact, along the lines of the "slow food" movement, is the *slow reading* movement, which while acknowledging that there is too much to read, nevertheless advocates a more moderate approach. Quantity and speed, these practitioners assert, is no substitute for the quality of the read. At root is the realization that not everything can, nor should, be read. By focusing only on the tasks at hand, one can slow down and conceivably learn far more about a subject, or oneself, than through skimming and picking at thousands of resources.

Role of Libraries: The Role of Information Literacy in Alleviating Cognitive Overload

Libraries do have a special role in helping to alleviate this problem. While existing as fault lines of information exchange, libraries create structure for the mass of information they hold, while also facilitating its exchange. Libraries have historically provided essential starting points for the creation, selection, and culling of collections. The essential service of evaluation and rating, which helps to narrow things down, provides users with a coping mechanism while searching and establishes a basic trust with the texts they are using. This long-standing activity of libraries remains their most well-known function.

But the most important ally, however, in the fight against information overload appears in the form of education itself. The American Library Association (ALA) and the Association of College and Research Libraries (ACRL) have created an extensive set of guidelines that explain information literacy, which they see as part of a much wider metaliteracy that "demands behavioral, affective, cognitive, and metacognitive engagement with the information ecosystem" (ALA, 2017). Librarians who teach are provided a clear set of rules, guidelines, and proficiencies that will help the library user navigate all aspects of information. Library users, scholars, students, and people in general are placed within this information ecosystem. Each element of the system impacts another:

- Authority Is Constructed and Contextual.
- Information Creation as a Process.
- Information Has Value.
- Research as Inquiry.
- Scholarship as Conversation.
- Searching as Strategic Exploration (ALA, 2017).

It should be argued, though, that the varied concepts of cognitive overload, information overload, and information anxiety each fall within this overarching concept of *metaliteracy*. If metacognition, cognition, and self-reflection are to be seen as pillars of the information literacy framework, it follows that anything impacting a user's ability to accomplish these things should be addressed as well. If one looks closely at how the ACRL has organized these headings and how they define their dispositions, or the way in which users demonstrate such information-literacy proficiencies, one can see information overload having direct impact upon them. As a result, greater awareness of information overload needs to be worked into this framework; as a result, librarians will be able to better address the obstacles to literacy itself.

Under the first main subheading, "Authority Is Constructed and Contextual," the ACRL defines a proficient disposition as the ability to "develop and maintain an open mind when encountering varied and sometimes conflicting perspectives" (ALA, 2017). It has been noted that when confronted with opposing viewpoints, or when shown too much information, people are likely to feel anxious. In some cases, people are likely to dig in and even maintain easily discredited positions. Obviously, it would be important then, for the sake of self-awareness, to realize the impact that information overload might have on a person's ability to conduct research and to ultimately make reasoned decisions. Cognitive dissonance is one of the causes of the worst traits in human beings. Information literacy could help to alleviate this along with information overload, which seems to exacerbate cognitive anxieties and the feelings of dissonance, as long as librarians are aware of its negative impact.

Later in the framework, under the section "Information Creation as a Process," the ACRL defines a positive disposition as one that accepts "the ambiguity surrounding the potential value of information creation expressed in emerging formats or modes" (ALA, 2017). Tolerance for ambiguity is not necessarily an easily acquired trait, and it has been notably absent in some circles, both public and private. Diego Gambetta and Steffen Hertog find that engineers, for example, despite being well trained within their discipline, are far more likely to espouse inflexible, even radical points of view that have led to participation in terrorist activities. Such a mind-set combined with frustrated economic expectations is hypothesized to be one of the main causes of this phenomenon (Farrell, 2015). The feeling of uncomfortable ambiguity is at the heart of information overload. Multiple viewpoints and multiple interpretations of the same set of information can cause issues with cognitive comfort levels, and might even cause very painful cognitive dissonance. *Information withdrawal* makes this tendency even worse. People will routinely shut out viewpoints that make them uncomfortable, leading to further isolation and extremism.

Finally, under the section "Searching as Strategic Exploration," the issue of information overload is danced around but never stated explicitly. Librarians are asked to encourage users to take positive actions in the face of problematic searches. This includes focusing on users' "mental flexibility and creativity," reinforcing the point that searches "do not always produce adequate results" (too much of something in this case), persisting "in the face of search challenges" (this could include anxiety or information withdrawal), and being able to recognize when there is "enough information to complete" the tasks at hand (ALA, 2017). While users could be considered literate in the ways of information if they do all these things, they might nevertheless feel overload in the process. Users might conceivably believe they have found enough information for their needs but are instead suffering from fatigue and information withdrawal. I recommend that information overload be explained clearly and addressed as a major roadblock to information literacy and a primary contributor to the problems users face when attempting to use library collections.

Obviously, the ALA/ACRL information literacy framework is an important guide to help evaluate users' levels of information literacy. However, it is clear to me that many of the symptoms of information overload, as posited by the researchers cited above, do appear in this list as unstated negatives or unevaluated assumptions in many of these positively reinforced behaviors. The opposite of persisting in the face of search challenges looks to me like the patron has given up. There may be various causes for this, but the role and frequency of information overload (especially mental and physical fatigue) should be considered one of the causes. It is debatable, too, whether techniques to alleviate information overload should be considered essential countermeasures to the condition. The unstated but assumed opposite of "mental flexibility and creativity" appears to be the information overload symptom of "shutting down," or digging-in in the face of contradictory information. Sometimes strategic exploration itself is sacrificed in the face of information overload and people find, despite their best intentions, they are unable to analyze or organize the information they've stumbled upon.

Ultimately, it is hoped that the ACRL information literacy standards can be applied to helping those suffering from information overload. However, as they are stated now, they might not be able to fully address these needs, especially as the assumptions stated in the framework might be missing the causes of these search pathologies. These pathologies may also lie at the heart of the technology's impact on the human psyche and may not be related whatsoever to any sort of educational program.

Librarian: A Word by Any Other Name . . .

On a final note, information overload does not impact only library users. It is also changing the concept of the librarian itself. New librarian positions are continually being devised to help patrons navigate the latest influxes of information. This is reflected in names such as databrarian, cybrarian, knowledge analyst, knowledge architect, knowledge integrator, knowledge management librarian, knowledge manager, knowledge network specialist, knowledge resource specialist, information advisor, info architect, info broker, info consultant, info officer, info specialist, metadata specialist, taxonomy librarian, webmistress, wired for youth librarian, and so on (Mach, 2003). It has become clear over the past ten to fifteen years that the term "librarian" does not fully do justice to all that is being done by these professionals.

While some of the job descriptions, such as cybrarian, may reflect wishful thinking along the lines of the full mind-body-machine interaction of the sci-fi anime *Ghost in the Machine*, many are merely descriptive of the types of tasks they are presently doing. The term "librarian," in that regard, no longer truly refers to what it used to. While librarians are still certainly working with print book technology and analog works while providing reference works and in the parlance of S. R. Ranganathan "every reader his book," the truth is that today digital resources and big data technology are the primary resources used in research. Even traditional paper-based archives are moving to digital finding aids and digitized collections at the item level. The ease and convenience with which we use these digital collections suggest a deep unease about the role of the librarian as reflected in these sudden name changes. "Every reader his book" is now "every user his web resource." If there was ever a clumsy attempt at trying to appear relevant, this is it. Our roles have changed but have not yet adapted to the technology. This likely scares not a few librarians.

The recent emphasis on information literacy as a priority for librarians speaks to this unease as well. We need to teach students, the argument goes, the ways in which to use information and to learn to trust us in the process of that learning. While I do not believe the goals were designed to be so self-serving, there is nevertheless some unease regarding our current role in dominating the ways in which the information literacy guidelines are being interpreted. Ultimately, time and technology will dictate how the world sees us and how we see ourselves as a profession. The impact of big data and information overload can't be relegated to just a few negative instances inferred by ACRL guidelines. It must be clear where librarians can teach useful methods to combat information overload. Without a clear understanding of the phenomenon, we will ultimately fail to help our users no matter how much we advocate for information literacy.

REFERENCES

Abdel-Khalik, A. R. (1973). The effect of aggregating accounting reports on the quality of the lending decision: An empirical investigation. *Journal of Accounting Research Supplement, 11*, 104–138.

American Library Association (ALA). (2017). ACRL framework for information literacy for higher education. http://www.ala.org.

Bartol, T. M., Bromer, C., Kinney, J., Chirillo, M. A., Bourne, J. N., Harris, K. M., and Sejnowski, T. J. (2015). Nanoconnectomic upper bound on the variability of synaptic plasticity. *ELife, 4*. https://elifesciences.org.

Bawden, D., and Robinson, L. (2009). The dark side of information: Overload, anxiety and other paradoxes and pathologies. *Journal of Information Science, 35*(2), 180–191.

Billboard. (2011). Business matters: 75,000 albums released in US in 2010—Down 22% from 2009. http://www.billboard.com.

Blair, A. (2003). Reading strategies for coping with information overload ca. 1550–1700. *Journal of the History of Ideas, 64*(1), 11–28.

Blair, A. (2010). *Too much to know: Managing scholarly information before the modern age.* New Haven, CT: Yale University Press.

Blair, A. (2011). Information overload's 2,300-year-old history. HBR. https://hbr.org.

Chewning, E. C., Jr., and Harrell, A. M. (1990). The effect of information load on decision makers' cue utilization levels and decision quality in a financial distress decision task. *Accounting, Organizations and Society, 15*, 527–542.

Christgau. R. (2008). *User's guide to the consumer guide* (blog). https://www.robertchristgau.com.

Cook, G. J. (1993). An empirical investigation of information search strategies with implications for decision support system design. *Decision Sciences, 24*, 683–699.

Dhawan, A. (2013). Searching mindfully: Are libraries up to the challenge of competing with google books? *Library Philosophy and Practice.* http://digitalcommons.unl.edu.

Eco, U. (2009). *The infinity of lists.* New York: Rizzoli.

Eppler, M., and Mengis, J. (2004). The concept of information overload: A review of literature from organization science, accounting, marketing, MIS, and related disciplines. *Information Society, 20*(5), 325–344.

Farrell, H. (2015). This is the group that's surprisingly prone to violent extremism. *Washington Post.* https://www.washingtonpost.com.

Galbraith, J. R. (1974). Organization design: An information processing view. *Interfaces, 3*, 28–36.

Good, A. (2017). The rising tide of aliteracy. Walrus. https://thewalrus.ca.

Griffeth, R. W., Carson, K. D., and Marin, D. B. (1988). Information overload: A test of an inverted U hypothesis with hourly and salaried employees. *Academy of Management Proceedings*, 232–237.

Hilbert, M. and López, P. (2011). The world's technological capacity to store, communicate, and compute information. Science, *332*(6025), 60–65. doi:10.1126/science.1200970.

Iselin, E. R. (1988). The effects of information load and information diversity on decision quality in a structured decision task. *Accounting, Organizations and Society, 13*, 147–164.

Iselin, E. R. (1993). The effects of the information and data properties of financial ratios and statements on managerial decision quality. *Journal of Business Finance and Accounting, 20*, 249–267.

Jacoby, J., Speller, D. E., and Berning, C. K. (1974). Brand choice behavior as a function of information load: Replication and extension. *Journal of Consumer Research, 1*, 33–43.

Keller, K. L., and Staelin, R. (1987). Effects of quality and quantity of information on decision effectiveness. *Journal of Consumer Research, 14*, 200–213.

Mach, M. (2003). Real job titles for library and information science professionals. *Beads and Books.* http://www.michellemach.com.

Malhotra, N. K., Jain, A. K., and Lagakos, S. W. (1982). The information overload controversy: An alternative viewpoint. *Journal of Marketing, 46*, 27–37.

Manguel, A. (2006). *The library at night.* Toronto: Knopf.

Meyer, J. (1998). Information overload in marketing management. *Marketing Intelligence and Planning, 16*, 200–209.

O'Reilly, C. A. (1980). Individuals and information overload in organizations: Is more necessarily better? *Academy of Management Journal, 23*, 684–696.

Owen, R. S. (1992). Clarifying the simple assumption of the information load paradigm. *Advances in Consumer Research, 19*, 770–776.

Quiroga, L., Crosby, M., and Iding, M. (2004). Reducing cognitive load. In *Proceedings of the 37th Annual Hawaii International Conference on System Sciences, 2004* (p. 9). Los Alamitos, CA: IEEE Computer Society Press.

Schick, A. G., Gorden, L. A., and Haka, S. (1990). Information overload: A temporal approach. *Accounting Organizations and Society, 15*, 199–220.

Schneider, S. C. (1987). Information overload: Causes and consequences. *Human Systems Management, 7*, 143–153.

Shenk, D. (1997). *Data smog: Surviving the information glut.* London: Abacus.

Tenopir, C. (1990). Online information anxiety. *Library Journal, 115*(13), 62.

Total Wine and More. (2017). Wine Store, Liquor Store, Buy Wine Online | Total Wine & More. http://www.totalwine.com.

Tuttle, B., and Burton, F. G. (1999). The effects of a modest incentive on information overload in an investment analysis task. *Accounting, Organizations and Society, 24*, 673–687.

Weiss, A., and James, R. (2014). *Using massive digital libraries: A LITA guide*. Chicago: ALA TechSource, an imprint of the American Library Association.

Wurman, R. (1989). *Information anxiety*. New York: Doubleday.

Part III

Library Shocks

Chapter Eight

Big Data, Libraries, and Collection Development

STATE OF THE LIBRARY: USE WHAT YOU KNOW, GIVE THEM WHAT THEY NEED

Up to this point this book has primarily concerned itself with the external factors and large-scale players involved with the multiple and sometime contradictory visions of data, big data, information and knowledge development, data collection, privacy and surveillance, and information overload. Certainly libraries impact and benefit from the macroscopic changes in the world at large, but aside from the development of massive digital library partnerships like the HathiTrust and Google Books, they have not quite morphed into large-scale engines of social change along the same lines as Silicon Valley startups or other technology companies. Yet libraries—performing their multiple roles as philosophies of information sharing, as embodiments of the hopes and dreams and utopian visions of information to all, as pragmatic organizations that impact people's lives in quantifiable ways, and as discrete, high-functioning information management systems—nevertheless have essential roles to play in the new era of big data collection.

Some questions arise amid all the cultural, structural, and philosophical realignment brought on by big data. For example, how exactly will library activities be impacted? What improvements to library services or missions might occur if big data is brought into the library sphere? Many wonder how big data can be harnessed in libraries. Others are interested in the ways in which big data could potentially enhance current library services.

We will examine these and other questions related to library services. But it might help to answer these questions if readers have a sense of what types of data libraries collect. The promise of big data collection is seen not only in service but also in the opportunity to understand the wider world and the changing role of libraries within it. Mark Bieraugel (2013) in his report on big data for the American Library Association asserts,

> Your library could be gathering big data for analysis to help make data driven decisions. What types of big data could you use to make better decisions about collection development, updating public spaces, or tracking use of library materials through your learning management system? Or you could be the thought leader on big data curation at your institution by providing guidance to storing and making accessible big data sets. Now is the opportunity for your library to understand the issues and opportunities big data offers to researchers, administration, and the librarians at your institution. (Bieraugel, 2013)

The exhortation is clear. Libraries need to somehow harness big data's potential; librarians need to evolve into leaders utilizing big data as their personal engines of change. The blog post raises a number of important questions, even as it leaves readers with vaguely outlined solutions. The main question at hand, though, is What types of data would help us make better decisions about the important trends in the field?

THE INTEGRATED LIBRARY SYSTEM MEETS BIG DATA

Axiell, one of many contractors for library services, identifies the following four areas likely to be enhanced by big data: resources, benchmarking, "react and predict" (their terminology), and service enrichment. Resources focuses on the funding and budgetary side of library management; benchmarking provides the chance for libraries to compare themselves to other institutions beyond mere anecdotes; "react and predict" allows libraries to anticipate and be ready for needs and changes occurring in their user populations; and finally, service enrichment sees the possibility of improving or honing in on the services that actually work.

Of course, speaking partly in the parlance of business-speak and partly in the parlance of libraries, Axiell's focus seems to combine the hollow naïveté of library institutional mission-speak and the crass opportunism of an IT startup company, especially in the following: "You can pick and choose the data that you can *exploit*," and "the *exploitation* of big data is driving literally £Billions in savings through efficiency gains across every industry that adopts practices that look to embrace it," and "the data doesn't *lie*" (Axiell, 2016). The poor choice of words aside, this still doesn't tell us much in terms of actual data usage or the impact that big data has on library strategic planning. On the other hand it does provide us with a look into the direction that libraries and library administrators might hope to go. An emphasis on return on investment (ROI), user satisfaction, streamlining services, performance tracking, and the like, read as if they come directly from the business world and not the library world. Ultimately, these contradictory viewpoints converge at the mutually beneficial exhortation "You can use what you know to give them what they want" (ibid.). Most libraries would agree that this platitude is a good thing. The trouble is how to do this and provide the subsequent evidence that it is working.

The good news is that libraries are not new to the concept of using data to justify services and evidence to inform policy-making decisions. One important source of collection-development data for the past thirty years has been library-use statistics from journal vendors, integrated library systems (ILS), and online catalogs. As these products have become more advanced, including the incorporation of linked data taxonomies, metrics, and citation analysis tools, they have expanded the detail and granularity necessary for making clear decisions on the use of library materials.

Libraries have used automated library systems since the late 1960s and early 1970s (OCLC in 1967, Research Library Group in 1974) to find out what patrons want and provide it to them. These systems have helped libraries manage the day-to-day functions of access, collection development, and resource sharing. Over time, these systems have also evolved from simple relational databases to full-service library management systems tapping into external controlled vocabularies and taxonomies, and linking to platforms that provide additional discovery and fulfillment services. The most current integrated library systems such as Alma tally information to track user preferences. They can be integrated with statistics counters and protocols to help librarians and library staff accurately track the usage of materials.

The types of information these systems gather are varied. The most common way that libraries collect data about their users is through the COUNTER project, based on the COUNTER code of practices, which aims to "facilitate the recording, exchange and interpretation of online usage data" (COUNTER, 2017). The types of information collected by this protocol include the major categories of e-resources "at an international level," such as journals, databases, books, reference works, and multimedia databases. These are bound to and defined by the National Information Standards Organization (NISO), the body for international standards. The main method of collecting this data occurs through the protocol known as SUSHI (Standardized Usage Statistics Harvesting Initiative), which helps with collecting/handling the information and repurposing it for the creation of reports. The potential for this is immense as libraries are able to quantify their usage of resources on ever-growing scales and ever-greater granularity.

While it is not necessarily the same as "big data," given its reliance on technology that is not embedded in social media or based on the 5Vs that have come to define it, the scale and increasing scope of the online catalog projects demonstrate that the library world is not far behind in terms of actual data creation and management with relation to the resources they collect. It is becoming obvious that the next generation of integrated library systems will surely build upon this strong base of international standards, especially as Software as a Service (SaaS) vendors like ProQuest, ExLibris, and the like, begin integrating with each other as SaaS Integration Platforms (SIPs) and providing aggregations of a full range of user-generated data, which "makes real-time data exchange and application integration possible" (Zhou, 2013). The dream, as ProQuest envisions it, "is a single, unified index" that allows them to analyze millions of users (ProQuest, 2013). This future is now, to paraphrase William Gibson; it's just not evenly distributed.

COLLECTION DEVELOPMENT STRATEGIES

Collections as a Mirror to and Aspiration for the Community

Libraries are often viewed as mirrors of their communities (Li and Rice, 2012). What this means is that they exist in order to serve the needs, goals, aspirations, and values of their communities. While outreach and reference services act as the most visible examples of this, collection development also provides an important component to this service. The collection of books and other resources represents the valuation of those items, based on the assumption that these choices will impact their immediate users. In numerous examples, librarians, information science researchers, and the like, find that most users expect their libraries to meet their basic information needs as well as reflect their values. By developing collections that mirror their users' values, libraries help to ensure their long-term visibility, impact, and sustainability.

But how are such collections evaluated with these values in mind? How is it clear that we are meeting the needs of our users? This is important to consider. What if an assumption of meeting user needs is actually wrong, or that specific needs are not being met in any tangible way?

The answers to these questions may not necessarily be obvious at face value and require some delving into the foundations of library science itself. We might consider going back to S. R. Ranganathan's five laws of the library, the essential and still-relevant pillars of the profession, to find some answers. These brief laws have remained unchanged over the past eighty-six years since he laid them out so succinctly and so clearly in 1931:

1. Books are for use.
2. Every reader his/her book.
3. Every book its reader.
4. Save the time of the reader.
5. The library is a growing organization.

Librarians and information science professionals have attempted to update these laws over the years in order to reflect the changes in book technology and the habits of contemporary library users. However, the primary functions that libraries are most widely known for nevertheless persist. Books and their contemporary analogues (i.e., journal articles, newspapers, e-books, internet blogs, etc.) remain in heavy use; every library user still has a potential resource waiting for him or her; there is still a place and need for all the resources found in the library; organizations will still strive for delivering information to users with speed and efficiency; and the library is always changing to reflect the needs of its users. These fundamental aspects of a library have not changed regardless of format collected or the names used to describe them.

Indeed, for every new technology being introduced and provided as an example of something that might disrupt the traditional services of reference, information literacy instruction, and collection development, they still remain the foundations of the profession. But there exists a dual tension of realities and needs and possible hopes for the future of a community. It appears that big data analytics might help librarians and administrators reach important clarity as they shape their collections for the future while remaining cognizant of their role as mirrors to their communities.

Patron-Driven Acquisitions

One of the current strategies for anticipating user needs is known as patron-driven acquisition (PDA); while much has been written and examined about this practice, its results remain mixed. The premise of PDA is to wait for patrons to express interest in a particular resource and provide it on demand. While it is useful in an anecdotal or one-on-one situation for meeting the needs of a small number of people, it may not always be backed up by specific metrics. Allowing large groups of people to ask for resources has the potential to be financially ruinous, especially if each person requested his or her own book or resource that was really only needed once. This could prove to be wasteful.

However, in conjunction with the tracking of user wants and behaviors, it might be possible to better anticipate user needs by improving the metrics associated with patron-driven requests. Marcia Thomas (2012) suggests moving away from collecting everything and being more mission focused through PDA, "collaboration across libraries, within institutions, and with non-library partners continued as a key management strategy. Libraries shifted from a just-in-case to a just-in-time approach to collection development, and subject specialists identified new areas of responsibility, such as data curation" (p. 183). In other words, libraries could spend more time on developing relationships and shaping the collections to meet the needs of specific *local* users in real time, making them more agile in providing unique services or emphasizing unique collections created by or closely associated with those users. PDA would work well with a tool that functions similar to the Amazon ads, which track the latest item a person has viewed. As advertisements, such tracking is annoying and creepy to many online users, but if it were a free service catering to specific information needs within the library, data collection on user habits might be worthwhile as a solicitation of book acquisition for a library collection. It is basically a method to track needs and an instrument to advertise the service meeting those needs.

Big data now becomes an essential tool for analyzing collections. "Patron-driven acquisitions," and "just-in-time collection development" become important aspects of the "big datalization" libraries. The implications of this would certainly have impact on the scope and type of data collection that libraries ought to be collecting. Of course, as seen in the chapter on privacy, this opens up the library to a number of ethical issues that are not fully addressed yet by the American Library Association or its subdivisions such as the Association of College and Research Libraries (ACRL), and the Library and Information Technology Association (LITA).

The Digital Library as Mirror and Method for Gap Analysis

In studies I've done on the intersection of digital libraries and mass digitization projects, it becomes obvious that one can determine how well a library might provide an accurate reflection of user needs by utilizing the massive amounts of data generated by these projects. In one study, Ryan James and I examined a tiny sample of the data provided by OCLC for digital books appearing in Google Books and the HathiTrust (Weiss and James, 2013). The findings suggest that, contrary to developing a true universal library, as espoused by Google, they have instead developed a collection of books reflecting the tastes, values, and needs of the academic community making up their primary body of users. We find, as shown in figure 8.1, that the collection in the aggregate skews in favor of specific academic library languages, emphasizing namely French, German, and even Japanese, far more than the Spanish language—which it should be noted represents nearly 12 percent of the population in the United States. In contrast, German, French, and Japanese speakers in toto comprise less than 1 percent of the US population. Chinese and Russian, which are comparable in collection size to Spanish, are also roughly combined at 1 percent. Looking at it in a slightly different way, we see that *more than 27 percent* of the HathiTrust is represented by languages that are spoken by only 2 percent of people living in the United States. This skew suggests that these massive digital libraries (MDLs) are not universal libraries reflecting the current population of the country. Ironically, however, due to its very comprehensive inclusion of millions of texts, they are incredibly accurate, if limited, mirrors of their intended, and imagined, audiences (Weiss and James, 2013).

Edgar Jones (2010) also looks at the Google Books digital library in terms of a "general research collection" and attempts to examine the limitations of its technology and the gap between the services promised and the services actually provided. The issue expands to one of actual access, as "full view" texts are primarily limited to those in the public domain. He writes, "The current study attempts to measure the extent to which 'full view' volumes contained in Google Books constitute a viable generic research collection for works in the public domain" (Jones, 2010, p. 77). Jones generously sees the collection as useful despite the limitations placed upon it by copyright restrictions. The interesting take from Jones's study is that despite the glaring gaps found in the comprehensive massive digital library collections in Google Books or the HathiTrust, there is still a possibility to use this massive corpus to identify with some accuracy the very areas that lack coverage for specific groups. Given the comprehensiveness of the collection, we can subsequently use it to identify where the gaps exist and take measures to ensure the collection is rounded out to meet the needs of local users. Librarians might also consider pairing this approach with crowd sourcing that solicits users to provide libraries with notifications of gaps. This workflow would also help librarians and collection developers identify the needs and wants of their users. It is a roundabout form of patron-driven acquisition, in a sense, applied in a way that transcends the specific needs of an individual user to

United States Census Bureau, "Top languages other than English spoken in 1980 and changes in relative rank, 1990-2010," *Census.gov*, February 14, 2013, http://www.census.gov/dataviz/visualizations/045/

	HathiTrust Corpus		US Census data (2010)	
Language	Count	Percent	Current Speakers in US	% of total population
German	572,990	9.21	1,083,637	0.34%
French	440,634	7.08	1,301,443	0.41%
Spanish	278,111	4.47	37,500,000	12%
Chinese	241,886	3.89	2,882,497	0.89%
Russian	230,835	3.71	905,843	0.29%
Japanese	187,713	3.02	436,110	0.13%

Figure 8.1. Comparison of collections in HathiTrust digital library to US Census data; comparisons show a skewed representation of books (4.5 percent of collection) in Spanish compared to speakers of the language (12 percent). *Source:* Census.gov, February, 2013, http://www.census.gov.

benefit the needs of a wider community. Ultimately, large crowds within the user base could function as the engines of collection development. Instead of atomized patron requests, though, libraries would be harnessing the "wisdom of the crowd" to develop the collection.

Using the Search Itself as an Indicator of Need: Big Data Analytics and User Queries

Apart from analyzing what exists or doesn't exist in a library's collection, libraries can also meet user needs for specific content by tracking how people conduct searches. It has been argued that search queries represent specific, real-time needs that patrons have for library resources. These are the written evidence of explicit information needs, formulated and written down in various forms of accuracy and skill by the users themselves. These represent potentially rich data libraries can mine to help with not only collection development but also information literacy instruction.

The library content vendor ProQuest argues that analyzing search behavior will help libraries tailor search results in order improve access and provide agile collections that better reflect granular needs. In their own research, ProQuest observes that "most common searches are 2–4 word queries with a long tail of much longer queries" (ProQuest, 2013). By examining these search queries, one can anticipate problems and obstacles in user searches and provide improvements in user experience such as suggestions for the ideal search and common search terms used for specific topics (ibid.). Ideally, the contents of the search terms will pair, just as Ranganathan suggested, the users to their resources.

As people often abandon searches at specific points, libraries and vendors have attempted to find ways of improving search results and retaining system users. For example, ProQuest has found that users who input more terms in their searches are less likely to abandon searches. Whether this is just evidence of more sophisticated preplanning by searchers or a recording of the enthusiasm a person is searching with at that particular moment in time is unclear. Obviously, knowing the factors that lead to search success and search abandonment will help libraries improve user satisfaction rates. Similar services have been developed to further increase the length of searches and reduce abandonment rates. Such services include the following: "Best Bets," for content recommendation; "Database Recommender," for other large databases to search; and "Related Search Suggestions," for a list of search queries to aid in finding information. Overall, the purpose of such widgets or programs is to provide better tie-ins and links to related and relevant content (ProQuest, 2013).

ProQuest is not the only service providing query analysis. Google Analytics (see figure 8.2) compiles similar metrics based on the user searches and browsing activity in library websites. Libraries have used these for some time now to provide snapshots of what users are seeking and to help with website redesign efforts. It becomes clear with these examples that by using such quantifiable measures to increase the user's satisfaction, libraries can easily harness big data to meet their ultimate missions, initiatives, and philosophical goals.

A RISING METRIC TIDE: BIG DATA AND CITATIONS, ALTMETRICS, AND LINKED DATA

Integrated library systems and digital libraries are not the only organizations generating quantified data for the sake of improving library reference and collection-development services. Publishers, often working in clear coordination with library and library user needs, have developed unique information-tracking schemas. Publishers now use and advertise a wide array of metric services to both improve findability and more accurately track user behavior. These services include author impact, journal impact, tracking and measuring impact, and author disambiguation.

Author impact metrics include the H-index, which measures both the productivity and citation impact of the publications of a scientist or scholar; the G-index, which quantifies scientific productivity based on the publication record; and the i10-index, which measures the number of publications with at least ten citations. Journal impact metrics include Journal Citation Reports (JCR) and Eigenfactors, which examine the overall citations of articles in a

Figure 8.2.   Screenshot of Google Analytics, providing the number of users, sessions, and duration of time spent at CSUN's Institutional Repository at http:// scholarworks.csun.edu. *Source:* Google Analytics, 2017.

particular publication. Article influence is also measured by Scimago Journal and Country Rank and Google Scholar Metrics, which provides the number of citations and a listing of those citations too. Tracking and measuring impact includes the Web of Science Citation Tools Google Scholar Citations and PLoS Article-Level Metrics. Finally, author disambiguation provides an important service by helping to sort names and link the appropriate papers to the actual authors; ORCID is perhaps the most well-known of these services.

Leading online academic journal publisher Elsevier appears to be taking big data and data-collection access services even further, having purchased bePress digital repository platform in summer 2017 and managing divisions such as Hivebench, Mendeley, Pure, and SSRN, each of which offer a wide range of data services to researchers "from study design and grant application to laboratory note-taking and file-sharing, to publication and post-publication assessment of effects" (Basken, 2017). The end result of their machinations appears to be an attempt at cornering the market in open-data services and creating a wedge in the open-access movement.

Delving into Citation Studies

The traditional types of metrics for collection development that have frequently been employed over the years in libraries—that is, anecdotal evidence, direct solicitation of needs, checkouts, downloads of articles, journal page views, and so on—are giving way to more sophisticated methods less clearly rooted in print bibliographic traditions and more aligned with online, digital social media culture. Although individual author statistics are not always essential to the decisions made by libraries and librarians, they might be worth examining in the aggregate. If a librarian were to examine the number of citations occurring by the faculty in their university or college, there might be a cause to reduce or expand the coverage for that particular resource.

However, journal impact metrics, such as Eigenfactor, along with basic journal rankings, have long provided academics and academic departments (as well as librarians) with more quantified indicators of an article's influence within a discipline. Stephanie Wical and Todd Vandenbark (2015) find that "combining an analysis of usage statistics with citation analysis provides a more strategic way to look at a Big Deal package" (p. 33). The combination of approaches would help librarians to determine if the costs they have sunk into particular resources are actually worthwhile. It might also help with setting specific benchmarks in order to evaluate the return on investment of the resource. If growth targets for use are not met, then librarians might more easily reach the decision of cutting a resource, especially if that resource is bundled with a large number of unused titles.

But there are significant issues with relying too heavily upon metrics to make decisions. Björn Brembs and colleagues (2013) find a strong correlation between the rank of the journal and its rate of error and article retraction. They note that the actual impact ranking is "negotiated, irreproducible, and unsound," meaning that it is subject to agreements between publishers and accreditors, and is as a result *a fundamentally unreliable metric*. Because of such practices, journal rankings actually impede the progress of science and slow down the dissemination of information rather than foster it. This should be damning enough on its own for the specific journals mentioned in the research, but when taken in the aggregate with thousands of other highly ranked journals, the potential for encountering ever-growing amounts of error and retracted articles increases. Much like with the glaring collection gaps found in massive digital libraries, the problems of error and retraction become magnified and amplified due to the large-scale aggregation of data.

There is also the issue of being overreliant on specific methodologies. The old cliché is that if you have a hammer, everything looks like a nail. In a similar fashion, many librarians and administrators are tempted to apply the same quantitative methods to things that might not be quantifiable. The impact of a painting or a poem, for example, cannot always be measured by objective means. The number of times a painting is cited or mentioned in tweets or in academic articles certainly demonstrates its notoriety but may not represent its value. As James Wilsdon (2015) suggests, "Some of the most precious qualities of academic culture resist simple quantification, and individual indicators can struggle to do justice to the richness and plurality of our research. Too often, poorly designed evaluation criteria are distorting behavior and determining careers" (p. 129). Not only is error a problem, but also, by this reasoning, the narrowing of disciplines based on an equally narrow conception of *impact* also negatively impacts the diversity of ideas found in a discipline. With narrower ideas of what constitutes success in a discipline, scholars and researchers are less likely to take risks or break with dominant theoretical paradigms. In the end such reliance on quantified methods can contribute to stagnation and a lack of progress in a field of study.

So ultimately, a word of caution needs to be extended to those tempted to quantify everything that can possibly be quantified in academic discourse. While STEM (science, technology, engineering, and mathematics) fields derive much benefit from the use of Eigenfactors to demonstrate impact, the rates of error that are associated with top journals due to the competitiveness of their selection process should give one pause to rely too heavily upon their meaning. Librarians involved in collection development would be well advised to remember, as Wilsdon suggests, that "metrics hold real power: they are constitutive of values, identities and livelihoods" (2015, p. 129). But lacking all-important context, such metrics lose their power. Providing the appropriate resources reliant not only on citations and impact factors but also on *qualitative* methods of citation and value analysis may prove to be the better approach.

Implementing Linked Data in Library Collections

The upside to linked data appears to be immense. Like much in the library world, the concept itself is not a new one, but the technology has finally arrived to make it feasible. Linked data essentially involves the linking of multiple taxonomies, controlled vocabularies, and name authorities so that they are automatically harvested from their sources and embedded into the display of online library systems' metadata records. Name authorities and controlled vocabularies have been in use by various organizations, including the Library of Congress, to provide precise information about resources in a library's collection. Used by the diligent cataloger, the well-constructed taxonomy creates a clean and easily searchable database. The concept, though, has been expanded in the online world so that these immense indexes can be aggregated and integrated into records constituted almost in real time when the need to retrieve them occurs. Instead of creating in-house solutions for standards, as invariably happens when siloed collections are created, the library or cataloger relies on these open standardized lists to generate accurate and universally adopted metadata.

Some researchers and librarians see no limits to the impact that linked data could provide. Philip Schreur, for example, writes that "by harvesting the entire output of the academy, an immensely rich web of data will be created that will liberate research and teaching" (2012, p. 227). The liberation, he argues, would occur in numerous tangible forms, impacting the way that research and scholarly communication are implemented and effacing the siloed approaches of the MARC-record-based online catalog system, which as we saw above was undergoing its own changes. Schreur sees linked data and open data sets bypassing the need for library catalog systems and MARC records altogether. Instead, he argues, the limits of the relational database would be surpassed and the main problem would not be the restriction of closed data systems but the "nearly infinite" amount of information that will potentially be "overwhelming" to the user.

Despite the optimism and advocacy of this manifesto from 2012, it appears that the shift toward more linked open-data modeling has not quite occurred in the five years since this piece was published. While it is an interesting and possibly prescient vision of the library's effaced and diffused role of the future, it hasn't quite come to pass. In fact many of the faults of libraries noted in the article—their insularity, their refusal to move beyond MARC, and their reliance on closed and siloed systems—remain in place, either through the inertia inherent to large institutions or by the decree of policies under the control of administrators.

Furthermore, it is not entirely clear how this model would alter the current information-searching landscape. Accrediting bodies remain in place, requiring libraries to continue subscribing to those journals essential to specific disciplines. Journal publishers remain in place, too, continuing to improve their metrics while at the same time offering hybrid open-access services. Integrated library systems keep generating added value that relies as much upon proprietary software as it does upon open data. It is also unclear how collection development is going to fit within this information ecosystem. If everything is gathered from elsewhere, how will we accurately track what our own users' needs actually are? If the metadata is developed by dozens of third parties, each with their own agendas and potentially contradictory needs, how will libraries ensure user privacy and confidentiality?

Also at stake is whether the development of increasing complexity in metadata systems is actually scalable. If these systems of information prove to be unwieldy or incompatible, then the whole "house of cards," so to speak, falls down. Schreur admits as much in his analysis too; the immense amount of data may prove to be overwhelming and could lead to greater confusion and information overload in users. However, if some of these issues are resolved, or if policy roadblocks and accreditation requirements change, the upside to opening up the data siloes will undoubtedly alter the information landscape.

Finding a Grain of Sand in the Sahara: RFIDs and Book Pathfinding

Despite the move toward e-books and electronic journals, print books remain vital components of any library's collection. One foundational study from the early 1970s suggests that print books help people remember the physical location of information, which aids information recall in readers (Rothkopf, 1971). In comparing print books to e-books, other researchers have found that the amount of information readers retain is greater when reading a print book (Wästlund et al., 2005). If these studies stand, there may be a resurgence, much like there has been a resurgence in the collection of vinyl records or other analog formats, of valuing paper/print media, especially if there are distinct differences in student success. Being aware of the impact of electronic screens on information retention might impact whether librarians in charge of collection development would purchase the electronic or print versions of a book.

However, even though books are still provided in print form, there are new strategies at play to help "datalize" them for use with electronic portable devices. Some libraries provide more digital markers for these physical books. Again, like many of the previous examples, this is not a new idea; bar codes have been in use on all library books since the 1970s. But the improve-

ment upon this concept includes new "location-sensitive tools for information engagement," including Foursquare, Facebook, augmented reality programs, QR codes, and other "apps" that provide users with a digital snapshot
of a book or information resource (Murphy and Kroski, 2012). Much of the
metadata about a book can be delivered to a user through QR codes, for
example, without requiring them to go back to a library PC terminal to
confirm basic information they might have forgotten or failed to consider.
This would be especially helpful for users who are seeking a book but are
unsure of its status (i.e., it's missing from the shelves due to loss or theft, or
it's a reference book that cannot be checked out). A library would be able to
procure use and handling statistics generated from the access of these QR
codes in ways that weren't possible before. It would certainly help in the
cases when a book is examined by a patron but never actually checked out.
Often patrons, in an effort to respect the library or be respectful of the
institution, return the book to the shelf in the exact spot that they found it,
even when the librarians ask that students leave such texts on a return shelf.

Along those lines of trying to figure out what books patrons have "unoffi-
cially" examined in one way or another, another strategy employs radio-
frequency identification (RFID) systems to create data profiles on print
books and collections in the aggregate. The use of an RFID system would
increase the efficiency of typical library reshelving and checkout workflows
(Coyle, 2005). RFID readers could examine a range of shelved books without having to pick up books individually to read them, allowing them to be
found more easily. Circulation is improved as individual titles would not
have to be scanned one by one. The increased granularity of metadata and
geographic location information about a specific book title will provide more
data about the book's usage and the book's user. It is hoped that the more
granular the digital information about a book, the more useful that book will
become for overall mass analytics about use, users, position within a collection, and position within the library itself.

DEFINING THE PURPOSE FOR DATA COLLECTING

There is clearly a lot of potential for big data in libraries to improve the
practices related to collection development, ranging from improved statistics
collection on user access and checkout behaviors to the use of citations and
alternative online metrics. There is potential in making each book a more
robust digitally identifiable object clearly tethered to user data. RFIDs, digital VR bookshelves, and other interesting areas of development would provide ever-growing data about a book and would be usable by both patron and
library system/administrator. But as amazing as these new possibilities
sound, the key is determining what statistics we truly need to collect and, by

doing so, determining what questions the data sets are actually going to be able to answer. It ultimately makes no sense to capture all data without understanding what it will be used for. Doing so will compromise the results, alienate the users when they find out about it, and result in much wasted effort that cannot be recovered. We must wisely choose the paths that need to be taken to reach our goals.

REFERENCES

Axiell. (2016). Big data and libraries: Getting the most from your library data. http://www.axiell.co.uk.

Basken, P. (2017). Elsevier is becoming a data company: Should universities be wary? *Chronicle of Higher Education.* http://www.chronicle.com.

Bieraugel, M. (2013). Keeping up with . . . big data. *American Library Association Blog.* http://www.ala.org.

Brembs, B., Button, K., and Munafò, M. (2013). Deep impact: Unintended consequences of journal rank. *Frontiers in Human Neuroscience, 7.* https://www.frontiersin.org.

COUNTER. (2017). Code of practice. https://www.projectcounter.org.

Coyle, K. (2005). Management of RFID in libraries. *Journal of Academic Librarianship, 31*(5), 486–489.

Google. (2017). Google Analytics Home. https://analytics.google.com/.

Jones, E. (2010). Google Books as a general research collection. *Library Resources and Technical Services, 54*(2), 77–89.

Li, H., and Rice, J. (2012). Libraries and the demographic shift. *Huffington Post.* http://www.huffingtonpost.com.

Murphy, J., and Kroski, E. (2012). *Location-aware services and QR codes for libraries: (THE TECH SET® #13).* Chicago: ALA TechSource.

ProQuest. (2013). Data mining "big data": A strategy for improving library discovery. http://www.proquest.com.

Rothkopf, E. (1971). Incidental memory for location of information in text. *Journal of Verbal Learning and Verbal Behavior, 10*(6), 608–613. http://dx.doi.org/10.1016/S0022-5371(71)80066-X.

Schreur, P. (2012). The academy unbound: Linked data as revolution. *Library Resources and Technical Services, 56*(4), 227–237.

Thomas, M. L. (2012). Disruption and disintermediation: A review of the collection development and management literature, 2009–10. *Library Resources and Technical Services, 56*(3), 183–198.

Wästlund, E., Reinikka, H., Norlander, T., and Archer, T. (2005). Effects of VDT and paper presentation on consumption and production of information: Psychological and physiological factors. *Computers in Human Behavior, 21*(2), 377–394.

Weiss, A., and James, R. (2013). An examination of massive digital libraries' coverage of Spanish language materials: Issues of multi-lingual accessibility in a decentralized, mass-digitized world. In *2013 International Conference on Culture and Computing* (pp. 10–14). Los Alamitos, CA: IEEE Computer Society. doi:10.1109/CultureComputing.2013.10.

Wical, S., and Vandenbark, R. (2015). Notes on operations: Combining citation studies and usage statistics to build a stronger collection. *Library Resources and Technical Services, 59*(1), 33–42.

Wilsdon, J. (2015). We need a measured approach to fmetrics: Quantitative indicators of research output can inform decisions but must be supported by robust analysis. *Nature, 523* (7559), 129.

Wilsdon, J. (2016). *The metric tide: Independent review of the role of metrics in research assessment and management.* Los Angeles: Sage. https://us.sagepub.com.

Zhou, B. (2013). Data integration as a service for applications deployment on the SaaS platform. In *Proceedings of the Sixth International Conference on Biomedical Engineering and
Informatics (BMEI), 2013* (pp. 672–676). Piscataway, NJ: IEEE.

Chapter Nine

Data Management Planning Strategies for Libraries in the Age of Big Data

THE GROWTH OF DATA ON COLLEGE CAMPUSES

"Databrarian" is arguably the newest moniker given to librarians, and it probably will not be the last alternative name deployed to describe the varied roles they take on. First appearing in 2013, the name implies that there is a new and unique set of conditions impacting library functions, and only those with sufficient training in handling data could manage them. But despite the novelty of the position name, the need for data management and the growth of data isn't necessarily a novel development. In fact, as Lynda Kellam and Kristi Thompson suggest, "data librarianship as a field is hardly new . . . it encompasses a diversity of forms, functions and specializations that are vital to academic research and teaching" (2016, p. 1). Of course, it should not be very surprising that there are new names invented for the changes occurring in the library field. They merely reflect the types of work that librarians are actually performing. Instead of focusing on the traditional services of reference, bibliographic instruction, collection development, and circulation, librarians are instead being asked to provide information services related to data, data management, and planning, while also navigating the ins and outs of federal-funder open-research guidelines.

Data management has become an especially important aspect of librarianship in the years since the Obama administration released its White House memo "Expanding Public Access to the Results of Federally Funded Research," based on the rationale that "citizens deserve easy access to the results of research their tax dollars have paid for" (Stebbins, 2013). The mandate covers federal agencies with operating budgets greater than one hundred million dollars annually and applies to researchers who have secured grant funding from these agencies. As seen in figure 9.1, the list is quite comprehensive and includes the National Science Foundation (NSF), the National Institutes of Health (NIH), and the Department of Defense (DoD). In their narratives, grant applicants are required to provide a data-management plan, or at least make mention of a plan, to provide both the data as well as resulting publications in an open-access repository.

As with many federal mandates, initiatives, and laws, the specifics are often left up to the agency to interpret and implement. For example, as shown in figure 9.1, the Department of Defense allows its grantees to submit data for public consumption in "established, publicly accessible institutional repositories"; NASA suggests archiving data into "existing data repositories"; and the NSF merely states "an appropriate repository" allowing the researchers/scholars to archive data in the place considered acceptable. But it should be noted that despite the relative vagueness and looseness in interpretation stipulated in these grant applications, they are nevertheless vital components to writing grants and sometimes the difference between being awarded and being passed over.

As result of these rising stakes regarding data management, librarians are being called upon to provide such data-management planning. I, for example, provide boilerplate language and data-management planning services for the faculty I serve. These plans are intended to ease the process of handling data during the life cycle of a project. The issues raised include privacy, appropri-

Figure 9.1.   Agency-funder mandates. *Source:* **Based on the 2013 White House memo "Expanding Public Access to the Results of Federally Funded Research" (Stebbins, 2013).**

ateness of releasing the data, ensuring the long-term preservation of the data, and so on.

This chapter will examine basic data-management plans (DMPs), data preservation and access methods, and discipline-specific approaches necessary to help libraries and librarians manage the deluge of data.

SIX ARGUMENTS FOR OPEN ACCESS AND DATA

The push for openly accessible, tax-funded data is driving many academic library administrators and librarians to adopt policies and procedures that help foster successful grant-funding initiatives. These policies for open data overlap in general with the open-access movement, which itself attempts to remove price and permission barriers to journal content and, in the words of the Public Library of Science (PLoS), "free availability and unrestricted use" of published articles and books (Suber, 2015). It is a movement that has seen great strides over the past sixteen years since the establishment of the Budapest Open Access Initiative (BOAI) in 2001 (BOAI, 2012). Overall growth in open access has seen the movement change from a niche initiative to one that dominates some disciplines, especially medicine and physics in the STEM fields. Indeed, the movement has since grown larger internationally through the Berlin Declaration on Open Access and its subsequent OA2020 initiative (Open Access 2020, 2017).

But what is the benefit of open access? What are the motivations that truly define it as a movement? Of course, as with all robust movements, there are numerous arguments that can be made on its behalf; numerous justifications provide the basis for its adoption. There are six main arguments related to open access that proponents regularly espouse to persuade others to adopt open-access measures.

First, open access clearly increases the rapidity of knowledge transfer, usually by cutting out the time-consuming peer-review step, a hallmark of traditional academic journal publishing. As is the case with physicists depositing preprints into arXiv, a long-established, green, physics open-access preprint repository, scholars can release their findings to peers as quickly as possible. The practice doesn't replace the peer-review system established for academic journals; it merely forgoes the initial peer-review step in order to release results immediately. Academic publishing is notoriously slow, with some journal articles taking years to go through the whole submission and publication process. As a result, depositing a preprint in arXiv, or similar subject repository, works to increase the speed of ideas reaching their counterparts at other institutions. One of the most compelling arguments related to this practice is that open access, as a result in part to the rapid and widespread dissemination of ideas, can lead to increased citations, a phenomenon known as the Open Access Citation Advantage (OACA) (Brody, 2004; Gentil-Beccot et al., 2009; Harnad and Brody, 2004; Lawrence, 2001; Wagner, 2010). Notably, as seen in figure 9.2, OACA research also suggests that not only do open-access articles provide more citations, but the open data sets associated with them will do so as well. Heather Piwowar and Todd Vision (2013) conclude that "authors published most papers using their own data sets *within two years of their first publication on the data set*, whereas data reuse papers published by third-party investigators continued to accumulate *for at least six years.*"

The second argument often made for open access is that it helps to bolster the "information commons," especially with regard to publicly funded research. Open-access mandates in the federal government, as seen in figure 9.1, often rely on this appeal. The public pays for it and therefore has the right to see and make use of it freely (Stebbins, 2013). The reasoning boils down to, in essence, the larger an information commons becomes, the more societies will benefit. Free and open access to information provides a clear public benefit in these arguments, though one must concede it may be difficult to calculate a specific return on investment.

The third argument, and one most espoused by those working in scholarly communications or in libraries, regards the transfer of copyright agreements often found in academic publishing. The argument in favor of open-access is that reputable open-access publishers will allow the author to maintain copyright, while reserving limited licenses for themselves in order to distribute the work under certain conditions. The problem with major academic publishers, such arguments go, is that the scholar, author, or researcher is expected to transfer the copyright of the article to the publishers, who in turn resell the content back to the institutions that originally funded it. When one thinks about it, it is an egregious situation for those librarians in collection development who see firsthand the rising costs of journals and the negative impact that copyright has on scholarly communication in general and on

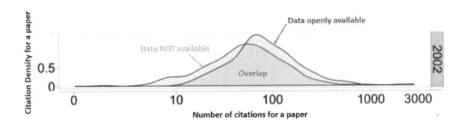

Figure 9.2.   An open-access citation advantage is also visible when data sets are provided online. *Source:* **Image adapted by the author. Piwowar and Vision, 2013.**

libraries specifically. John Willinsky's (2002) research into copyright's impact on scholarly communication has found that academic publishing functions contrary to the original wording of the constitution on copyright (i.e., "to promote the progress of the science and useful arts"). He describes current copyright law as a "system that reduces public access to knowledge." Additionally, Paul Heald's (2014) research shows evidence of this lack of access through his own research conducted on copyright, orphan works, and the "hole in our culture" exacerbated by excessively long copyright terms. In one notorious example, Heald demonstrates that books from the 1980s and 1990s are less available through new editions than books printed seventy years earlier in the 1910s and 1920s.

Along the same lines, librarians have continually noted the rise of journal prices as a result of publishers' increased control over the copyright of this material as well as the artificially created scarcity model they have developed for electronic journal access. According to one recent estimate, journal subscription package prices have been increasing by 5–6 percent annually, nearly double the current rate of inflation (Bosch and Henderson, 2017). Additionally, Harvard University has mentioned that "large journal publishers have made the scholarly communication environment fiscally unsustainable and academically restrictive" (Sample, 2012). This fourth argument for open access asserts that open-access publishers can help to alleviate some of the ongoing problems found with traditional academic publishing, by allowing access at no cost as well as by "flipping journals" from traditional publishing to gold open access (Solomon et al., 2016).

Since open access is concerned primarily with reducing the barriers to access raised by traditional publishing practices, it opens up information to those in need, not only in local or regional areas within the United States, but also in impoverished regions in other parts of the world. It is argued that third-world countries in Africa or Asia would benefit the most from being able to access vital health information. With the growing *physical* connectivity of the modern world through transportation systems that link people directly to regions of the world historically isolated from each other, the threat of pandemics greatly increases. Risks can possibly be mitigated if the latest techniques and information for disease control are made available, especially to such places that have served as ground zeroes and incubators for dangerous diseases.

Finally, researchers have found that open-access publishing models are cheaper to run and cost less to manage than their traditional publishing counterparts (Pinfield, 2010). Michael Lesk (2012) finds in his research that publishing-behemoth Elsevier spends close to $10,000 per article published, while PLoS spends $1,500 per article, which is notably the exact cost of their article processing charge (APC). ArXiv was found to have spent roughly $7 per article self-submitted by scholars. It should be noted that the cost of publishing these articles does not appear to have very much to do with the editors, peer reviewers, or authors of the content, since they are typically *not compensated* by the big publishers for their efforts. One wonders, then, what actually accounts for such a discrepancy in cost. The likelihood is that expenses not directly associated with the actual costs of publishing (i.e., advertising, legal costs, royalty payments, shareholder dividends, administrative and staffing costs, etc.) have inflated the prices of publishing traditional journal articles. The cheaper open-access models seem to be more efficient at and dedicated to their primary mission, which is to publish and disseminate knowledge. Indeed, some open-access publishers such as the University of California Press's online megajournal *Collabra* (similar in structure and mission to PLoS) actually set aside part of the APC to pay peer reviewers and editors, making the costs associated with Elsevier and the other major publishers—especially if they offer their misleading "hybrid open-access" options—even harder to fathom or justify (Chalwa, 2015).

Ultimately, these six main arguments for open access are varied, interlocking, and compelling. Notably, data has more recently been folded into the movement's philosophy. The citations researchers can gain from open data are notably persuasive too. The mandates put forth by the US federal government and the Obama administration have also increased participation in open access. Finally, the increase of green open-access institutional repositories and their subject repository counterparts for specific disciplines at numerous research organizations and universities provide a growing foundation for the movement.

As libraries and librarians begin to establish services in data-management planning, it will be important to keep in mind the philosophical foundations for the open-access movement. For as the open-access movement becomes more prominent, the stakes will get higher and the pushback from traditional publishing, even greater.

DATA-MANAGEMENT PLANNING AND DATA LIFE CYCLE MANAGEMENT

The specific tools of data-management planning are as varied as the stipulations written into the grant-funding mandates and grant applications. Most academic libraries these days have taken at least minimal steps to provide services related to data management. One of the leaders in the field of data-management planning is the California Digital Library, which developed the DMPTool (https://dmptool.org) as a method to help faculty researchers and scholars in the University of California (UC) system plan for the data life cycle. Along with DMPTool, Merritt provides a suite of services for all UC faculty to help them plan, archive, and preserve the data generated by their scholarly and research activities. Unique to their mission, Merritt utilizes a series of "micro-services," which they describe as "digital curation based on devolving curation function into a set of independent, but interoperable, services that embody curation values and strategies" (UC3 Merritt, 2017). The result of this approach is that each "micro-service" is independent from others and therefore easier to manage and subsequently integrate as necessary. The services include the following discrete areas: creation and acquisition, appraisal and selection, preservation planning, preservation intervention, and service brokerage (UC3, 2010).

Looking at each service specifically, we find that *creation and acquisition* provide best-practice guidance for creating digital objects and data, while also incorporating the appropriate technical specifications and providing the best edition among multiple versions of a digital object. *Appraisal and selection* helps scholars to determine the factors for curating content, especially the value (be it intellectual, aesthetic, economic, or artifactual) and the rarity of the digital object. *Preservation planning* and *preservation intervention* are very much two sides of the same coin. *Planning* allows scholars to determine future needs and wants, while *intervention* focuses on what steps need to be taken to ensure preservation can persist long after the plan has been implemented. Finally, *service brokerage* pairs scholars with appropriate venues or providers for data and digital object management (UC3, 2010).

Other academic libraries have developed innovative tools for improving the data-management process. These tools range from specific data life cycle planners to data-submission checklists and repository deposit services. What they mainly have in common is the desire to ensure that the data that can and should be archived is done so in an efficient and ethical manner. One good example of a data life cycle planner, designed by Katy McKen at the University of Bath, UK, provides a clear description of the changes and steps that data goes through during the research process (McKen et al., 2012). In figure 9.3, the user can see that as data is generated it is subsequently utilized in research projects and publications, and then finally preserved. The cycle runs this gamut from planning and project design, collection and data capture, interpretation and analysis, and management and preservation, to finally release and publication. The final part in this cycle returns back to the beginning: discovery and reuse. This cyclical understanding is in many ways the key concept for providing data-management planning to scholars. Librarians need to press upon researchers that a library's ultimate goal is providing access points and searchability for users to discover and reuse data. Ultimately the "life cycle" will provide justification as well as reassurance that data can be accessed later.

In addition to schematic life-cycle diagrams and workflows, data-management planning templates can also help librarians and library staff with aiding data preservation. It is important for librarians to find a way to assess

UNIVERSITY OF **BATH**

Research360: Data in the Research Lifecycle

Katy McKen
(K.E.McKen@bath.ac.uk)
Catherine Pink
Matt Davidson
Liz Lyon

 JISC

Data is an important product of research that should, as far as possible, be accessible for re-use. This requires key stakeholders from across the institution to develop mechanisms that enable data management throughout the research lifecycle.

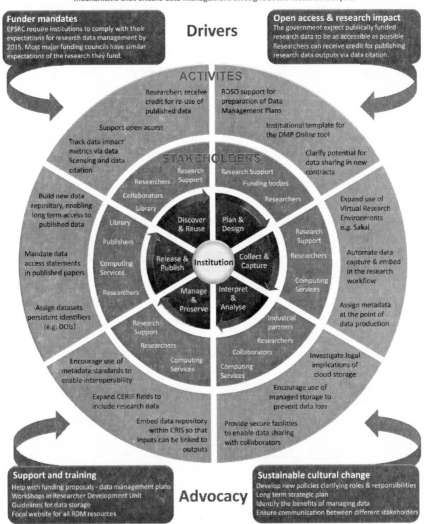

Figure 9.3.   The data life cycle as divided by drivers and advocacy, and activities and stakeholders. *Source:* University of Bath, UK. McKen et al., 2012.

what is coming at them. DMP tools allow both librarians and their faculty and researcher clients to focus on the important questions related to data management.

The most important question to consider is whether the data being generated is appropriate for an open-access repository. This is determined by considering the types of data created by a project and whether the data includes private or sensitive information. They also need to determine what file formats are used and the tools that might be necessary to render the data understandable to humans (i.e., scripts, databases, user interfaces, etc.). Additionally, librarians and researchers need to know how the data would be generated and acquired. Quality-control standards severely impact how data is organized and stored, and lacking these might compromise future access. Finally, documentation, descriptive standards, and metadata need to be applied to the raw data sets. As we discovered in previous chapters, without context, data loses meaning and utility. Librarians and their researcher clients would need to determine what necessary metadata standards should be applied to the data, or whether the metadata will be generated by hand or automatically through machinery. Ancillary to this standardization of description, scholars will also need to determine their disciplines' overall best practices for file naming, and project and data identifiers.

Among specific storage and preservation practices, librarians and scholars will need to consider who would be responsible for data backup and where it would occur. Perhaps scholars will save data on local PCs and send it to servers elsewhere, in the cloud or otherwise. Along with that, though, comes the issue of cybersecurity, authentication, and overall stability of the storage systems. Ultimately, long-term digital storage will need to be arranged with reputable and stable systems. Though university repository systems or third-party systems are available, it is unclear sometimes whether appropriate digital-preservation practices are in place. Too often people, including librarians, confuse the practice of data backup, which is but one small action, with the series of interlocking steps and policy guarantees essential to ensure true digital repository preservation as espoused in ISO 16363, an international standard for trusted digital repositories (TDR) (Center for Research Libraries, 2017). Ultimately, it comes down to who is actually responsible for policy that preserves the data and what functions are actually provided by repositories, libraries, and other knowledge organizations.

Finally, data retention and data sharing become bigger issues the longer the data is stored and the larger the data set. Retention schedules are well known to those who work in archives. Records management for specific state institutions, for example, dictate what documents must be retained and for how long. Failure to comply with such regulations opens up organizations to specific liabilities. One might argue that data needs to follow specific retention guidelines too. Often, institutional review boards will require such retention schedules to ensure that old data is not kept for too long and not misplaced from carelessness or failure to delete when necessary. In other cases, the data generated may be mandated for sharing with the public—as with many federally funded grants; as a result, understanding and implementing data sharing and dissemination methods becomes essential. It is important to note also that even if grant funders mandate data sharing, some data cannot be released due to regulatory and legal constraints. The Health Insurance Portability and Accountability Act (HIPAA), for example, stipulates that it is illegal to share medical data beyond the specific purposes outlined in its regulations (US HHS, 2003). Aside from this, the scope of who accesses data is also necessary to consider. Would the data be restricted to merely those involved in the project, or is it opened to a wider audience? Privacy remains an utmost concern for data. But is there anyone else who might also claim some ownership on the data or have a stake in its future? Finally, if one does allow the data to be reused, what policies actually exist that will proscribe or regulate how it might be used in the future? Although creative commons licensing often helps with describing how people can use creative works after they are released, sometimes it is not clear if a person or entity has any legal copyright control over generated data. If one does own the data in that sense, what specific ways will one determine how others can use that data later? These are all difficult questions that librarians and libraries need to wrangle with as they begin to provide services and tools for managing data.

Libraries have also been providing support for scholars whenever they begin their grant-writing process. Many of the federally mandated open-access grant funders require data-management planning sections within their grant narratives. One way that libraries and librarians can provide support for this is by writing language specifically for a grant as well as providing "boilerplate" or "template" paragraphs for scholars to insert into the narratives. One such example might read, in part, as follows:

> CSUN ScholarWorks Open Access Repository (SOAR; http://scholarworks.csun.edu) is California State University Northridge's open-access institutional repository (IR). Its mission is to organize, distribute, and permanently preserve CSUN student and faculty research, publications, and instructional materials. By default, items added to the repository are publicly accessible but can be restricted to specific users or groups at the collection or file level when needed.
>
> ScholarWorks is based on the well-established open-source software platform DSpace, which was developed in the early 2000s by Hewlett Packard and MIT. Since 2007, a DSpace implementation has been hosted by the California State University Chancellor's Office, which provides technical support and ongoing digital preservation strategies. A ScholarWorks DSpace instance is offered to all campuses in the CSU system at no direct cost. As a result, repository services at CSUN are provided by the university library to the faculty without charge.

The system utilizes the Dublin Core metadata scheme to ensure interoperability with other repositories and external content indexers such as Google. Through the Handle System every item is provided with a persistent URI, a vital component of Digital Object Architecture as defined by the Corporation for National Research Initiatives (CNRI). Data integrity is confirmed through checksum validation routines, and although any file type is acceptable, the system will recognize forty-one standard MIME types. The repository is backed up daily, with copies of data stored offsite by established cloud-based services. The CSU Chancellor's Office also provides cloud storage, enabling the long-term storage of data in the petabyte range, and streaming server capabilities.

Additionally, librarians and staff members can provide letters of support for grant narratives explaining exactly what they would do to help researchers archive, preserve, and share appropriate data. Similar in content to the boilerplate language above, letters of support would describe the repository system, its location on the web, the services provided by the repository, the digital preservation strategies taken by repository staff, and the basic philosophy of the practitioners involved. Ultimately, the letter of support provides clear documentation of who will fulfill certain roles and obligations for the long-term preservation and access of the data.

On a final note, the growth in the amount of data sets and their file sizes is spurred by the wider technological and social developments related to big data. Additionally, the impact of the open-access and open-data movements on libraries should not be underestimated. These movements are contributing to the increase in data handled and managed by libraries, not only making it findable and reusable but also increasing the profile of data so that more researchers feel the normative pressures to save data as well. Changing disciplines and their adoption of digital tools has also contributed to the need for creating management tools where none existed in the past. Ultimately, libraries will need to develop more robust ways of handling the data brought to them. While checklists and templates for data are helpful, the most important aspect, preservation, must be framed in terms of specific long-term, sustainable services. Libraries with their long histories of organizing information, structured or otherwise, have an essential role to play.

REFERENCES

Bosch, S., and Henderson, K. (2017). New world, same model: Periodicals price survey 2017. *Library Journal.* http://lj.libraryjournal.com.

Brody, T. (2004). *Citation analysis in the open-access world.* Southampton, UK: University of Southampton, School of Electronics and Computer Science. http://eprints.ecs.soton.ac.uk.

Budapest Open Access Initiative (BOAI). (2012). Budapest open access initiative: Frequently asked questions. http://legacy.earlham.edu.

Center for Research Libraries. (2017). Digital preservation metrics. Global Resources Network. https://www.crl.edu.

Chalwa, D. (2015). New open-access journal plans to pay peer reviewers. *Science.* http://www.sciencemag.org.

Gentil-Beccot, A., Mele, S., and Brooks, T. C. (2009). Citing and reading behaviours in high-energy physics: How a community stopped worrying about journals and learned to love repositories. ArXiv. http://arxiv.org.

Harnad, S., and Brody, T. (2004). Comparing the impact of open-access (OA) vs. non-OA articles in the same journals. *D-Lib Magazine, 10*(6). http://www.dlib.org.

Heald, P. J. (2014). How copyright keeps works disappeared. *Journal of Empirical Legal Studies, 11*, 829–866. doi:10.1111/jels.12057.

Kellam, L., and Thompson, K. (Eds.). (2016). Introduction. In *Databrarianship: The academic data librarian in theory and practice* (pp. 1–6). Chicago: Association of College and Research Libraries, a division of the American Library Association.

Lawrence, S. (2001). Free online availability substantially increases a paper's impact. *Nature, 411*(6837), 521–521.

Lesk, M. (2012). A personal history of digital libraries. *Library Hi Tech, 30*(4), 592–603.

McKen, K., Pink, C., Lyon, L., and Davidson, M. (2012). Research360: Data in the research lifecycle. Poster presentation, University of Bath, UK. http://opus.bath.ac.uk.

Open Access 2020. (2017). Home page. https://oa2020.org.

Pinfield, S. (2010). Paying for open access? Institutional funding streams and OA publication charges. *Learned Publishing, 23*(1), 39–52. https://doi.org/10.1087/20100108.

Piwowar, H., and Vision, T. (2013). Data reuse and the open data citation advantage. *Peer Journal, 1*, e175–e124. http://www.ncbi.nlm.nih.gov.

Sample, Ian. (2012). Harvard University says it can't afford journal publishers' prices. *Guardian.* https://www.theguardian.com.

Solomon, D. J., Laakso, M., and Björk, B. (2016). Converting scholarly journals to open access: A review of approaches and experiences. https://dash.harvard.edu.

Stebbins, M. (2013). Expanding public access to the results of federally funded research. White House. https://obamawhitehouse.archives.gov.

Suber, P. (2015). Open access overview. MIT Press. https://mitpress.mit.edu.

UC3. (2010). Curations foundation document. https://confluence.ucop.edu.

UC3 Merritt. (2017). Home page. https://merritt.cdlib.org.

US Department of Health and Human Services (HHS). (2003). HIPAA health information privacy minimum necessary requirement. https://www.hhs.gov.

Wagner, A. (2010). Open access citation advantage: An annotated bibliography. *Issues in Science and Technology Librarianship.* http://www.istl.org.

Willinsky, J. (2002). Copyright contradictions in scholarly publishing. *First Monday, 7*(11). doi:http://dx.doi.org/10.5210/fm.v7i11.1006.

Chapter Ten

Academic Disciplines, Their Data Needs, and How Libraries Can Cater to Them

While the last chapter focused primarily on how libraries can provide support for the broad measures and large-scale (national and international) initiatives driving the development of data management, this chapter will focus on the approaches to harnessing and managing data in specific disciplines. As all disciplines are becoming impacted by digital technology and its ability to generate large amounts of data at an ever-quickening pace, we will examine not only STEM (science, technology, engineering, and mathematics) fields, which have admittedly been the historical drivers of quantitative data genera-tion, but also the social sciences and the humanities. These so-called soft sciences are moving more toward quantified data-analysis techniques, using them in tandem with or in place of tried-and-true qualitative methods devel-oped for their disciplines.

THE DISCIPLINES AND THEIR SPECIFIC NEEDS

It is no secret that every discipline is unique. Each holds its own normative values for the development and dissemination of new knowledge. While these normative values can assist the rapidity of communication among the scholars within that discipline, it can also hinder potential collaboration and cooperation with those outside that group. This inability or unwillingness to communicate with others contributes to the siloed approaches that many disciplines face as they converge upon similar problems and research agen-das. Central to the normative values of research communities are "knowledge infrastructures" developed by those operating within a discipline. As Christine Borgman and colleagues (2015) point out, "The design of successful knowledge infrastructures for science depends on successful explication of the socio-technological structures embedded in research data practices, technical configurations, and policies" (p. 209). Seeing how these infrastructures exist for specific disciplines can help libraries and librarians insert themselves within the scholarly workflows and practices of the discipline. As data becomes central to all disciplines, it becomes imperative that librarians find ways to become central to these normative values and knowledge infrastructures. Librarians, it is constantly argued, have specialized skills and distinct roles that lend themselves well to the structures and strictures of scholarly communication, but they are sometimes notoriously ignored or passed over by the practitioners within the disciplines affected.

It is important to also note that the incorporation of open access within these normative practices plays a large role in the development of knowledge infrastructures as well. As we can see in Elisabetta Poltronieri and colleagues (2016), each discipline's adoption of open access remains disparate and cuts along the edge of STEM versus the social sciences and humanities. It even cuts along the edges of specific disciplines within STEM as well, as noticeable in figure 10.1. The health and biological sciences, for example, dominate the open-access field even among their other STEM counterparts. Their frequency of publishing within an open-access publication is a testament to the impact that the federal-funder mandate has had upon these fields. It is worth noting, too, that the important journals within these disciplines are also moving toward open access. In medicine, for example, approximately 60 percent of the titles designated as open access are listed in the first quartile of journal rankings. In biology the rate is approximately 55 percent. In comparison, chemistry overall has far fewer open-access journals, and a much smaller percentage of these rank among the first quartile. Interestingly, natural science and mathematics have nearly all of their journals within the top quartile, demonstrating that the longevity of their working with open access remains a potent factor in estimating the degree to which a discipline has adopted open-access practices.

Obviously, other disciplines in the humanities and social sciences over time have shown far less adoption of open-access practices. Ross Mounce (2012) demonstrates that economics and business journals are "less well developed" in open access than are STEM journals. Humanities have been slower to adopt the open-access/open-data model as well but appear to be gradually moving toward it with digital humanities' use of open data sets, crowdsourcing, data mining, and citation analysis. The social sciences have also been slower but are steadily adopting the workflows of a healthy open-access movement. Despite the well-documented split between the humanities and the sciences occurring in the 1950s (cf. C. P. Snow's *The Two Cultures*,

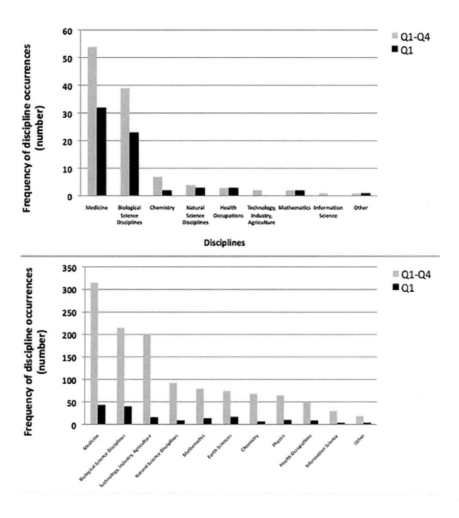

Figure 10.1. Adoption of open access by STEM discipline; the black bars show the amount of first-tier open-access journals compared to all open-access journals in a discipline. *Source:* Poltronieri et al., 2016.

1959), the quantitative digital methods being adopted by both suggest that this is the time for reconciliation. Many in the digital humanities have begun to adopt the quantitative and open-data approaches long adopted by the STEM fields. It remains to be seen if such a reconciliation provides opportunity for new approaches and fruitful collaborations.

However, regardless of the saturation of the open-access movement or the normative values dominant within a specific discipline, access to data itself remains an unresolved problem among academics. First, while open-access has found a general foothold in the publishing world as a useful antidote to rising journal costs or to speed up knowledge transfer, the goals of open data are not necessarily the same. As authors usually own the copyright to the open-access articles they have published, they retain a modicum of control over the expressions written in them. While the ideas are obviously not restricted by copyright, there is nevertheless a greater demand in disciplines to police how others' work is shared, cited, and evaluated within this framework of the law. The incentives are clearly in the favor of authors retaining their rights. Data, on the other hand, is often not copyrightable given its numeric or factual basis. Fear of scooping is extreme. Those sharing data with its limited contexts and weaker legal protections may feel they will lose control over their work if it is shared. A sense of proprietorship lingers long after a project ends, and many researchers can be fearful of allowing their data to be released "into the wild," so to speak.

Second, as scholars write journal articles or books as methods of persuasion and make a case for their particular theories, the results of their labors are best shared widely. But with data sets, the issue of "ownership and control of data remains among the intractable problems of eResearch" (Borgman et al., 2015, p. 211). By sharing their data widely, in contrast to sharing an article widely, researchers may actually be serving to rebut their own assertions and theories. While the replication of results is the gold standard of experimental research, the fear of having to retract or revise works can create disincentives to sharing data sets. Ultimately, unless it has been specifically mandated, who owns and controls the data and for which purposes remains a central unresolved problem leading to depressed participation rates among practitioners in many disciplines.

To combat this problem, replication policies, along with open-access mandates, have been proposed. These should contribute to the development of data repositories and ensure their long-term relevance. The *European Economic Review*'s (*EER*) replication policy, for example, states that it will

> publish papers only if the data used in the analysis are clearly and precisely documented and are readily available to any researcher for purposes of replication. Authors of accepted papers that contain empirical work, simulations, or experimental work must provide to the EER, prior to publication, the data, programs, and other details of the computations sufficient to permit replication. (Elsevier, 2017)

The policy clearly advocates a need for sharing data in order to open areas of inquiry and to foster truth and accuracy in academic disciplines. Other organizations beyond the *EER* are adding replication clauses or policies to their publications or funding requirements, including the Data Access and Research Transparency (DA-RT) initiative (DA-RT, 2015; Jensen, 2015; Population Studies Center, 2017).

Libraries, of course, can contribute to open data by helping to alleviate fears of scooping, rebuttals, or forced retractions. Providing digital platforms, metadata management, and even authentication for access to the information, if so desired, will help to foster a life cycle of data-management within a specific discipline. Notably, faculty researchers at traditionally non-research-centered universities, such as state comprehensive schools or master's-granting institutions, are now more likely to apply for federal grant funding. As a result, the stakes are higher than they have ever been not only for campuses and individual departments but also for the libraries that support them.

But how can libraries contribute to data management for specific disciplines? In the case of some universities that have moved from the typical master's-granting university to a quasi-R1-type model (San Diego State University, for example), the libraries struggled to provide support as the institutions became entirely more research intensive. The following sections will examine how data is created and managed in the STEM fields, social sciences, and the humanities. The ways in which libraries contribute will be examined as well.

STEM Fields

Generally speaking, the data life cycle in STEM fields follows patterns unique to the disciplines comprising this area of scholarship. Borgman separates the fields into two distinct sections, defining a small-scale (or "little science") approach to research and a large-scale (or "big science") approach, which she outlines as "large, ambitious, long term, and requiring substantial social and economic investment" (2015, p. 86). Genomics and astronomy often represent the "big science" side of the STEM fields, dealing with sets reaching into the petabyte and beyond. The implication is that "little science" is practiced on a less ambitious scale, through shorter terms, and requires less social and economic investment. As she describes it, little science is "carried out by individuals or small teams of scientists working in either a single laboratory or at distributed sites" (Borgman et al., 2015, p. 210). The little science side of STEM might include any discipline, but with more modest means. The practitioners in all of these fields, regardless of the size, nevertheless generate data that needs to be preserved as part of the life cycle of the research.

All practitioners in both big and little science rely significantly upon the most current information technologies available to collect, parse and analyze, and present the data. As a result the size of the data sets being generated within the STEM fields ranges from gigabytes on the lower end to terabytes and petabytes on the upper, depending on the size of the laboratory, the methods of data collections, and the number of participants in the research. A 2011 survey in *Science*, for example, found that 20 percent of respondents

dealt with data sets larger than one hundred gigabytes while 7 percent handled data sets larger than one terabyte. So it becomes obvious that even if the
averages are relatively modest in comparison to "big data" generated by the
likes of Facebook, the overall amount of data represents a significant amount
in the aggregate (Grigg, 2016).

Libraries and librarians can provide data-management support for the
STEM fields, though it is more often in their abilities to refer scholars to
existing resources than to archive and collect raw information from them.
Libraries tend not to have the necessary information infrastructures in place
to handle and organize the largest data sets created by the European Organization for Nuclear Research (CERN). Librarians also tend not to have as a
profession the strong quantitative skills associated with parsing or visualizing
data. They do, however, have the expertise in place to provide certain data-
management services that best plan how to organize this data, whether
through a local repository or through a third-party repository designed to
collect, describe, and preserve it. Ultimately, the scope impacts the abilities
of the librarians to cope with the data sets. It could be argued that small
science STEM projects might work best with libraries, while big science
endeavors might work best with third parties that can better create tools and
storage systems designed specifically for them.

Genomics and Biomedical Sciences

Biomedical and genomic data is often generated in huge amounts and has
been notably expensive over the years due to the costs of the technology and
process of mapping the human genome itself. But the cost for generating data
has reduced drastically over the past half decade, with the average raw genome in 2009 costing over $154,000 lowered to less than $5,000 by 2014
(Grigg, 2016). As part of the "big science" movement, genomic data employs
large-scale data-management tools and yet, as it is often funded federally or
among international funders, open access to the data remains an essential but
complicated requirement. Privacy rules and ethics concerns remain strong
barriers to allowing open access for data generated by genomic and biomedical experimentation. But opportunity exists for those willing to help alleviate
these issues. The necessary balance between funder requirements and the
need to respect the privacy of individuals represents an area where librarians
could provide essential advice and support. Librarians have historically provided information within a framework of moral and ethical control, most
recently manifested in the Association of College and Research Libraries'
(ACRL) information literacy framework, but also perpetuated as the role of
information protectors throughout the centuries since the age of the Enlightenment.

There are several movements within the health and biological sciences that overlap regarding their handling of data and inquiry yet remain distinct in their approaches. Bioinformatics on the one hand attempts to solve research questions in biology and biomedical sciences by using computational methods. This includes processing genomics and proteomics (the large-scale study of proteins) data for basic biology research. The computational approach relies on computer modeling and data mining to reach its conclusions. At the same time, health informatics focuses on data and its use in decision-making processes—especially for health administration, doctoring, health care, and insurance.

While bioinformatics is primarily driven by theoretical research concerns, the data generated might also be of practical use in the health-care fields as well. The complex relationships between the researcher and practitioner sides are also where libraries and information managers would come into primary support roles. Medical librarians could provide essential health and genomic data-management services, while also serving as essential gatekeepers and guides versed in the ethical handling of data.

Data repositories developed and hosted by medical librarians help to serve these specific ends. They have been implemented to help researchers archive data, preserve it, and provide access so that it can be reused or reexamined to test the reproducibility of conclusions. The major challenge for this area of librarianship is managing the balance between the need to share new research results and the ethical handling of the data. Some of the primary repositories in this field include the following:

- cBioPortal for Cancer Genomics (2017): "provides visualization, analysis and download of large-scale cancer genomics data sets."
- Dryad Digital Repository (2017): a "resource that makes the data underlying scientific publications discoverable, freely reusable, and citable. Dryad provides a general-purpose home for a wide diversity of datatypes."
- GenBank (2017): "NIH genetic sequence database, an annotated collection of all publicly available DNA sequences."
- National Center for Biotechnology Information Gene Expression Omnibus (NCBI GEO, 2017): "a public functional genomics data repository supporting MIAME-compliant data submissions. Array- and sequence-based data are accepted. Tools are provided to help users query and download experiments and curated gene expression profiles."
- 1000 Genomes: "established to ensure the ongoing usability of data generated by the 1000 Genomes Project and to extend the data set" (IGSR, 2017).

Astronomy

Astronomy is perhaps the oldest science and has relied the most heavily over the past several centuries upon data collected through observations. The foundational work of Galileo, itself built upon Persian and Greek astronomy, remains one of the most famous early examples of this reliance upon measured observations. Obviously the scope of experimentation and the sophistication of the equipment observing the universe have greatly increased since these early times. Though there are always notable amateur and small independent endeavors in astronomy—and varying sizes of laboratories and observatories ensure that varying sizes of data and evidence will always be generated—it is primarily the universities and other large-scale research organizations (i.e., CERN, NASA, etc.) that contribute the most to the flood of data in this discipline. As Borgman observes, astronomy "is a big data field" that has shifted "from local control over instruments to shared international resources" (2015, p. 85). However, in contrast to other technology-driven disciplines, astronomy is also one of the most open fields in terms of data sharing among institutions.

Overall, astronomy remains a model in terms of open access. Their decades of working with digital media and digital information management, especially in sharing and reusing data and depositing preprint works into repositories, remain a constant reminder of the cutting edge of research for all disciplines. Some of these important repositories are as follows:

- Earth observing system data and information system (EOSDIS, 2017): "provides end-to-end capabilities for managing NASA's Earth science data from various sources—satellites, aircraft, field measurements, and various other programs."
- NASA/IPAC Extragalactic Database (NED, 2017): "a comprehensive database of multiwavelength data for extragalactic objects."
- NASA Space Science Data Coordinated Archive (NSSDCA, 2017): "serves as NASA's permanent archive for space physics mission data. It provides access to several geophysical models and to data from some non-NASA mission data."
- Sloan Digital Sky Survey (SDSS, 2017): a major multifilter imaging and spectroscopic redshift survey collecting and providing open data.

Ultimately, the major challenge facing a discipline like astronomy boils down to an ability to provide the provenance of the data through sufficiently descriptive metadata that would allow researchers to share it since "the advance of astronomy frequently depends on the comparison and merging of disparate data" (Grigg, 2016, p. 183). Some of these frameworks for allowing this merger would involve incorporating Darwin Core and the Integrated

Taxonomic Information System (IT IS), the Standard for the Exchange of Earthquake Data (SEED), and the Geospatial Interoperability Framework (GIF). Time will tell if these attempts at providing clear interoperable standards are effective. At any rate, many disciplines can learn much from the currently standard best practices employed in astronomy.

Chemistry

In contrast to the public-facing missions of many in the health sciences or the culture of sharing central to the astronomy field, chemistry remains somewhat more cloistered in terms of its scholarly communication normative values. Given that the research tends to be based in smaller-sized laboratories in universities, or is heavily proprietary, especially among research and development sections of businesses like Dow Chemical, the openness of chemistry-related data tends to be stunted. Copyright restrictions and a lack of adoption of open-access journals within chemistry also contribute to the lower participation in open data relative to the other STEM fields. One study cited by Grigg reports that 67 percent of responding chemists "never utilized an online repository" (2016, p. 184). It is notable to mention that while there's no discipline norm to share data among their peers, researchers will do so when requested by other researchers. Some of the primary repositories in this field are as follows:

- Cambridge Structural Database (CSD, 2017): "the world's repository for small-molecule organic and metal-organic crystal structures. Containing over 875,000 entries from x-ray and neutron diffraction analyses." As seen in figure 10.2, its number of data sets has increased significantly since the early 1970s.
- PubChem Project: "a component of NIH's Molecular Libraries Roadmap Initiative. It provides information on the biological activities of small molecules. PubChem is organized as three linked databases . . . PubChem Substance, PubChem Compound, and PubChem BioAssay" (PubChem, 2017).

The major challenge facing a discipline like chemistry is the adoption of open data as a vehicle for spurring the science. The obstacles mentioned above contribute to the slowness of adoption, yet at the same time education seems to be a primary way of altering the views of chemists. Librarians and libraries might make great inroads with chemistry by focusing on the need to provide long-term preservation services for data. What would be especially helpful for chemists would be the assurances that perhaps the data, while not primarily open, would certainly be available upon request from researchers.

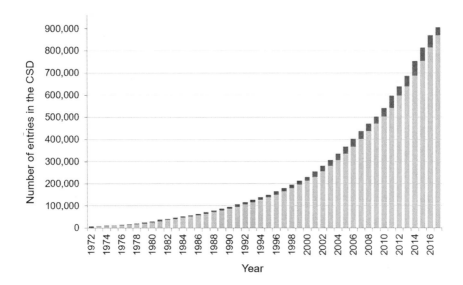

Figure 10.2.   The growth of chemical structure data from 1972 to 2016 increased from almost nothing to nearly 900,000 items. *Source:* **Cambridge Structural Database, 2017.**

Allowing a space to provide the data would help librarians provide this important service model and may ultimately provide catalyst for change.

Social Sciences

The social sciences encompass the study of human society and social relationships. The disciplines include economics, political science, geography, psychology, sociology, anthropology, archaeology, and linguistics, to name but a few. As such, they have generated their own legacy data and attendant philosophies for handling it. Due to the limitations of quantitative methods, the discipline also utilizes qualitative methods. The social sciences tend to fall along two divisions. The first, *positivism*, attempts to use more quantitative methods to define human society, while the second, *intrepretism*, tends to use less quantitative and more qualitative—even holistic and symbolic— methods to understand their subjects. Multiple methodologies, however, are routinely used and often combine quantitative and qualitative approaches to the generation of their data and evidence.

The major challenge facing the social sciences will be ensuring that data that might have been generated using differing methods can be accessed and reused. As social sciences often employ mixed methodologies in their research, it becomes necessary to provide ever more documentation of that data. Without the necessary contextual information and metadata to provide a standardized data framework, the aggregation of all this data may ultimately be compromised. Repositories preserving this data will need to employ methods to ensure this context and provenance persists. Currently, the following repositories providing such essential services in this field include the following:

- openICPSR (2017): "a research data-sharing service for social and behavioral sciences. It allows the public to access research data at no charge."
- Dataverse Project: "an open source web application to share, preserve, cite, explore, and analyze research data. It facilitates making data available to others, and allows you to replicate others'" work more easily" (Dataverse, 2017).
- National Center for Educational Statistics (2017): "the primary federal entity for collecting and analyzing data related to education."
- National Data Archive on Child Abuse and Neglect (NDACAN, 2017): "promotes secondary analysis of child abuse and neglect data by providing researchers with high quality data sets, documentation, and technical support, and encourages collaboration within the scientific community."

It is clear that libraries and librarians need to meet the challenges offered by the mixed approaches in the social sciences. The skills related to metadata development and information organization can provide essential service to alleviating this problem with data in the social sciences, especially as the fields incorporate such disparate subjects and require methods unique to their areas of inquiry.

Humanities

Stereotypically the humanities have been seen as lagging behind the other disciplines for their willingness to participate in the open-data/data-archiving movement. As the humanities generally deal with how people process and document the human experience, and as this is incredibly varied in approach and method, being able to codify and create data standards for these disciplines is nearly impossible, "drawing" as it does "on all imaginable sources of evidence" (Borgman, 2015, p. 161). The main difficulty in defining humanities, however, is the wide breadth of the subjects covered by them and the seemingly blurred and hard-to-discern boundaries that are supposed to separate them. Of course, the humanities overall include such wide-brushed areas as music, art, literature, history, education, and language. Each discipline focuses on gathering evidence in its own way, ranging from quantitative to qualitative and mixed, similar to the social sciences.

The major development of the past fifteen to twenty years in the humanities has been the incorporation of digital tools and digital analysis methods. Though bibliographic controls have been just as rigorous in the humanities as they have been in the sciences and social sciences, the humanities are also starting to adopt the language of information science to "think in terms of data, metadata, standards, interoperability, and sustainability" (Borgman, 2015, p. 162). In other words, they are beginning to adopt a digital culture and implement the quantitative methods traditionally found in more computational-intensive fields. Many of the key supports libraries play are in those very areas, especially the use of metadata, the implementation and enforcement of standards, the fostering of interoperability, and the concern for sustainability.

The development of data repositories has also improved the overall conditions in the discipline. Some of the more important data repositories in humanities have been developed over the past several years. These include the following:

- Association of Religion Data Archives (ARDA, 2017): "strives to democratize access to the best data on religion."
- Commons Open Repository Exchange (MLA CORE): provides "permanent, open-access storage facility for their scholarly output, facilitating maximum discoverability and encouraging peer feedback" (Humanities Commons, 2017).
- Cultural Policy and the Arts National Data Archive (CPANDA, 2017): "the world's first interactive digital archive of policy-relevant data on the arts and cultural policy in the United States."
- Institute for Advanced Technology in the Humanities (IATH, 2017): "offers consulting, programming, and data services to academic, cultural, non-profit, government, and business organizations."
- Isidore (2017): a "platform of search allowing the access to digital data of Humanities and Social Sciences. Open to all and especially to teachers, researchers, PhD students, and students, it relies on the principles of Web of data and provides access to data in free access (open access)."
- UCL Centre for Digital Humanities (UCLDH, 2017): endeavors to collect data "in information studies, computing science, and the arts and humanities."

Librarians, though, still need to find ways to adapt to the change in the discipline by providing platforms and services for the digital humanities while at the same time avoiding alienating practitioners in the humanities who do not rely on such methods. It is clearly a tricky balance to uphold. Researchers in the humanities are also coming to realize that not everything can and should be digital. It is unclear sometimes whether the adoption of digital tools compromises the results found. Certainly new doors are open with new tools, but will adopting a hammer require that every problem need a nail to be solvable? What is missing with reliance on digital information methods in a subject area so inherently subjective? Some forms of evidence work best as physical objects. The long-standing support of the humanities is evidenced by the strength of our archives and historical records management efforts. There is no danger of these disappearing, but the forms of data and evidence need not be altered into digital information just for the sake of appearing contemporaneous. Libraries overall will need to adopt policies on data and evidence sharing that still keep the role of analog materials in mind.

MULTIPURPOSE DATA SERVICES PROVIDERS

Despite the stubborn persistence of the schism among disciplines—especially between the STEM fields and the humanities—there is nevertheless a conscious effort by many organizations to provide data-management services across all areas. Even though discipline-specific data repositories may best represent the normative values of a certain discipline such as astronomy and provide services necessary for the practitioners in such a field, others see the boundaries among disciplines as the cause of problems in modern scholarship. As a result, some organizations such as the California Digital Library's MERRITT service, the US federal government Data.gov, and the Data Archiving and Network Services (DANS) are beginning to provide multidisciplinary approaches to handling data.

The Netherlands-based DANS, for example, provides services that "are centered around 3 core services: data archiving, data reusing and training and consultancy" (DANS, 2017). But they are also cognizant of the fact that different disciplines will approach the same questions in different ways. This diversity in viewpoint fuels innovation and progress in science:

> Datasets collected for a certain research purpose can also contain answers to research questions from very different research in the same or in another research discipline. This is certainly the case for historical data. Furthermore, new insights are gained by combining data sets, which is impossible if the data are not sufficiently described and available. The availability of research data finally facilitates the reproduction of research, which is an important condition for science. (DANS, 2017)

As a result of this clear, overarching mission to open up data to cross-disciplinary research, DANS provides support for a number of national and international data-sharing/data-archiving projects that range from the STEM fields to the social sciences and to humanities (DANS, 2017). Such projects include the following:

- Council of European Social Science Data Archives (CESSDA)
- Digital Collaboratory for Cultural Dendrochronology (DCCD)
- Digital Research Infrastructure for the Arts and Humanities (DARIAH)
- European collaboration in visualising knowledge (KNOWeSCAPE)
- European data infrastructure for scientific research (EUDAT)
- European Holocaust Research Infrastructure (EHRI)
- Humanities at Scale (HaS-DARIAH)
- Knowledge Complexity (K-PLEX)
- Open Access Infrastructure for Research in Europe (OpenAIRE2020)
- Pilot European Open Science Cloud (EOSC pilot)
- Pooling Activities, Resources and Tools for Heritage E-research (PAR-THENOS)
- Portable Antiquities of the Netherlands (PAN)

Obviously DANS is but one example of these developing multidisciplinary data service providers. Their recent growth suggests that data will become less siloed over time and will begin to be aggregated regardless of the somewhat arbitrary boundaries found between disciplines. The breakdown of such disciplines can provide an important catalyst for generating new ideas. Combining data sets in new ways suggests possible innovations for future disciplines. At the same time, as with any data generated, the normalization as well as the standardization of such data remains imperative. Without standardized documentation and description, all the data in the world may be useless for research. Data.gov, as a primary example of the foresight the US federal government has shown in terms of public health and research, provides clear examples of how to make sure that government data are open and machine readable so that they can be reused in numerous scenarios. Their philosophy of open government includes mandates to be as transparent as possible with government-related activities (Data.gov, 2017).

COMMON POINTS: DATA AS A LINGUA FRANCA

It becomes clear from examining the methods and basic normative values of the areas of STEM, social sciences, and the humanities that despite the disparate approaches, the need for a data-management specialist in each discipline and subdiscipline is essential. While the paths taken to final peer-reviewed publication differ within the scholarly norms and practices of each discipline, the evidence and generation of data remain common points. Though methodologies could be quantitative, qualitative, or mixed, the need to provide provenance and sustainability for the data is essential, especially as more disciplines begin a push for replication of that data and reduplication of conclusions. Libraries and librarians can provide the essential services for all the needs of data, ranging from advising the best house for the data to metadata policy development and provenance, to enforcing standards, and finally providing suites of services and platforms that will meet the current needs of any subject.

REFERENCES

Association of Religion Data Archives (ARDA). (2017). About ARDA. http://www.thearda.com/about.

Borgman, C. (2015). *Big data, little data, no data: Scholarship in the networked world.* Cambridge, MA: MIT Press.

Borgman, C., Darch, P., Sands, A., Pasquetto, I., Golshan, M., et al. (2015). Knowledge infrastructures in science: Data, diversity, and digital libraries. *International Journal on Digital Libraries, 16*(3), 207–227.

Cambridge Structural Database (CSD). (2017). Home page. https://www.ccdc.cam.ac.uk.

cBioPortal for Cancer Genomics. (2017). Home page. http://www.cbioportal.org.

Cultural Policy and the Arts National Data Archive (CPANDA). (2017). About CPANDA. http://www.cpanda.org.

Data Access and Research Transparency (DA-RT). (2015). Home page. https://www.dartstatement.org.

Data Archiving and Network Services (DANS). (2017). DANS projects. https://dans.knaw.nl.

Data.gov. (2017). Open government. https://www.data.gov/open-gov.

Dataverse Project. (2017). About the project. http://dataverse.org/about.

Dryad Digital Repository. (2017). The organization. http://datadryad.org.

Elsevier. (2017). Mandatory replication policy. https://www.journals.elsevier.com.

EOSDIS. (2017). About EOSDIS. https://earthdata.nasa.gov/about.

GenBank (2017). Home page. https://www.ncbi.nlm.nih.gov/genbank.

Grigg, K. (2016). Data in the sciences. In L. Kellam and K. Thompson (Eds.), *Databrarianship: The academic data librarian in theory and practice* (pp. 179–192). Chicago: Association of College and Research Libraries, a division of the American Library Association.

Humanities Commons. (2017). Welcome to CORE—MLA commons. https://mla.hcommons.org/core.

Institute for Advanced Technology in the Humanities (IATH). (2017). About IATH. http://www.iath.virginia.edu.

International Genome Sample Resource (IGSR). (2017). 1000 Genomes Project home page. http://www.internationalgenome.org.

Isidore. (2017). Home page. http://www.rechercheisidore.fr.

Jensen, N. (2015). Data access and replication policies in management. Nathan M. Jensen. http://www.natemjensen.com.

Mounce, R. (2012). Review of open access in economics. *Open Economics* (blog). https://openeconomics.net.

NASA/IPAC Extragalactic Database (NED). (2017). Introduction to NED. https://ned.ipac.caltech.edu.

NASA Space Science Data Coordinated Archive (NSSDCA). (2017). About the NSSDCA. https://nssdc.gsfc.nasa.gov.

National Center for Educational Statistics (NCES). (2017). Home page. https://nces.ed.gov.

National Data Archive on Child Abuse and Neglect (NDACAN). (2017). About NDACAN. http://www.ndacan.cornell.edu.

NCBI Gene Expression Omnibus (NCBI GEO). (2017). Home page. https://www.ncbi.nlm.nih.gov/geo.

openICPSR. (2017). Home page. https://www.openicpsr.org.

Poltronieri, E., Bravo, E., Curti, M., Ferri, M., and Mancini, C. (2016). Open access publishing trend analysis: Statistics beyond the perception. *Information Research, 21*(2), paper 712. http://www.webcitation.org.

Chapter 10

Population Studies Center. (2017). University of Michigan Institute for Social Research. http://www.psc.isr.umich.edu.
PubChem. (2017). PubChem FAQ. https://pubchem.ncbi.nlm.nih.gov.
Sloan Digital Sky Survey (SDSS). (2017). Home page. http://www.sdss.org.
UCL Centre for Digital Humanities (UCLDH). (2017). Home page. http://www.ucl.ac.uk/dh.

Part IV

Future Shocks

Chapter Eleven

Libraries and the Culture of "Big Assessment"

One of the main goals for this book has been to explore the ways in which the shocks of the big data era have changed us as people, as citizens, as consumers of content, and as producers of trackable digital information. The impacts of these changes can have serious negative consequences as well as beneficial developments in the quality of our lives. Another goal for the book has been to examine these widespread changes in terms of libraries and librarianship. As a profession, librarians have much to be concerned about as "big data" begins to morph into "big assessment," which points for better and for worse toward an all-encompassing culture of monitoring and constant surveillance of library users. Both the impetus and the desire to capture the information of students and patrons have become increasingly normalized within "libraria" at large, not just within academia and in the wider world. Yet, even as assessment and analysis of students and patrons has become more widely adopted over time, many librarians fear they are ironically missing what their communities and constituents truly need.

So how might libraries meet user needs? More to the point, how do librarians meet the needs of students and patrons when they are not always accurately reflected in the profession and the strategies needed to accomplish this not clearly understood by practitioners? Already libraries are morphing the terminology of the professional to add "assessment librarian" to the ranks in order to help meet such unresolved issues. The Association of College and Research Libraries (ACRL) has in turn devised a set of clear criteria to help define the roles and scopes of the proficient "assessment librarian" (ACRL, 2017a). The areas that assessment librarians are expected to understand include general assessment in libraries and academia; ethics; assessment methods and strategies; research design; data collection and analysis; communication and reporting; advocacy and marketing; collaboration and partnerships; leadership; management; and mentoring, training, and coaching (ibid.). Obviously, this book will not examine each of these areas in significant depth. Instead, it will focus on the issues related to big data, specifically what all librarians might need to begin learning in order to better understand their place within the big data and big assessment eras. As Siva Vaidhyanathan (2013) suggests, "Big data offers [librarians] an opportunity to examine the very nature of knowledge both historically and instrumentally." But how librarians trained in these methods actually implement such examinations remains unclear. Taking things a step further, though, one might argue that *all librarians*, regardless of their current stripe, inclination, or area of specialization, will need to be "assessment" and "big data" librarians as part of their core professional competencies.

This chapter, then, will use the ACRL proficiencies for assessment librarians as a starting point to begin further speculation on what librarians will need to do in the future to facilitate, generate, and manage the imminent change to big data practices in libraries. In other words, *What future shocks are in store for us?* For a librarian wrangling with the *new-ish* paradigm that is big data, what knowledge and skill sets will be essential? How exactly will librarians wrangle with even *bigger* data, should it come to dominate the information landscape?

This is all hard to fathom since the current state of the world itself is shocking enough, and speculating on the future is always risky business—just ask Francis Fukuyama whether history really ended. However, indulge me for a while as we examine the future of libraries, the library profession, and the role of the librarian itself. The areas that libraries might consider employing the tools and methods of big data analytics will involve the following: student learning, facilities management and development, return on investment, and future librarian job relevancy. It is worthwhile examining how they will come to impact library policies and practices.

TOWARD UNIVERSAL BIG DATA AND "BIG ASSESSMENT" PROFICIENCIES FOR LIBRARIANS

Knowledge of Assessment in Libraries and Higher Education

Obviously, librarians need to have a basic understanding of the purpose and theories guiding assessment and the evaluation of libraries. The important skill librarians need to improve upon is the ability to see how the assessment ties or connects to wider university and community goals. Importantly, librarians need to understand the changing and mutable concept of assessment itself as it pertains to specific disciplines and groups within even the same organization. Assessment as interpreted and practiced by a university English department will be very different than a library's conception of the same. Within this wider context, too, it should be noted that regional, national, and international concepts of assessment vary as well.

Results of assessment will vary too. In the same way that data is a protean concept, so too is assessment. Its value can be interpreted or extrapolated in different ways by different stakeholders, depending upon the intended goals. To better wield assessment tools and to more fully understand the potential for inherent bias within intended goals, assessment librarians should understand and be familiar with "current national initiatives . . . methods . . . and standards" (ACRL, 2017a); these include the following: LibQUAL+, ROI, NSSE, IPEDS/NCES, Ithaka, EBLIP, SAILS, RAILS, Conspectus, ACRL standards, and so forth. Each of these assessment initiatives, methods, and standards provides avenues for librarians and libraries to evaluate and generate data on different aspects of library activity and service, but each also has its flaws. As the culture of assessment becomes ever more permeated and permanent within an institution, the greater amount of data generated increases the necessity to be familiar with these tools and their limitations. The big data era is nudging libraries into the adoption of such initiatives, methods, standards, and tools, limited and purpose specific as they are, and being unaware of them is no longer an acceptable excuse for librarians.

Ethics for Assessment

Previous chapters examined how generating vast amounts of information impacts the decisions people must make in order to handle it. Librarians proficient in assessment and the use of data will need to respect *and* protect the welfare of their human subjects, usually library patrons or community users, as established by institutional review boards (IRBs). The mantra for all librarians, not just ones that engage in assessment activities, ought to be "maximizing benefits and minimizing harm," to ensure that data is analyzed and reported with integrity and honesty.

Another hallmark of ethical behavior is displaying impartiality and maintaining a sense of objectivity. This is especially important during the analysis phase. The results of the experiment can often end in a null hypothesis, or the evidence examined is inconclusive, or the results flat-out refute initial assumptions. Under pressure from peers or administrators to express desired outcomes, assessors might find themselves tempted to manipulate the statistics or alter the results. This is especially dangerous in the big data era as some of the big data "gurus" have suggested that a hypothesis is no longer essential. Enough data exists, in their mind, to provide hidden patterns not just targeted results. With this danger clearly possible, it is therefore very important to use data with a specific purpose in mind and not manipulate the results just to meet certain agendas.

Assessment Methods

The types of methods essential for librarians proficient in assessment include quantitative and qualitative methods, and implementing multiple methods as well as mixed methods. The key, of course, is determining what would be appropriate for specific assessment activities and goals, and what standards would be relevant to the intended data gathering.

Another key concern librarians should consider now is whether the standards applied in libraries will hold up in the era of big data. What will the increased scope, speed, and size (i.e., the "5Vs") do to our current standards? Are they able to handle such large scopes in data gathering? Instruments such as surveys, interviews, rubrics, and scorecards may not hold as much weight compared to the automated data gathering of social media platforms and electronic monitors, or even compared to data sets aggregated by entities across the whole student body.

Finally, assessment and big data will include the development of action research projects, ethnographic studies, user-centered designs, collection and use analyses, examination of the use of citations, usability studies of web pages and e-books, the evaluation of web and floor-plan designs, and last but not least, evaluations of the impact of library services. Again, it is unclear how the use of large data sets impact libraries and users' views of libraries. Big data will surely improve data-logging benchmarks, but it may also exacerbate the encroachment of privacy and the erosion of public trust.

Research Design

Research design is essential for librarians because it establishes clear-cut routes of inquiry to help answer the primary research questions. Librarians need to know what types of problems and questions can be answered by the type of data at hand. They also need to know what types of tools and knowledge will help them complete their designs, including databases, spreadsheets, statistics and statistical analysis, qualitative and quantitative methods, and data visualization. Librarians will need to know about data-management and how to share, secure, and preserve research ethically.

The design of the research project determines what we can actually ask of and find within our data. In turn, the experiment generates the data necessary to answer our essential research questions. Without knowing what questions to ask, though, librarians will not be able to use the new data in meaningful ways. This is also essential as the data sets become larger and larger. Reams of data may not matter if they are not usable to answer our essential questions.

At the same time, big data complicates this by not allowing us to truly know all the provenance of the data, and as Vaidhyanathan (2013) suggests, big data can help us with understanding knowledge from a historical perspective as well as an instrumental one. We can approach data not only from a long-term perspective to examine the patterns of the past found within them but also from a new pragmatic perspective to apply them in new ways for improving future services.

Data Collection and Analysis

Data collection and analysis are two of the most important aspects of assessment. Research and scholarship require gathering and analyzing data to draw meaningful conclusions. Librarians will need to move away from the purely service role that has been in fashion in librarianship since the later nineteenth century—since the development of open stacks and the reference revolution in particular—and into a more research-intensive analytical role that uses library-generated data for specific purposes. Rather than rely on the ubiquitous "case study" reportage that passes for much of library research, data should be employed in more pure research to inform the profession in more quantified ways on how to make decisions for current or future services.

However, more than just tallying reference statistics at a service desk, the new data age in libraries will require that librarians devise ways to automate data collection and integrate it all from multiple, even disparate, sources. Various data sources need to be utilized as well, including time-stamp data, library data, institutional data (i.e., student outcomes, grades, etc.), and third-party generated data (i.e., Google Analytics and other Web 2.0/social media vendors). Importantly, librarians will need to identify and define the important metrics and data sets necessary to measure the outcomes prioritized by individual institutions.

Finally, sharing the data with appropriate stakeholders is essential for its impact and for its ensured objective analysis. Third parties and tangentially related stakeholders may have more to add to the decision-making process than ever before. If users were aware, for example, of their own usage patterns (or even a lack of patterns), they might be able to participate by providing suggestions on how to better improve services. Greater transparency regarding the release and sharing of library-related metrics will also serve to help the greater public understand exactly what libraries do and how the public receives benefits from them.

Communication and Reporting

To build upon this new sense of transparency, big data librarians will need to improve upon their abilities to communicate and report the amounts of data being generated. Change will likely come from within, so to see this change, librarians must provide the impetus for it. Part of this change would include sharing the data generated as a visualization for those unfamiliar with the data set to see some of the clear conclusions derived from it.

One of the important aspects to assessment in academic libraries is the concept of "closing the loop" (CTL), a term that refers to implementing the information generated in assessment through praxis or initiatives to improve student learning outcomes (CSUN Mike Curb College of Business, 2017). In the case of university campuses, as seen in figure 11.1, closing the loop involves the completion of a set of assessment efforts, which in turn circle around to better inform the development (or revision) of student learning outcomes. Such activities are meant to be iterative in process, allowing for both repetition and ongoing revisions. The types of activities associated with CTL include ensuring that improvements to teaching, courses, or curricular programs are implemented; that assessment results are conveyed to the campus community; that the assessment process itself is evaluated and then revised as necessary; and, finally, that professional development activities related to assessment are planned and implemented.

Obviously, librarians have a very important role to play in this process. The campus would benefit from librarians finding ways to improve student learning outcomes as well as refining and revising them through the development of ongoing assessment activities. In the era of big data, with larger data available about students, the importance of closing the loop becomes ever greater. The greater the data available, the more potential there will be to usher effective change for more accurate and attainable student learning outcomes.

Collaboration and Partnerships

The bigger the data and assessment activities, the greater impact they will have on an ever-growing number of people. As a result, more than ever, the data- and assessment-oriented librarian will need to develop joint initiatives with multiple library and nonlibrary stakeholders. Partnerships and collaborative efforts will become essential activities for librarians in the big data era. Developing partnerships and collaborative efforts to recruit and hold interest in assessment activities becomes an essential skill. Librarians in the big data era have to cultivate these relationships. Otherwise, they will lose not only the moral edge for their activities but also the practical trust of their target audiences.

What is also essential will be the development of "strategic communication," which will ensure that messages to constituents and stakeholders necessary to the success of assessment projects are sent and that the rationale for sometimes-intrusive assessment activities will be understood. While it is relatively easy to get the buy-in of small groups of people to participate in surveys or the analysis of their behaviors, especially when small incentives

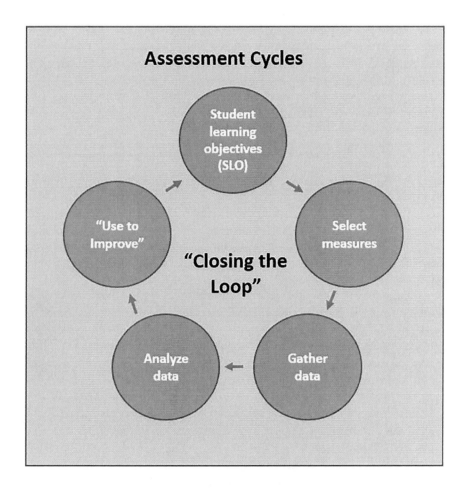

Figure 11.1. A typical diagram that demonstrates the concept of "closing the loop." *Source:* **Jankowski, 2014. Redrawn by author.**

are offered, it becomes more difficult to get sufficient participation rates when larger groups of people are involved.

Leadership, Management, and Training for a "Culture of Assessment"

What would leadership look like in the coming era of big data and big assessment? The ACRL sees leadership as a "shared vision of assessment," capable of incorporating views from multiple perspectives while leveraging institutional politics in order to persuade management and administrators on the value of the assessment activities. They ultimately see leadership of assessment projects as systems-oriented activities, "recognizing that the library is part of a larger institution with a shared mission and goals" while at the same time pushing for their own needs and "a place at the table" within governance (ACRL, 2017b). In other words, librarians must be far more assertive in their approaches to their partners, constituents, and users. They must rub shoulders with and act on the same level as their counterparts in different departments within a university, or in the wider communities outside the university.

Librarians will also need to become better managers of data collection across the whole field—not just technical services and systems librarians but *all* librarians, including reference and instruction librarians. One of the important aspects in this new era will be the development of systematic data-collection and data-analysis initiatives. Librarians will need to determine what types of data should be part of recurrent data-collection tasks, what data should be collected on a case-by-case basis, and what data should be collected irregularly. This also includes the development, adoption, and even invention of the necessary tools for gathering the data one wants to collect. Internal as well as external data-collection procedures, perhaps along lines similar to archival document collection and retention processes, will need to be developed. To do this successfully, essential priorities need to be identified, established, and managed through policies and resolutions.

All of these actions undertaken by librarians will result in a stronger "culture of assessment." While this term is essentially vague, it does help to push the library profession into a better-managed, analytical direction. The culture of assessment starts with leadership and management but succeeds or fails through training. Librarians have long been the service workhorses of the academic world, but now that data, data analysis, and assessment have become essential aspects to the profession, librarians need to cultivate the skills for this new culture of assessment. If they are to remain relevant to changes within the wider world, all librarians will need to be trained in the development, generation, analysis, and implementation of data and assessment projects.

STUDENT LEARNING OUTCOMES

Aside from the proficiencies outlined by the ACRL, one of the most important aspects of librarianship has always been—and always will be—education. This area now includes the concept of information literacy. We previously examined information literacy in chapter 7 as one potential method of alleviating information overload, especially as it has direct impacts on how students utilize and incorporate information found in a library's own resources. Yet, despite the academic librarian's near obsessions with information literacy via the ACRL IL Framework, notable gaps persist in the ability of librarians to both ensure as well as measure student success and the attainment of student learning outcomes.

One idea currently permeating higher education is the belief that big data approaches can be harnessed for student success in addition to improving information literacy. Some are calling this "learning analytics," which allows institutions the ability to keep track of the specific, physical actions students take during their time attending and studying for a class. The ultimate goal in "using these data-infused pictures [is] to build more effective courses," argues Jeffrey Young (2016). The end result of this approach, as seen in figure 11.2, is to examine "teaching with an engineering mind-set, not just a curatorial one. If it's done right, proponents argue, the average student will learn more than ever before—which will not only help individual learners expand their minds, but also improve an institution's retention rate" (Young, 2016). Another trending idea is to track any and all user behavior online. According to Sarah Brown (2017), "Virtually every student interaction at WGU—collaborating with classmates, using course resources, submitting assignments—is tracked online." But limitations with these quantified approaches nevertheless persist, especially in the analysis and interpretation of the generated data. Some faculty who are teaching and analyzing their students' actions and behaviors find it hard to interpret the data or to apply any of the results to real-life teaching.

Of course, such problems exist within any framework or set of initiatives and guidelines. Librarians for their part are well aware of the limitations of the ACRL framework, which seem to some as an incoherent set of ideas that doesn't translate to specific action. The same can be said for any set of guidelines that suddenly needs to be quantified in order to show evidence of results. California State University, Northridge, is experiencing this dilemma through its Graduate Initiative 2025, which is meant to improve the four-year graduation rates for its students (Oh, 2016). To facilitate the development and sharing of important data about the university, its faculty, and its students, the university's Office of Student Success Innovations has recruited faculty in all departments across the campus to serve as data champions, who would each "facilitate data-informed decision making about how [the university] can better support student success" (CSUN Office of Student Success, 2017).

Determining ways to reach this goal as well as to evaluate and assess the student activities meant to accomplish this represents a real problem both in methodology and in practical solutions. While it may be helpful to have students graduate on time or faster than average, the solution may end up reducing requirements or lowering standards. To make things worse, the pressure to produce results in the face of declining or arbitrary funding is immense. Such limits do not necessarily test the veracity of the data itself,

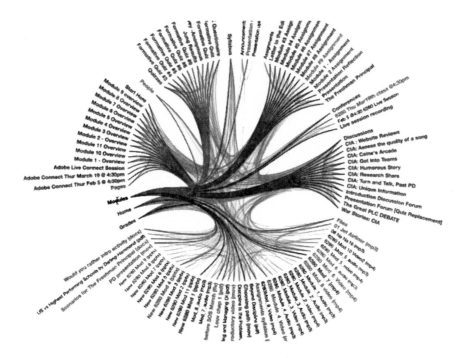

Figure 11.2.   This data visualization produced by Utah State University depicts all the possible categories of student activity in one online course. *Source:* **Young, 2016.**

but they surely put the onus on the researchers attempting to construct meaning or narrative from data that may not give the much-desired answers.

In another telling example of the limits of "learning analytics" and the big "datalization" of student success, Barbara Fister (2016) observes from a study on student satisfaction that "the large majority [of more than 1,500 students surveyed or interviewed] believed that formulating and asking their own questions was the one skill that they had not developed in college but found they needed in their post-college lives." Academic institutions have long attempted to define and quantify what represents student success and often pride themselves on their ability to do so. But the students in this example are essentially reporting on a huge gap in their preparation for the world outside academia, demonstrating the danger of focusing on the wrong things. While it is surely important that universities prove that students learned specific content, or that librarians know which databases were used and how long students studied in their spaces each week, sometimes students' essential needs lie outside the scope of the actual institution or its accreditation-driven policies. Librarians as data and assessment experts will increasingly need to hone in on and anticipate such gaps that invariably occur in student learning.

But how could this be done? Some recent studies and practices in these areas might show us the way (Hall et al., 2014; Wilde and Level, 2011). Certainly for future library contributions into the big data tracking of student success, libraries will need to examine their target user groups and pinpoint those areas of information literacy that translate into specific outcomes. Obviously this is easier said than done, but studies have begun to examine this. Faculty, for example, are beginning to "use textual-analysis programs, facial-recognition software, and even smartphones or Apple Watches to capture data about how students go about learning" (Biemiller, 2017). Nicole Johnston and colleagues (2016) demonstrate how students read and process information in the form of print journal articles in contrast to electronic journals. At the same time, research might examine how the reading behaviors of beginning students contrast with expert behavior (which might include faculty, advanced graduate students, researchers, and scholars).

For some researcher-educators, "every student becomes a potential data point" (Brown, 2017). At California State University, Northridge, data sets are provided by the CSUN Counts initiative offered through its Office of Institutional Research. The website provides a statistics digital dashboard covering topics such as student demographics, continuation and graduation rates, faculty demographics, enrollment levels, and statistics related to feeder community colleges and high schools. The breakdown of information is incredibly rich and varied and provides potential for developing evidence-based approaches to student success and improving learning outcomes (CSUN Office of Institutional Research, 2017).

Librarians should take a similar approach, utilizing these types of data sources at their respective institutions as well as developing their own benchmarks for measuring student success. As in the case measuring student outcomes from classroom assignments, examining student papers in the aggregate, for example, would help instructors find areas of weakness across multiple years, ages, and other demographics. Analyzing first-year papers written by students of various abilities and backgrounds might help to determine typical areas of grammatical or rhetorical weakness. As students use mobile devices more frequently, it might be helpful for faculty members and librarians to harness the data of their computer usage to improve student learning as well.

Ultimately, though, student learning can benefit much from big data learning analytics. The key, of course, will be to determine how and when to utilize it and for what purpose. All of these are gigantic questions that every librarian, regardless of primary skill sets, will need to be able to answer in the near future.

JUSTIFICATION OF ROI TO ADMINISTRATORS

Establishing the return on investment of a library has been notoriously difficult, especially as the services provided to communities often resist a clearcut financial value. However, tools have been devised to help administrators devise simple estimates of their impact on a community. The American Library Association (ALA), for example, provides a useful library value calculator (http://www.ala.org) to help administrators demonstrate costs versus impact (ALA, 2017). However, the number of newspapers read or CDs borrowed, while easily translated into an equivalent dollar value in terms of saved costs for patrons, hardly represent the true values of libraries—their ability to satisfy information needs, whatever they might be.

Assessment and big data raise the expectations for demonstrating the library's return on investment (ROI) even further. Current technologies also make it easier to assess a library's value using specific, but limited metrics. As data visualization becomes more prevalent, the ability to convey expenses, time used, student success, and learning outcomes met can be communicated more easily to administrators in charge.

For academic libraries, too, the need to examine student success or demonstrate an impact on specific student learning outcomes is again difficult to pin down and is not merely the aggregated sum of all journal articles read, the number of books checked out (or held in the stacks), or the number of information literacy sessions attended.

But new approaches and metrics are being developed. Instead of focusing on typical content and service transactional metrics, Carol Tenopir and colleagues (2010), as shown in the equation in figure 11.3, suggest that return on investment could be determined through the number of grants awarded to a university, and the subsequent role that libraries would play during the process of meeting the needs of the grant—especially in terms of research output and the amount of money spent by the library to this end. It is ultimately "a model that draws upon institutional data, the library budget and responses to a faculty survey to help articulate the library's value to research" (Elsevier, 2017).

Other ROI calculators include the Valuing Library Services Calculator, which is provided by the University of Utah's National Network of Libraries of Medicine/MidContinental Region as a way to establish the "cost to replace . . . library services on the retail market" (NN/LM-MCR, 2017c); they also provide the CBA/ROI Calculator for books and journals, which helps to determine the annual return an institution realizes on what it spends on a collection (NN/LM-MCR, 2017a). Finally the institution's Database Calculator provides clear cost-and-benefit analyses for the databases that a library subscribes to (NN/LM-MCR, 2017b). Other institutions such as the Library

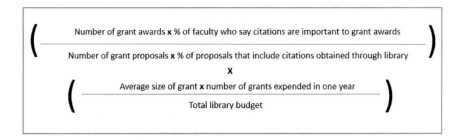

Figure 11.3.   One method of calculating the return on investment (ROI) for an academic library providing support for grant awards. *Source:* **Tenopir et al., 2010.**

Research Service (LRS) provide ROI calculators as well, for example, the Personal ROI Calculator (Library Research Service, 2017).

As of the writing of this chapter in June 2017, the Global Facility for Disaster Reduction and Recovery's (GFDRR) Open Data for Resilience Initiative (OpenDRI) published what it calls a "bombshell report" on the return on investment of contributing to open-source software solutions (GFDRR, 2017). According to a third-party analysis of the report, this "win-win" relationship between funder and open-source solutions created a 200 percent return on investment for GFDRR in its "open source software efforts" (Deparday and Soden, 2017). There appear to be great possibilities in this announcement for libraries, especially those that have adopted the philosophies of both open access and open source. While they are not the same, it appears that the benefits of examining such endeavors and the long-term investment of these open-source and open-access solutions would help the library as well. As libraries foster similar "open" philosophies, they may be able to rely on similar studies to justify their efforts.

Aside from these pragmatic attempts at quantifying the various service actions of a library, something intangible nevertheless persists when trying to establish the value of a library. Something persists beyond the quantified, even clichéd, actions of students or researchers. How would one be able to quantify, for example, the time spent inside the library, either studying or conducting group activities? If a student hypothetically enters the library and merely purchases a cup of coffee from the in-library coffee shop, sits down, and then proceeds to drink it while checking Facebook, does that action constitute a meaningful return on investment? On the one hand, it could be argued that the setting itself, and the mind-set in which the student is situated, contributes to student learning, or that because the library exists as a viable and useful learning space contributes to this student's learning potential. But this is in no way easily quantified, and causation may remain impossible to determine.

Yet, with specific and more intrusive data-collection methods, it might be possible to make these connections. The next step in the future might be to analyze brain-wave patterns, one could argue, to get a sense of the student's well-being and whether the library's ambient conditions contribute to this. Perhaps the combination of all things within a library—its stacks, tables, chairs, others students, ambience, and mental spaces—contributes to the student's success. The student might enjoy the coffee on this particular day while waiting for his class to begin; then, after the class ends, the student may be more inclined to revisit the library again to complete homework, to write out notes, or even to begin basic research into a longer-term project. Analyses of a student's biorhythmic metrics may someday provide librarians with the holy grail of ROI derived specifically from how much money spent on a library and how much time spent in the library using its resources and spaces equates to specific grades and learning outcomes.

The problem remains to find ways to isolate all of the incredibly complex and even contradictory variables in such situations. As librarians, it is difficult to consider where to draw the line. Of course, like much of the real world, many of these bright lines are dictated by external forces in form of directives, policies, and state and federal laws. The library exists within this web of culture and will not necessarily be the entity solely determining how intrusive the data analysis librarians implement can be. We may find that students, upon entering the university in the next generation, will need to sign away their rights to privacy in order for us to guarantee, and groom them for, their later success.

BIG DATA AND LIBRARY ASSESSMENT: TO WHAT END?

To what end do we enter into this era of big data and big assessment? While it is clear that assessment and big data now permeate the objectives and initiatives of almost all libraries, and impact all librarians at least tangentially, it remains to be seen whether librarians can keep themselves relevant in the face of these changes. I argue that *all* librarians regardless of their focus or background need to know assessment and need to know the impact that big data will have on their careers. Librarians without a clear understanding of how they do things—and ultimately why they do things—will very quickly find themselves out in the cold, not only from the profession itself, but also from the communities they serve or the campuses they support.

Yet being familiar with assessment and big data should also hardly be seen as the ending point of the transformation of libraries and librarians. Libraries will change as the technologies change. Librarians will change as the technologies impact them in ever more unimaginable ways. Librarians must adopt big data as another tool in their arsenals, and it must become part of the core competencies and proficiencies of not just these newfangled "databrarians," or assessment librarians, but all librarians. It starts at library schools. They must ensure that the students in classes are facile with not just metadata for bibliographic and digital objects but also data, data sets, and assessment activities.

REFERENCES

American Library Association (ALA). (2017). Library value calculator. http://www.ala.org.

Association of College and Research Libraries (ACRL). (2017a). ACRL proficiencies for assessment librarians and coordinators. http://www.ala.org.

Association of College and Research Libraries (ACRL). (2017b). Assessment in action: Academic libraries and student success. http://www.ala.org.

Biemiller, L. (2017). Big data for student success still limited to early adopters. *Chronicle of Higher Education.* http://www.chronicle.com.

Brown, S. (2017). Where every student is a potential data point. *Chronicle of Higher Education.* http://www.chronicle.com.

CSUN Mike Curb College of Business. (2017). Suggestions for closing the loop. California State University, Northridge. http://www.csun.edu.

CSUN Office of Institutional Research. (2017). CSUN Counts. https://www.csun.edu/counts.

CSUN Office of Student Success. (2017). Student success initiatives. California State University, Northridge. http://www.csun.edu.

Deparday, V., and Soden, R. (2017). Leveraging open sources as a public institution: New analysis reveals significant returns on investment in open source technologies. World Bank. https://blogs.worldbank.org.

Elsevier. (2017). Calculating return on investment for academic libraries. Library Connect. https://libraryconnect.elsevier.com.

Fister, B. (2016). The (lasting?) value of libraries. *Inside Higher Ed.* https://www.insidehighered.com.

Global Facility for Disaster Reduction and Recovery (GFDRR). (2017). *Open data for resilience initiative and geonode: A case study on institutional investments in open source.* Washington, DC: GFDRR. https://opendri.org.

Hall, M., Ogier, A., Bailey, A., Gilmore, T., and Stovall, C. (2014). Data management—It's for libraries too! In *Proceedings of the 2014 Library Assessment Conference: Building Effective, Sustainable, Practical Assessment.* Seattle, WA, August 4–6, 2014.

Jankowski, N. (2014). Closing the loop: Using assessment results to enhance student learning. National Institute for Learning Outcomes Assessment. http://www.learningoutcomeassessment.org.

Johnston, N., Salaz, A., and Alsabbagh, L. (2016). Print and digital reading preferences and behaviors of university students in Qatar. In S. Kurbanoğlu et al. (Eds.), *Information literacy: Key to an inclusive society* (pp. 247–255). ECIL 2016. Communications in Computer and Information Science 676. Cham, Switzerland: Springer.

Library Research Service. (2017). Individual return on investment calculator. http://www.lrs.org.

National Network of Libraries of Medicine/MidContinental Region (NN/LM-MCR). (2017a). Cost benefit and ROI calculator. https://nnlm.gov/mcr.

National Network of Libraries of Medicine/MidContinental Region (NN/LM-MCR). (2017b). Cost benefit and ROI calculator for databases. https://nnlm.gov/mcr.

National Network of Libraries of Medicine/MidContinental Region (NN/LM-MCR). (2017c). Retail value calculator. https://nnlm.gov/mcr.

Oh, H. (2016). CSUN implementing strategies to elevate graduation rates, student success. *CSUN Today*. https://csunshinetoday.csun.edu.

Tenopir, C., Love, A., Park, J., Wu, L., et al. (2010). University investment in the library, phase II: An international study of the library's value to the grants process. Bepress. http://works.bepress.com/carol_tenopir/76.

Vaidhyanathan, S. (2013). Library assessment and big data: The need for ethical legal and philosophical analysis. Library Assessment Conference 2012. http://libraryassessment.org.

Wilde, M., and Level, A. (2011). How to drink from a fire hose without drowning: Collection assessment in a numbers-driven environment. *Collection Development, 36*(4). http://dx.doi.org/10.1080/01462679.2011.604771.

Young, J. (2016). This chart shows the promise and limits of "learning analytics." *Chronicle of Higher Education*. http://www.chronicle.com.

Chapter Twelve

Building the "Smart Library" of the Future

UTOPIANISM AND THE STRIVING FOR A "SMART SOCIETY"

This chapter will examine things that don't quite exist yet, or if they do, they are not yet universally adopted or recognized. To paraphrase author William Gibson, *the library's future is already here—it's just not evenly distributed.* In that light we will examine things that may or may not catch on in all places at the same time; things that may or may not have widespread positive impact on our world and our profession; things that may reflect the desire for a perfect future but fall short of their intended goals. What is a library, in some sense, if not an institution meant to instill hope and trust in its users by preserving *future* access to the past regardless of how well preserved it actually is?

Widening the scope a little further, utopian and dystopian visions extend beyond single institutions to wider societies—and often as idealized urban areas—to help define and evaluate the lives of people. We can see this utopian push—that *Winthropian* shining city on a hill, in a sense—finding its way into the rhetoric dominating the intersection of big data and the internet of things (IoT). Smart cities, as the most recent manifestation of this ideal, have been hypothesized (and fantasized) as the ultimate melding of technology, human behavior, and big data analysis; they are an amalgam of the clean, predictable algorithm with irrational, confounding human behavior, and a mixing of our animal selves with our digital avatars to create the perfect inhabitants. It is that age-old "covenant of grace" replaced by a "covenant of works" conveniently tracked by the latest technology to ensure that our better selves prevail.

One of the current outgrowths of this centuries-long strain of speculation and idealism is the area of foresight. Martin Hilbert and colleagues (2009) have done some excellent work in the use of data to hone predictions of human behavior in the political realm. In particular his research team has developed a method of "participatory policy making," which entails soliciting participation and input from various stakeholders in a community. For Hilbert, big data can contribute to "e-democracy," and its open nature will allow for greater foresight and better planning to improve people's basic living conditions and status. Tellingly, many of the current tech giants are also employing similar approaches to the development of predictive technologies and the implementation of utopian ideals. Smart societies are not far beyond these explorations. It remains to be seen whether smart societies and their cities wind up more like present-day *über-exclusive* San Francisco where only the super-rich can afford to live, or like Hilbert's vision of the *"e"-qualized* society, where all are given equal voice and live in mutually beneficial cooperation.

To address the issue of urban areas central to our modern societies (smart or otherwise), some researchers have suggested a quantified "science of cities" to better meet these utopian goals. These quantified big data approaches would help to "describe and model the networks and flows that make up an urban city" (Pierson, 2017), allowing cities to grow and evolve in ways that can avoid current pitfalls of crime, poverty, and overcrowding, especially as populations move from rural to urban and suburban areas (Deakin, 2013).

From a practical point of view, a number of information technology corporations are beginning to develop nascent solutions and best practices for the science of cities. Institute of Electrical and Electronics Engineers (IEEE), for example, has developed a set of standards for creating and documenting "smart cities," which "address preservation, revitalization, livability, and sustainability . . . [via] the integration of IoT technologies, such as mobile crowdsourcing and cyber-physical cloud computing" (IEEE, 2017). Such cities, it is envisioned, would see improved living conditions for residents through connectivity and efficient living methods (ibid.).

Cisco Systems, additionally, envisions the move from our current state of digital connectivity to more efficient "fog computing" and "mist computing," which allows the networks to be extended further into more devices (Janakiram, 2015). Cisco defines this as "a system-level horizontal architecture that distributes resources and services of computing, storage, control and networking anywhere along the continuum from Cloud to Things" (Cisco Systems, 2015; OpenFog Consortium, 2017), allowing ever more possibilities of data collection and observation.

One of the problems with current data tracking and surveillance, however, is its lack of "immediacy"; as explained in Cisco's OpenFog whitepaper, "By the time the data makes its way to the cloud for analysis, the opportunity to act on it might be gone" (Cisco Systems, 2015). Figure 12.1 shows this need for more granular insertions of sensors to gather data. While we have a significant amount of data being collected as it is, this push for ever more granular observations and data collection promises to open the door to this vision of the "smart city." Barcelona, Spain, is one such city attempting to create a "smart city" based on the structure of fog computing (Kranz, 2015).

Dubai is another city attempting to harness data collection to make it "the smartest and the happiest city . . . by utilizing innovative technologies to achieve our goal" (Milliken, 2017). To accomplish this goal, the city planners are attempting to gather as much data as possible on the actions, desired services, and so forth, that the people in the city would need. As Dr. Aisha Butti Bin Bishr asserts, "To run these smart cities we need smart people. Today cities are run by data. If you don't have proper knowledge about how to read data it will be very difficult for you. Because nowadays, it's the data economy. It's not even knowledge economy" (Milliken, 2017). Their goals, though, are somewhat nebulous and focused on the "happiness" of their residents. By focusing on the data and information created by their residents, the city planners hope to improve the well-being of their residents. Of course,

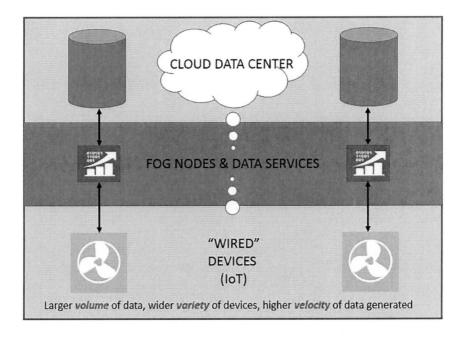

Figure 12.1.   A visualization of how "fog computing" intermediary services provide more responsive and comprehensive data gathering. *Source:* **Cisco Systems, 2015.**

Dubai's city planners are hardly the only ones to hold this sentiment about how data will improve lives. Others in the IT industry echo this fixation with data. Jack Ma, billionaire founder of Alibaba, considers data to be the "electricity of the 21st century" (Sharma, 2017), something so fundamental to modern smart society that it would cease to exist without it. As smart cities develop, the economies will develop with them.

Ultimately, though, beyond the buzzwords and catchphrases of Silicon Valley corporate-speak, the endpoint for these initiatives is presumably the development of that utopian-tinged "smart society" that might better understand itself through the monitoring and analysis of its own actions on a much larger scale than currently implemented. The granularity and handling of such data becomes ever more atomized, providing services and monitoring never before imagined.

Extending this a little further, it may be necessary to focus on these more granular components of such a society. These more granular institutions, such as public housing, roads, infrastructure, markets, and individual building, would comprise bit by bit the edifice of the smart society, though the problem is being able to integrate all these disparate elements and provide them with standardized, interoperable service.

From Smart Cities to Smart Libraries

Along these lines, then, libraries of the future might fit in within a "smart" society as one of its cornerstone organizations. This chapter will draw upon many of the topics discussed in previous chapters, including library development, student assessment, data itself, surveillance, and anticipation of behaviors to envision what such a "smart library," for lack of a better term at this time, might look like in ten, twenty, or thirty years' time.

As Nova Spivack (2007) predicts (see figure 2.3), the changes to information technology will push us beyond the semantic web, which we might argue is our current state, and into the Web 3.0 and Web 4.0 in which we are ultimately assisted and nudged by intelligent personal agents. Information and people become more and more interconnected, Spivack argues, and the more elaborate those connections, the more potential there exists for an intelligent web, but the backbone for this remains the development of the data and the way in which it is interoperable (Spivack, 2007). Currently, organizations such as MIT and the Bayerische Staatsbibliothek, for example, are testing out a "semantic" web search called Yewno, which "allow[s] users to explore connections between concepts" (Botsford, 2016; see also Breeding, 2017; and Yewno, 2017).

At the same time, even as libraries continue to exist within the developing track toward the semantic web and beyond, the roles of these libraries will need to change and adapt to the increase in information and the connections between people. The potential areas for a smart library to delve into would include the library and librarian as evaluator and educator for communities and individuals. The smart library will become, along with the K–12 and university infrastructure, one of the many monitors of and contributors to student success, by tracking behavior and results in the long term at potentially unimagined levels of granularity and comprehensiveness.

THE SMART LIBRARY AS EVALUATOR AND EDUCATOR FOR COMMUNITIES AND INDIVIDUALS

In the same vein as a smart city, whose end goal is seen as providing for the happiness and well-being of its inhabitants, the "smart library" would use data analysis to improve the well-being of its users. In many ways, the smart library might be envisioned as the ultimate evaluator of its users, providing big data analytics to help determine, even predetermine or target, the needs of the users both individually and within a specific community. Using a combination of demographic information as well as the real-time social media data generated by users within a community, libraries might be better able to position themselves as complete and accurate mirrors to their communities as well as accurate content providers, anticipating needs within a community.

Of course a number of important questions arise, then, if the smart library is to be tied in with community and user evaluation and subsequent education. For example, what standards exist to regulate and to determine what would be evaluated, and what would be considered off-limits? What standards need to be developed by libraries to ensure that they are contributing to the "smart" development of their users and communities? Furthermore, how might this adoption of standards actually work? The real-world examples that currently exist for smart cities might help to show the way. The set of standards established by the IEEE for smart cities, for example, might be adopted and altered for use with libraries and library patrons. Of course, such standards would need to be altered depending upon the type of the library too— be it be academic, public, or special.

The Association of College and Research Libraries (ACRL) framework on information literacy exists to help determine ways in which the uses of information can be best taught, but how might big data be inserted into this framework? How might big data analytics inform both librarians and library users on the best methods for improving literacy in this area? The effort would need to include linking the education efforts of smart libraries to specific policies on information literacy and the possibility of using big data analytics to help determine and drive the efforts of information literacy.

Tools would also need to be developed to help foster the role that a smart library might play in the evaluation and education of users and user communities. This would include improved semantic search capabilities (along the lines of the semantic search engine Yewno, for example), personal digital reference assistants (along the lines of Apple's SIRI, Amazon's Echo, Microsoft's Cortana, or Google Home), and online facilitators of information consumption and use. Other tools would need to be developed within the framework of information literacy philosophies and pedagogies, especially as a way to help alleviate information overload and facilitate cognitive development and student learning.

Ultimately, the smart library would be situated amidst a wired community tracking the real-time data usage of its members while providing and anticipating the most relevant, on-demand resources. One can imagine the smart library as an "agile" organization, capable of pivoting quickly or altering collections in real time based on the ongoing changing aspects of its user communities. Public libraries serving in college towns, for example, might alter their collections for the summer months or for the beginning of the small semester in order to anticipate specific community needs and reflect the swift changes in local demographics. This is currently done, of course, on a much smaller scale and in slower response times based on anecdotal or partial data, and meant to serve a narrower constituency. One imagines that more nuanced but widespread approaches could occur if more specific and voluminous data were made available to librarians.

THE SMART LIBRARY AS MONITOR OF STUDENT SUCCESS AND DATA-ANALYSIS ENGINE

Measuring student success is arguably the most important goal in college undergraduate and K–12 education. Knowing whether students have actually learned what they are supposed to is an essential metric. This importance was noted in a recent Wiley/*Chronicle of Higher Education* white paper: "Measuring Student Success: The Importance of Developing and Implementing Learning Outcomes for Continuous Improvement in Higher Education." The report poses two difficult questions: first, it asks, "Can [an] institution produce data on which students have mastered particular learning outcomes and provide evidence (e.g., assessed student work) for that determination?" and second, "Can students and instructors articulate the desired learning outcomes?" (Wiley, 2010; see also Richards and Coddington, 2010). These questions point out the dual role of education to provide evidence of subject mastery and to communicate the importance of that mastery not only to others but also to the teachers and the students themselves. While a reliance on standardized testing and traditional grades has been the most typical approach for creating data to measure student success through subject mastery, newer metrics have come to the fore that focus on the other areas that promote or impede student progress. Some of the metrics administrators now focus upon include retention rates (and the factors that impact them), graduation rates (and the factors that impact them too), the time taken to completion, and tracking educational goals and postgraduation hiring rates.

Yet, despite the obvious importance of student success and student learning for universities, there are nevertheless significant persistent gaps in student evaluation, especially as "there is no accepted measure of performance that allows students, faculty, employers and the public to understand who's succeeding in the teaching and learning realm" (Wiley, 2010). As seen in a detailed examination of the thirty measures of quality used by the six major university rating systems—including *US News and World Report*, *Forbes*, and Academic Ranking of World Universities—none of the measures could directly gauge "student learning outcomes" (Wiley, 2010). If major evaluative and accrediting bodies are not directly examining student success or student learning outcomes, then new measures and new evaluative processes will need to be devised and implemented to meet these obvious needs.

The smart library might have an ability to help answer these specific questions and to help both monitor student success as well as generate data and evidence to help with evaluation. Of course this raises the question of what indicators smart libraries would be able to monitor beyond what libraries currently offer. Certainly with the development of big data analytics projects, libraries and librarians might be able to gather more usage data on their subjects. Perhaps librarians will be able to observe the "typical day" of a library user and tie it to specific grades and work outputs. The holy grail of library assessment is to be able to draw a clear causal relationship between library usage and grade outcomes. Perhaps a smart library equipped with monitoring and evaluative technologies would be able to provide this specific information to university and community administrators. Likewise a smart library for the K–12 levels would be able to tie student library use to better grades and higher standardized test scores.

However, another question that inevitably arises as a result of this discussion is what student success should *look* like in the age of big data. Additionally, how would big data analytics be applied to help students truly become more successful? If we could tie in the various metrics of information about student performance, including grades, time spent studying, time spent on other activities, library usage, and other important parts of campus life—that is, interpersonal and family relationships—students with such performative "red flags," so to speak, could be easily identified and assisted to prevent failing grades, dropping out, or delayed graduation.

Even the amount of time a student spent studying could be analyzed to better help students pass and master materials. As mentioned in chapter 11, eye-tracking studies by library researchers show how neophyte students process information in journal articles. Establishing this technology as part of a student-assistance service would be a promising pedagogical aid. If it were possible to employ eye tracking to observe students as they read, they might be advised in real time on how to master their materials or essential learning objectives for each class. Questions might be posed as students interact with texts once they have reached certain document headings or key words within the article or book they are reading. A library-centered digital personal assistant fueled by the latest artificial intelligence might aid in the comprehension of information necessary to complete assignments or to become knowledgeable in a field of study.

Finally some more specific technologies and studies might be undertaken to aid in student learning. Digital personal web 3.0/4.0 personal monitors might be created to help with ideal study times for students. Perhaps the library itself will be set up for individuals based on their ideal relaxation environments; libraries could also be equipped with smart technologies to determine the best lighting at certain times of the day for optimal study and relaxation conditions; opening and closing hours could be adjusted to student use based on more detailed analytics, leading to more appropriate staffing decisions; and lighting and furniture arrangements could be developed that change automatically based on the needs and stated preferences of the students using the facilities. Another development would be related to mobile and screen technologies that adapt to student needs. If student identification cards are tied to library usage, personalized information windows (similar to targeted ads) could be created. In contrast to targeted ads, though, these information windows would not be used to sell baubles or services but would appear as recommendations of articles or books that are related to current classes or assignments that appear in a syllabus. Such personalized screens might serve as reminders and as aids to the completion of tasks and assist in time management.

It remains to be seen how far libraries are willing to go to monitor students and users. It is not so far-fetched to assume that people could be using wearable or embedded body technologies in the next ten to twenty years. Indeed, recent news has reported upon companies providing readable microchip technologies for their employees that can be inserted under the skin, not unlike the microchips inserted in dogs and cats (Marks, 2017). The use of such technologies may be so widespread among businesses and corporations that colleges and universities would be forced to utilize such systems to help find employment for their graduates, raising again the issue of whether libraries would be willing to harness and access this potential glut of data. If everyone is already doing it and privacy policies are robust enough to clearly protect users and students, the ethics of gathering the data may be a nonissue. But as seen in previous chapters, such guarantees of privacy and protection have been hard to come by, and overreach has been especially tempting to IT companies.

THE SMART LIBRARY AS CONTENT PROVIDER

In the midst of a big data–smart libraries era, what would collection development look like? We've already examined in chapter 8 how big data is having an impact on content development in libraries. The basics of this involve providing on-demand content to users and improved user fulfillment experiences in the form of suggestions and "also read" lists. But it is likely the library will at some point become part of the internet of things. It is possible, as a result, that physical books themselves will become "wired" to the internet without having to be digitized. Previous generations of technology have attempted this connectivity by using radio-frequency identification (RFID) tags. The smart library would obviously be more granular in its approach, perhaps being able to detect the difference between reading a book (and what pages were actually perused) and the mere removing of a book from its shelf. OpenFog data analytics, as mentioned above, might be able to better track how a book is accessed and whether a duplicate copy would be necessary to purchase or if the original should be removed.

Overall, as Spivack has predicted, the connections between people and information continue to grow and become ever more elaborate. One important development of the past several years is the adoption of blockchain, a digital ledger technology that tracks the changes to the ledger resulting in a newly possible sense of provenance for digital objects. Jason Griffey (2016) describes the benefits of blockchain contributing to distributed networks that are immutable and thus verifiable, based upon the consensus of all partners. He sees three important developments coming from the adoption of blockchain: provenance, digital provenance, and bibliographic metadata (Griffey, 2016). This is important because it allows for a more enforceable concept of ownership and preserves the provenance of digital objects. Prior to this, digital objects were essentially inexhaustible content streams reborn once they were copied from their originals. This has resulted in the loss of provenance and verifiability.

The adoption of blockchain technology, which is also notably the base technology for digital currencies such as Bitcoin and the new standard for digital contracts, will result in a new digital era where copies are no longer endlessly uncontrollable. The smart library could conceivably become a true clearinghouse and archive for exclusive and original digital information; second, the metadata generated by blockchains of digital objects would create gigantic ledgers full of data in need of preservation. Libraries would therefore become essential parts of the information infrastructure. Libraries would be generating metadata upon metadata, nearly ad infinitum, contributing to a mushrooming but richly documented context; in other words, libraries would feed back into those growing connections found in Spivack's prescient analysis.

Finally, within this environment of on-demand digital objects and blockchain ledgers providing important provenance for digital information, the library has an opportunity to become a seamless part of a scholarly communications infrastructure awash in the brokerage and sharing of the information economy. The smart library as an information hub will truly come to fruition, especially as they morph from print-based collections to consortium-based online collections of e-books along the lines of massive digital libraries. In other words, the "big datalization" of the library will have commenced. In a sense, then, the connections to and about information will embed the smart library even further in the smart society and provide essential services for the well-being of its constituents.

THE SMART LIBRARY AS PERSONNEL MANAGER

Finally, the smart library might be able to implement important cost savings through targeted and efficient employment practices. It is no secret that the coming automation of the workforce through robotics will have a profoundly challenging impact on our society. Even though employment in May 2017 was at near capacity (4.3 percent), this is not a permanent condition. Indeed, the future poses great risks in terms of not only manufacturing but also service jobs, especially driving and transportation, cashiers, fast food service, and the like, which will possibly see up to 47 percent of US jobs lost to automation over the next twenty years (Clifford, 2016). The Pew Research Center predicts "that robotics and artificial intelligence will permeate wide segments of daily life by 2025" (Smith and Anderson, 2014), while a more recent study from 2015 concludes that "robots are to blame for up to 670,000 lost manufacturing jobs between 1990 and 2007 . . . and that number will rise because industrial robots are expected to quadruple" (Miller, 2017). Another well-known prediction suggests roughly 50–75 percent unemployment will occur in the age of robots (Nisen, 2013). Serious proposals for a universal basic income, especially from tech industry billionaires like Elon Musk and Mark Zuckerberg, is a direct result of this pending economic bombshell.

In the face of declining employment possibilities in a "postlabor" world, what would staffing look like at a smart library? What jobs would become automated by "bots" or replaced by machines capable of AI? Such questions don't appear to have reassuring answers.

On one hand, it's quite easy to imagine book reshelving and collection organizing, which is often a primary staffing need in libraries, being replaced by robots capable of returning books to specific locations within stacks or to warehouse spaces. On the bright side, this could potentially open up funding for other types of jobs in a library but may ultimately curtail the staffing in medium-sized libraries from a few hundred student employees to a few dozen. Other types of positions, especially those related to digitization of archive materials, appear to be also easily replaced by automation technologies. Certainly the mass scanning of books has already been semiautomated by Google, the HathiTrust, and the Internet Archive projects. Humans are still necessary for page turning and manning the scanning equipment, but it is likely that full automation is but a few years away on these projects. It's also possible to imagine this kind of mass-digitization project occurring in smaller libraries as well, contributing to the unique content findable "in the cloud." In consortia, digital e-books of current physical holdings replace shelf copies in growing numbers, resulting in consortia-wide, nearly universal digital libraries. At the same time the automation of the technology would further reduce staffing and cut overall personnel costs almost to the bone.

It is, on the other hand, a lot more difficult to imagine the replacement of less repetitive, highly idiosyncratic positions that rely on the expertise and institutional knowledge of real people. This includes faculty, librarians, highly skilled library paraprofessionals, well-trained student assistants, and volunteers. It is still possible to believe at this point that these types of labor and skills-intensive jobs will be immune to the coming robot "invasion." At the same time, even such positions as reference librarian might be curtailed by the widespread implementation of personal digital assistants that anticipate questions and user needs while giving basic answers to reference and research questions. Are we ready for this? Would automation, robotics, and personal digital assistants truly be able to replace educators? One would hope not, but this is unclear.

PARTING THOUGHTS: ON THE LIMITATIONS OF A "SMART SOCIETY"

We have all imagined at some point or another what utopia or paradise might look like. Each century in the United States has envisioned utopia as a uniquely American ideal. For John Winthrop in the eighteenth century it was "the shining city on the hill"; in the nineteenth century it was the rags-to-riches stories of Ragged Dick or Horatio Alger mingled with the teachings of the gospel of wealth; and in the twentieth century it was the pre-Depression gilded age of American wealth and then the American postwar dream of economic suburban prosperity. There has always been a strain of deep religious utopianism, too, as seen with the Quakers, the Shakers, the Mormons, and all others wishing to worship and live in their own fashion.

The New World, in short, has been awash in the dreams of utopianism for centuries. The smart society is one more addition to this long list of ideals. Libraries, which I would position as central pillars to that smart society, represent the best of human nature, the utopian instincts for a fair and just society. The public sphere and the sense of public service—not yet dead even in the era of alternative facts, internet trolls, and manipulative "bots"—fuel the missions of all our libraries. They propel us toward big data collection as a tool to foster these new utopian, neohumanist societies. The Silicon Valley tech leaders occasionally border on this zealotry and idealism; politicians of all stripes believe in this impulse, or at least cynically attempt to exploit this urge, in their partisan divides and pushes for a just society.

But, again, Marx's main criticism of capitalism has always been that it has the power to eventually destroy itself by its own innate "creative destruction." Joseph Schumpeter, a mid-twentieth-century economist, now largely forgotten, suggests that capitalism will eventually "eat itself"; the faster and more efficient capitalism becomes, the more easily it will displace people and throw them for good off the table. Ultimately, as we see with the efficiency of robots, there may be no one working because there will be no jobs available for anyone. As a result, the capitalist mantra of "hard work; high returns" will morph into something completely different. People will no longer work to accumulate capital, and the system will be compromised and overthrown (Magadh, 2015). In this hypertechnological era, it should come as no surprise, then, that the smart society may ironically contain the seeds of its own discontent and unraveling.

Yet, as anyone who has read the previous chapters will realize, there are also limits to the benefits of big data and relying too heavily upon quantities and algorithms for making decisions. As there are clear limits to the "smart society," the smart library would also be in turn limited in its ability to follow through on some of the proposed promises. Not all things can be automated, quantified, or predicted. Endeavors such as education, for example, resist the pull of big data's predictions and the automation of the industrial and information age. While we can certainly find quantitative methods that will help us to identify weak students and the factors leading to student success, actual classroom teaching nevertheless remains a labor-intensive and time-consuming endeavor. As Jonathan Rees (2017) argues, "Education involves a lot more than just conveying information." Good teaching, he suggests, is just one long series of "edge cases," in which educators constantly tool and retool the information they convey in real time, adjusting their approach when students fail to grasp the tasks or information conveyed.

But this also leads us to the question of what else along with learning and education cannot be automated, quantified, or predicted? If we take things far enough, we can argue that consciousness itself may be impossible to quantify. Religious experiences cannot be quantified either. While neuroscientists have certainly been able to see the processes of the brain and can indicate when someone is in a specific state of mind, it remains difficult to pin down both the state of consciousness itself and the concept of the mind. Fundamental limits on the ability to quantify our lives appear even at the most basic levels of reality itself. Quantum spookiness confounds us with its ability to transcend our typically experienced physical and time-bound realities. While we are able to manipulate matter, understand patterns, and learn from these actions and experiences, it is truly the case that we cannot quantify it all. Additionally, while it is true that simulations of reality can help us to learn about the patterns of life and predict some outcomes, such as in computer-simulated sports matchups or in election results, the probabilities can still be wildly off. There is no substitute, sometimes, for experience itself. Not all is analytics, and not all can be analyzed. We have much to lose when we assume it can be or, worse, if we lose trust in anything that cannot be measured. As the Dubai smart-city planners admit, "When it comes to cognitive and deeper needs, we don't fully understand them" (Milliken, 2017).

In the end, this is far from the final word on the development of the connections between people, the connections between intelligence, and the development of big data. It may be that events will nevertheless prevent us from reaching a fully automated connection between information and people. The push toward the smart library may eventually be considered as quaint as an eight-track recording studio, full of lessons about the hubris of technological advancement, the illusions of modernity, and the inevitable decline into the dustbin of history. People may flock to old ruins of libraries, wondering how anyone could survive without being plugged in, or wondering exactly what it is we were seeking there. But who is to say that by quantifying everything and being in full connection with each other we are also not missing out on one of the best things about life: serendipity. Change and chance are lost when every whim or desire can be anticipated and treated as the "fulfillment" of desires. We want for nothing, it is true, but we may lack the ultimate satisfactions of perpetual change, surprise, and wisdom.

REFERENCES

Botsford, F. (2016). Yewno: A new way to discover. MIT Libraries. https://libraries.mit.edu.

Breeding, M. (2017). Smart libraries. ALA Tech Source. http://about.yewno.com/.

Cisco Systems. (2015). Fog computing and the internet of things: Extend the cloud to where the things are. https://www.cisco.com.

Clifford, C. (2016). Elon Musk says robots will push us to a universal basic income—here's how it would work. CNBC. https://www.cnbc.com.

Deakin, M. (2013). *Smart cities: Governing, modelling, and analysing the transition.* Abingdon, UK: Routledge.

Griffey, J. (2016). Blockchain for libraries (presentation slides). Speaker Deck. https://speaker-deck.com.

Hilbert, M., Miles, I., and Othmer, J. (2009). Foresight tools for participative policy-making in inter-governmental processes in developing countries: Lessons learned from the eLAC Policy Priorities Delphi. *Technological Forecasting and Social Change, 76*(7), 880–896. http://www.martinhilbert.net.

Institute of Electrical and Electronics Engineers (IEEE). (2017). Smart cities standard. http://smartcities.ieee.org.

Janakiram, M. (2016). Is fog computing the next big thing in internet of things? *Forbes*. https://www.forbes.com.

Kranz, M. (2015). Building scalable, sustainable, smart+connected communities with fog computing. *Cisco Blogs*. https://blogs.cisco.com.

Magadh. (2015). Capitalism will eat itself. Souciant. http://souciant.com.

Marks, G. (2017). A Wisconsin company offers to implant remote-control microchips in its employees. *Washington Post*. https://www.washingtonpost.com.

Miller, C. (2017). Evidence that robots are winning the race for American jobs. *New York Times*. https://www.nytimes.com.

Milliken, G. (2017). Dubai wants to use data to become the "happiest city on earth." Motherboard. https://motherboard.vice.com.

Nisen, M. (2013). Robot economy could cause up to 75 percent unemployment. *Business Insider*. http://www.businessinsider.com.

OpenFog Consortium. (2017). OpenFog insights: White papers. http://www.cisco.com.

Pierson, L. (2017). Big data analytics in smart cities: You can't have one without the other. LinkedIn. https://www.linkedin.com.

Rees, J. (2017). You can't automate good teaching. *Chronicle of Higher Education*. https://chroniclevitae.com.

Richards, A., and Coddington, R. (2010). 30 ways to rate a college. *Chronicle of Higher Education*. http://chronicle.com.

Sharma, R. (2017). When will the tech bubble burst? *New York Times*. https://www.nytimes.com.

Smith, A., and Anderson, J. (2014). AI, robotics, and the future of jobs. Pew Research Center. http://www.pewinternet.org.

Spivack, N. (2007). Web 3.0: The best official definition imaginable. *Nova Spivack* (blog). http://www.novaspivack.com.

Wiley. (2010). Measuring student success: The importance of developing and implementing learning outcomes for continuous improvement in higher education. Wiley Education Services. https://edservices.wiley.com.

Yewno Discover. (2017). Discover what's been missing (white paper). http://about.yewno.com.

Index

About the Author

Andrew Weiss is a digital services librarian at California State University, Northridge, with more than ten years of experience working in an academic library. He focuses primarily on issues of scholarly communication, especially open access, copyright policy in academia, institutional repositories, and developing better strategies for data curation. His current and prior research examines the impact of massive digital libraries such as Google Books and the HathiTrust on libraries and library users, the future directions of open-access publishing, information overload, and of course the intersection of big data and assessment in libraries.